TEACHER'S EDITION 1

English
No Problem!

The **LITERACY CONNECTION**
270 North Grove Avenue • Elgin IL 60120

Trish Kerns
Old Marshall Adult Education Center
Sacramento City Unified School District, CA

Patty Long
Old Marshall Adult Education Center
Sacramento City Unified School District, CA

New Readers Press

English—No Problem!™
English—No Problem! Level 1 Teacher's Edition
ISBN 1-56420-351-4

Printed in the United States of America
9 8 7 6 5 4 3 2 1

All proceeds from the sale of New Readers Press materials
support literacy programs in the United States and worldwide.

Acquisitions Editor: Paula L. Schlusberg
Developer: Mendoza and Associates
Project Director: Roseanne Mendoza
Project Editor: Pat Harrington-Wydell
Content Editor: Rose DeNeve
Production Director: Heather Witt-Badoud
Designer: Kimbrly Koennecke
Cover Design: Kimbrly Koennecke
Cover Photography: Robert Mescavage Photography

Authors

Trish Kerns
Old Marshall Adult Education Center
Sacramento City Unified
  School District, CA

Patty Long
Old Marshall Adult Education Center
Sacramento City Unified
  School District, CA

Contributors

National Council Members
Audrey Abed, *San Marcos Even Start Program, San Marcos, TX*
Myra K. Baum, *New York City Board of Education (retired), New York, NY*
Kathryn Hamilton, *Elk Grove Adult and Community Education, Sacramento, CA*
Brigitte Marshall, *Oakland Adult Education Programs, Oakland, CA*
Teri McLean, *Florida Human Resources Development Center, Gainesville, FL*
Alan Seaman, *Wheaton College, Wheaton, IL*

Reviewers
Sabrina Budasi-Martin, *William Rainey Harper College, Palatine, IL*
Linda Davis-Pluta, *Oakton Community College, Des Plaines, IL*
Patricia DeHesus-Lopez, *Center for Continuing Education, Texas A&M University,*
  Kingsville, TX
Gail Feinstein Forman, *San Diego City College, San Diego, CA*
Carolyn Harding, *Marshall High School Adult Program, Falls Church, VA*
Debe Pack-Garcia, *Manteca Adult School, Humbolt, CA*
Pamela Patterson, *Seminole Community College, Sanford, FL*
Catherine Porter, *Adult Learning Resource Center, Des Plaines, IL*
Jean Rose, *ABC Adult School, Cerritos, CA*
Eric Rosenbaum, *Bronx Community College Adult Program, Bronx, NY*
Laurie Shapiro, *Miami-Dade Community College, Miami, FL*
Terry Shearer, *North Harris College Community Education, Houston, TX*
Abigail Tom, *Durham Technical Community College, Chapel Hill, NC*

Pilot Teachers
Connie Bateman, *Gerber Adult Education Center, Sacramento, CA*
Jennifer Bell, *William Rainey Harper College, Palatine, IL*
Marguerite Bock, *Chula Vista Adult School, Chula Vista, CA*
Giza Braun, *National City Adult School, National City, CA*
Sabrina Budasi-Martin, *William Rainey Harper College, Palatine, IL*
Wong-Ling Chew, *Citizens Advice Bureau, Bronx, NY*
Renee Collins, *Elk Grove Adult and Community Education, Sacramento, CA*
Rosette Dawson, *North Harris College Community Education, Houston, TX*
Kathleen Edel, *Elk Grove Adult and Community Education, Sacramento, CA*
Margaret Erwin, *Elk Grove Adult and Community Education, Sacramento, CA*
Teresa L. Gonzalez, *North Harris College Community Education, Houston, TX*
Fernando L. Herbert, *Bronx Adult School, Bronx, NY*
Carolyn Killean, *North Harris College Community Education, Houston, TX*
Elizabeth Minicz, *William Rainey Harper College, Palatine, IL*
Larry Moore, *Long Beach Adult School, Long Beach, CA*
Lydia Omori, *William Rainey Harper College, Palatine, IL*
Valsa Panikulam, *William Rainey Harper College, Palatine, IL*
Kathryn Powell, *William Rainey Harper College, Palatine, IL*
Alan Reiff, *NYC Board of Education, Adult and Continuing Education, Bronx, NY*

Brenda M. Rodriguez, *San Marcos Even Start Program, San Marcos, TX*
Juan Carlos Rodriguez, *San Marcos Even Start Program, San Marcos, TX*
Joan Siff, *NYC Board of Education, Adult and Continuing Education, Bronx, NY*
Susie Simon, *Long Beach Adult School, Long Beach, CA*
Gina Tauber, *North Harris College, Houston, TX*
Diane Villanueva, *Elk Grove Adult and Community Education, Sacramento, CA*
Dona Wayment, *Elk Grove Adult and Community Education, Sacramento, CA*
Weihua Wen, *NYC Board of Education, Adult and Continuing Education, Bronx, NY*
Darla Wickard, *North Harris College Community Education, Houston, TX*
Judy Wurtz, *Sweetwater Union High School District, Chula Vista, CA*

Focus Group Participants
Leslie Jo Adams, *Laguna Niguel, CA*
Fiona Armstrong, *New York City Board of Education, New York, NY*
Myra K. Baum, *New York City Board of Education (retired), New York, NY*
Gretchen Bitterlin, *San Diego Unified School District, San Diego, CA*
Patricia DeHesus-Lopez, *Center for Continuing Education, Texas A&M University, Kingsville, TX*
Diana Della Costa, *Worksite ESOL Programs, Kissimmee, FL*
Frankie Dovel, *Orange County Public Schools, VESOL Program, Orlando, FL*
Marianne Dryden, *Region 1 Education Service Center, Edinburgh, TX*
Richard Firsten, *Lindsay Hopkins Technical Center, Miami, FL*
Pamela S. Forbes, *Bartlett High School, Elgin, IL*
Kathryn Hamilton, *Elk Grove Adult and Community Education, Sacramento, CA*
Trish Kerns, *Old Marshall Adult Education Center, Sacramento City Unified School District, Sacramento, CA*
Suzanne Leibman, *The College of Lake County, Grayslake, IL*
Patty Long, *Old Marshall Adult Education Center, Sacramento City Unified School District, Sacramento, CA*
Brigitte Marshall, *Oakland Adult Education Programs, Oakland, CA*
Bet Messmer, *Santa Clara Adult School, Santa Clara, CA*
Patricia Mooney, *New York State Board of Education, Albany, NY*
Lee Ann Moore, *Salinas Adult School, Salinas, CA*
Lynne Nicodemus, *San Juan Adult School, Carmichael, CA*
Pamela Patterson, *Seminole Community College, Sanford, FL*
Eric Rosenbaum, *Bronx Community College, Bronx, NY*
Federico Salas, *North Harris College Community Education, Houston, TX*
Linda Sasser, *Alhambra District Office, Alhambra, CA*
Alan Seaman, *Wheaton College, Wheaton, IL*
Kathleen Slattery, *Salinas Adult School, Salinas, CA*
Carol Speigl, *Center for Continuing Education, Texas A&M University, Kingsville, TX*
Edie Uber, *Santa Clara Adult School, Santa Clara, CA*
Lise Wanage, *CASAS, Phoenix, AZ*

Special thanks to Kathryn Hamilton for her help in the development of this book.

Contents

Warm-Up Unit Are You Ready? 10

◆ Vocabulary: Information • Days and months • Weather • Time • Transportation • Classroom directions • School supplies • Money
◆ Language: Subject pronouns with *be* • Contractions with *be* • Possessive nouns and adjectives • *Need, need to* • Plurals of regular nouns
◆ Pronunciation: Syllable stress
◆ Culture: Class rules in the US

Unit 1   My Life Is Changing! 22

◆ Vocabulary: Relatives • Neighborhood places • Job ads
◆ Language: Negative contractions with *be* • Yes/no questions and answers with *be* • Commands • Prepositions of location
◆ Pronunciation: Question and answer intonation
◆ Culture: Job interviews in the US

Unit 2   I Need to Plan a Party 34

◆ Vocabulary: Party plans • Work schedules
◆ Language: Present-tense verbs • Prepositions of time • Frequency adverbs • Present-tense yes/no questions and answers
◆ Pronunciation: Present-tense ending sounds • Long and short *a* sounds
◆ Culture: Birthday parties in the US

Scope and Sequence

Unit Number and Title	Global Unit Theme (across all levels)	Unit Topic/Skill	Lesson-Specific Life Skills	Vocabulary	Language
Warm-Up Unit Are You Ready?	NA	Starting in English	L1: Talk about the time and weather Talk about transportation L2: Follow classroom directions L3: Count money	Information Days and months Weather Time Transportation Classroom directions School supplies Money	Subject pronouns with *be* Contractions with *be* Possessive nouns and adjectives *Need, need to* Plurals of regular nouns
Unit 1 My Life Is Changing!	Life stages: personal growth and goal setting	Helping your family	L1: Talk about family members L2: Find places in your neighborhood L3: Complete a job application	Relatives Neighborhood places Job ads	Negative contractions with *be* *Yes/no* questions and answers with *be* Commands Prepositions of location
Unit 2 I Need to Plan a Party	Making connections	Planning an activity	L1: Read a schedule Write a note L2: Talk about asking for advice L3: Change plans	Party plans Work schedules	Present-tense verbs Prepositions of time Frequency adverbs Present-tense *yes/no* questions and answers
Unit 3 How Do You Feel?	Taking care of yourself	Getting medical help	L1: Ask for sick leave L2: Fill out a medical form L3: Read medicine labels	Common illnesses and symptoms Question words Medicine labels	Object pronouns Present-tense *Wh-* questions with *be* Present-tense *Wh-* questions with other verbs
Unit 4 I Need a Budget!	Personal finance	Making a budget	L1: Learn ways to save money L2: Talk and write about needs and wants L3: Read shopping ads	Money problems Job skills Shopping for clothes	Present continuous statements and questions *Like, like to, need, need to, want, want to* *This, that, these, those*

Pronunciation	Culture	Tasks and Unit Project	EFF Skill/Common Activity (The basic communication skills— read with understanding, convey ideas in writing, speak so others can understand, listen actively, and observe critically— are taught in every unit.)	SCANS Skills (The basic skills of reading, writing, listening, and speaking are taught in every unit.)	Technology
Syllable stress	Class rules	T1: Make a class list T2: Make a name card T3: Get ready to buy school supplies UP: Make a new student booklet	Take responsibility for learning	Manage time Manage materials and facility resources	Make a cover for the new student booklet on the computer.
Question and answer intonation	Job interviews	T1: Draw your family tree T2: Draw a map T3: Interview a partner/write the information on a job application UP: Prepare a personal information sheet	Plan Solve problems and make decisions	Decision making Problem solving	Photocopy the personal information sheet.
Present-tense ending sounds Long and short *a* sounds	Birthday parties	T1: Trade a favor T2: List people who can give you advice T3: Talk about changing plans UP: Plan a class party	Plan Solve problems and make decisions	Manage time	Make a party invitation on the computer and photocopy it.
Intonation with *be* and *Wh-* questions	Home remedies	T1: Ask to leave work or school early T2: Give medical information T3: Talk about medicines UP: Complete a family medical information form	Solve problems and make decisions	Responsibility Self-management	Call and leave a message for the teacher saying you are sick today.
Long and short *e* sounds	Customer service	T1: Make a poster about how to save money T2: Give and write advice about making changes T3: Write and role-play a conversation about returning clothing to a store UP: Make a budget	Plan Use math to solve problems and communicate Take responsibility for learning	Manage money Serve clients/customers Arithmetic Self-management	Go to a web site to find the price of something you want to buy.

Scope and Sequence

Unit Number and Title	Global Unit Theme (across all levels)	Unit Topic/Skill	Lesson-Specific Life Skills	Vocabulary	Language
Unit 5 What's for Dinner?	Consumer awareness	Choosing good food	L1: Ask for help L2: Read coupons L3: Order food in fast-food restaurants	Foods Coupons	Count and noncount nouns *There is* and *there are* Questions and answers with *or*
Unit 6 Call the Police!	Protecting your legal rights	Reporting a crime	L1: Take a home inventory L2: Report a crime L3: Describe people	Home inventory words Police report words Describing people	Past-tense statements with *be* Past-tense statements with regular and irregular verbs Past-tense questions with *be* and other verbs
Unit 7 Succeeding at School	Participating in your new country and community	Talking to teachers	L1: Read a report card L2: Decide what's most important L3: Plan for school success	School words Report cards After-school activities	Possessive adjectives Compound sentences with *and* Future tense with *going to*
Unit 8 I Want a Good Job!	Lifelong learning	Improving your skills	L1: Talk about job skills L2: Talk about future goals L3: Read flyers	Employment words Educational opportunities	*Can* and *can't* Compound sentences with *but* *A, an, the*

Pronunciation	Culture	Tasks and Unit Project	EFF Skill/Common Activity (The basic communication skills—read with understanding, convey ideas in writing, speak so others can understand, listen actively, and observe critically—are taught in every unit.)	SCANS Skills (The basic skills of reading, writing, listening, and speaking are taught in every unit.)	Technology
Intonation with words in a list	Fast food	T1: Write a grocery list T2: Look for specials and coupons T3: Find fast-food restaurants UP: Plan a meal	Reflect and evaluate	Negotiate to arrive at a decision Acquire and evaluate information	Write a recipe on the computer and make copies for the class.
Long and short *i* sounds Past-tense ending sounds	Neighborhood Watch programs	T1: Take a home inventory T2: Fill out a report T3: Describe a person UP: Make a home safety packet	Reflect and evaluate	Understand systems Reasoning	Make a chart on the computer for your home inventory.
Long and short *o* sounds	Parent participation in schools	T1: Write your and your child's school information T2: Make an activities chart T3: Make a poster showing how you can succeed in school UP: Make a school information chart	Guide others Advocate and influence	Manage time Exercise leadership Monitor and correct performance Decision making	Photocopy the school information chart.
Long and short *u* sounds	Education can increase income	T1: List your skills T2: Make a goals chart T3: List places for adult education in your community UP: Make a time line and a resume	Plan Take responsibility for learning	Understand systems Select technology Decision making Self-management	Make a class jobs and skills chart on the computer. Type your resume on the computer and photocopy it.

About This Series

Meeting Adult Learners' Needs with *English—No Problem!*

English—No Problem! is a theme-based, performance-based series focused on developing critical thinking and cultural awareness and on building language and life skills. Designed for adult and young adult English language learners, the series addresses themes and issues meaningful to adults in the United States.

English—No Problem! is appropriate for and respectful of adult learners. These are some key features:
- interactive, communicative, participatory approach
- rich, authentic language
- problem-posing methodology
- project-based units and task-based lessons
- goal setting embedded in each unit and lesson
- units organized around themes of adult relevance
- contextualized, inductive grammar
- student materials designed to fit into lesson plans
- performance assessment, including tools for learner self-evaluation

Series Themes

Across the series, units have the following themes:
- Life Stages: Personal Growth and Goal Setting
- Making Connections
- Taking Care of Yourself
- Personal Finance
- Consumer Awareness
- Protecting Your Legal Rights
- Participating in Your New Country and Community
- Lifelong Learning
- Celebrating Success

At each level, these themes are narrowed to subthemes that are level-appropriate in content and language.

English—No Problem! Series Components

Five levels make up the series:
- literacy
- level 1 (low beginning)
- level 2 (high beginning)
- level 3 (low intermediate)
- level 4 (high intermediate)

The series includes the following components.

Student Book

A full-color student book is the core of each level of *English—No Problem!* Literacy skills, vocabulary, grammar, reading, writing, listening, speaking, and SCANS-type skills are taught and practiced.

Teacher's Edition

Each teacher's edition includes these tools:
- general suggestions for using the series
- scope and sequence charts for the level
- lesson-specific teacher notes with reduced student book pages
- complete scripts for all listening activities and Pronunciation Targets in the student book

Workbook

A workbook provides contextualized practice in the skills taught at each level. Activities relate to the student book stories. Workbook activities are especially useful for learners working individually.

 This icon in the teacher's edition indicates where workbook activities can be assigned.

Reproducible Masters

The reproducible masters include photocopiable materials for the level. Some masters are unit-specific, such as contextualized vocabulary and grammar activities, games, and activities focusing on higher-level thinking skills. Others are generic graphic organizers. Still other masters can be used by teachers, peers, and learners themselves to assess the work done in each unit.

Each masters book also includes scripts for all listening activities in the masters. (Note: These activities are not included on the *English—No Problem!* audio recordings.)

 This icon in the teacher's edition indicates where reproducible masters can be used.

Audio Recording

Available on CD and cassette, each level's audio component includes listening passages, listening activities, and Pronunciation Targets from the student book.

This icon in the student book and teacher's edition indicates that the audio recording includes material for that activity.

Lesson-Plan Builder

This free, web-based *Lesson-Plan Builder* allows teachers to create and save customized lesson plans, related graphic organizers, and selected assessment masters. Goals, vocabulary lists, and other elements are already in the template for each lesson. Teachers then add their own notes to customize their plans.

They can also create original graphic organizers using generic templates.

When a lesson plan is finished, the customized materials can be printed and stored in PDF form.

This icon in the teacher's edition refers teachers to the *Lesson-Plan Builder,* found at www.enp.newreaderspress.com.

Vocabulary Cards

For literacy, level 1, and level 2, all vocabulary from the Picture Dictionaries and Vocabulary boxes in the student books is also presented on reproducible flash cards. At the literacy level, the cards also include capital letters, lowercase letters, and numerals.

Placement Tool

The Placement Test student booklet includes items that measure exit skills for each level of the series so that learners can start work in the appropriate student book. The teacher's guide includes a listening script, as well as guidelines for administering the test to a group, for giving an optional oral test, and for interpreting scores.

Hot Topics in ESL

These online professional development articles by adult ESL experts focus on key issues and instructional techniques embodied in *English—No Problem!,* providing background information to enhance effective use of the materials. They are available online at www.enp.newreaderspress.com.

Addressing the Standards

English—No Problem! has been correlated from the earliest stages of development with national standards for adult education and ESL, including the NRS (National Reporting System), EFF (Equipped for the Future), SCANS (Secretary's Commission on Achieving Necessary Skills), CASAS (Comprehensive Adult Student Assessment System) competencies, BEST (Basic English Skills Test), and SPLs (Student Performance Levels). The series also reflects state standards from New York, California, and Florida.

About the Student Books

Each unit in the student books includes a two-page unit opener followed by three lessons (two at the literacy level). A cumulative unit project concludes each unit. Every unit addresses all four language skills—listening, speaking, reading, and writing. Each lesson focuses on characters operating in one of the three EFF-defined adult roles—parent/family member at home, worker at school or work, or citizen/community member in the larger community.

Unit Opener Pages

Unit Goals The vocabulary, language, pronunciation, and culture goals set forth in the unit opener correlate to a variety of state and national standards.

Opening Question and Photo The opening question, photo, and caption introduce the unit protagonists and engage learners affectively in issues the unit explores.

Think and Talk This feature of levels 1–4 presents questions based on classic steps in problem-posing methodology, adjusted and simplified as needed.

What's Your Opinion? In levels 1–4, this deliberately controversial question often appears after Think and Talk or on the first page of a lesson. It is designed to encourage lively teacher-directed discussion, even among learners with limited vocabulary.

Picture Dictionary or Vocabulary Box This feature introduces important unit vocabulary and concepts.

Gather Your Thoughts In levels 1–4, this activity helps learners relate the unit theme to their own lives. They record their thoughts in a graphic organizer, following a model provided.

What's the Problem? This activity, which follows Gather Your Thoughts, encourages learners to practice another step in problem posing. They identify a possible problem and apply the issue to their own lives.

Setting Goals This feature of levels 1–4 is the first step of a unit's self-evaluation strand. Learners choose from a list of language and life goals and add their own goal to the list. The goals are related to the lesson activities and tasks and to the unit project. After completing a unit, learners revisit these goals in Check Your Progress, the last page of each workbook unit.

First Lesson Page

While the unit opener sets up an issue or problem, the lessons involve learners in seeking solutions while simultaneously developing language competencies.

Lesson Goals and EFF Role The lesson opener lists language, culture, and life-skill goals and identifies the EFF role depicted in that lesson.

Pre-Reading or Pre-Listening Question This question prepares learners to seek solutions to the issues presented in the reading or listening passage or lesson graphic that follows.

Reading or Listening Tip At levels 1–4, this feature presents comprehension and analysis strategies used by good listeners and readers.

Lesson Stimulus Each lesson starts with a reading passage (a picture story at the literacy level), a listening passage, or a lesson graphic. A photo on the page sets the situation for a listening passage. Each listening passage is included in the audio recording, and scripts are provided at the end of the student book and the teacher's edition. A lesson graphic may be a schedule, chart, diagram, graph, time line, or similar item. The questions that follow each lesson stimulus focus on comprehension and analysis.

Remaining Lesson Pages

Picture Dictionary, Vocabulary Box, and Idiom Watch These features present the active lesson vocabulary. At lower levels, pictures often help convey meaning. Vocabulary boxes for the literacy level also include letters and numbers. At levels 3 and 4, idioms are included in every unit.

Class, Group, or Partner Chat This interactive feature provides a model miniconversation. The model sets up a real-life exchange that encourages use of the lesson vocabulary and grammatical structures. Learners ask highly structured and controlled questions and record classmates' responses in a graphic organizer.

Grammar Talk At levels 1–4, the target grammatical structure is presented in several examples. Following the examples is a short explanation or question that guides learners to come up with a rule on their own. At the literacy level, language boxes highlight basic grammatical structures without formal teaching.

Pronunciation Target In this feature of levels 1–4, learners answer questions that lead them to discover pronunciation rules for themselves.

Chat Follow-Ups Learners use information they recorded during the Chat activity. They write patterned sentences, using lesson vocabulary and structures.

In the US This feature is a short cultural reading or brief explanation of some aspect of US culture.

Compare Cultures At levels 1–4, this follow-up to In the US asks learners to compare the custom or situation in the US to similar ones in their home countries.

Activities A, B, C, etc. These practice activities, most of them interactive, apply what has been learned in the lesson so far.

Lesson Tasks Each lesson concludes with a task that encourages learners to apply the skills taught and practiced earlier. Many tasks involve pair or group work, as well as follow-up presentations to the class.

Challenge Reading

At level 4, a two-page reading follows the lessons. This feature helps learners develop skills that prepare them for longer readings they will encounter in future study or higher-level jobs.

Unit Project

Each unit concludes with a final project in which learners apply all or many of the skills they acquired in the unit. The project consists of carefully structured and sequenced individual, pair, and group activities. These projects also help develop important higher-level skills such as planning, organizing, collaborating, and presenting.

Additional Features

The following minifeatures appear as needed at different levels:

One Step Up These extensions of an activity, task, or unit project allow learners to work at a slightly higher skill level. This feature is especially useful when classes include learners at multiple levels.

Attention Boxes These unlabeled boxes highlight words and structures that are not taught explicitly in the lesson, but that learners may need. Teachers are encouraged to point out these words and structures and to offer any explanations that learners require.

Remember? These boxes present, in abbreviated form, previously introduced vocabulary and language structures.

Writing Extension This feature encourages learners to do additional writing. It is usually a practical rather than an academic activity.

Technology Extra This extension gives learners guidelines for doing part of an activity, task, or project using such technology as computers, photocopiers, and audio and video recorders.

Assessment

Assessment is completely integrated into *English—No Problem!* This arrangement facilitates evaluation of class progress and provides a systematic way to set up learner portfolios. The pieces used for assessment are listed below. You may use all of them or select those that suit your needs.

Check Your Progress

Found on the last page of each workbook unit, this self-check is tied to the goals learners set for themselves in the student book unit opener. Learners rate their progress in life and language skills.

Unit Checkup/Review

For each unit, the reproducible masters include a two-page Unit Checkup/Review. You can use this instrument before each unit as a pretest or after each unit to assess mastery. If it is used both before and after, the score differential indicates a learner's progress.

Rubrics for Oral and Written Communication

The reproducible masters include a general rubric for speaking and one for writing (Masters 6 and 7). You can use these forms to score and track learner performance on the unit tasks and projects. Copy the rubric for each learner, circle performance scores, and include the results in the learner's portfolio.

Forms for Evaluating Projects

For the unit projects in Unit 2 and Unit 8, the reproducible masters include a form on which you can evaluate learner performance. Make a copy for each learner, record your assessment, and add the form to the learner's portfolio.

Peer Assessment

Peer assessment helps learners focus on the purpose of an activity. Encourage learners to be positive in their assessments of each other. For example, ask them to say one thing they liked about a presentation and one thing they did not understand. Use the Peer Assessment Form (Master 10 in the reproducible masters) when learners are practicing for a performance. Peer assessment is best used to evaluate groups rather than individuals and rehearsals rather than performances.

Self-Assessment

Self-assessment is a way for learners to measure their progress. Use the self-check masters (Masters 8 and 9 in the reproducible masters) at the beginning of Unit 1 and at the end of Units 4 and 8. Then save them in learners' portfolios.

Ongoing Assessment

These minirubrics and guidelines for assessing Task 1 and the unit project in Unit 3 are integrated into the teacher notes. You can include the pieces you evaluate in learners' portfolios. You will probably develop similar ways of assessing learners' progress on other activities, tasks, and projects.

Teaching Effectively with English—No Problem! Level 1

The following general suggestions for using level 1 of English—No Problem! can enhance your teaching.

Before beginning a unit, prepare yourself in this way:
- Read the entire set of unit notes.
- Gather the materials needed for the unit.
- Familiarize yourself with the student book and workbook pages.
- Prepare copies of masters needed for the unit.

Look for ways to express meaning clearly, using objects, pictures, gestures, and the most basic language structures and vocabulary. Avoid idioms and two-word verbs, which do not translate well. Help learners by slowing the instructional pace. Don't hesitate to repeat, recycle, and explore material in depth.

Materials

The notes for each unit include a list of specific materials. These lists do not include the following, which are recommended for all or most units:
- large sheets of paper (butcher or flip-chart).
- magazines, newspapers, catalogs (to cut up).
- art supplies (scissors, glue, tape, colored pencils, markers, colored and plain paper, etc.).
- a "Treasure Chest" box or other container of prizes (new pencils, pens, erasers, rulers, stickers, hard candy, small candy bars, key chains, and things collected at conferences or found at dollar stores).
- *yes/no* cards. Create a *yes* card and a *no* card for each learner to use when you need to check comprehension. The cards are referred to throughout the teacher notes.

Grouping

Working in groups increases learner participation and builds teamwork skills important in the workplace.

Learners can be grouped randomly. Four or five on a team allows for a good level of participation. For increased individual accountability, assign roles to group members. These commonly include
- group leader, who directs the group's activities
- recorder, who writes group responses
- reporter, who reports the group's responses to the whole class
- timekeeper, who lets everyone know how much time is left for an activity

Groups and roles within groups can be changed as needed.

Talking about the Photos

Contextualized color photos are used as starting points for many unit activities. Talking about the photos with learners is a good way to assess prior knowledge and productive vocabulary. For every photo, follow one or more of these suggestions:

- Before you talk about the photo, ask learners questions relating to their own lives.
- Discuss the photo with learners. Ask the open-ended question "What do you see?"
- Ask *yes/no, true/false,* and simple *wh-* questions about the photo.
- As learners name items in the photos, write new words on the board or an overhead transparency. Before erasing them, point to each word and have learners point to the item in the photo.
- If a photo has a lot of detail, groups can compete to list the most items or write the most simple sentences. Make this more challenging by showing the photo for 30 seconds and asking the groups to work from memory.

Reading Titles and Captions

Focusing on titles and captions helps learners create a context for the unit or lesson.

Lesson Titles Discuss vocabulary that appears in lesson titles. Ask learners to talk about how the titles relate to the lessons. In some cases, you can ask learners to predict what will happen in the story.

Captions Use the captions to discuss the characters and the story. Ask questions like these: Do you know anyone like this/in this situation? What do you think the character will do?

Identifying and Analyzing Problems

The questions in What's the Problem? set up the central issue for the unit. Model responses by talking about how *you* would answer the question. Learners may think about the questions individually or discuss them with a partner or group. If they discuss the questions, ask volunteers to share ideas from their small groups. Then follow up with a class discussion.

The grammar structures taught in the unit often appear in the opening discussion. You can use the structures yourself in talking about the problem, but do not expect learners to use them yet.

Setting Goals

Follow these steps:
- Read each goal and explain unfamiliar vocabulary by miming or pointing to pictures or objects.
- Ask which goals are important for learners.
- Have learners use their *yes/no* cards as you read each goal again.
- Ask learners if anyone has another goal.
- Ask if anyone already has achieved some of the goals.
- Ask learners to check their personal goals.

Listening Comprehension

One lesson in each unit is driven by a listening passage that is a realistic conversation. There are also other listening activities.

Ideally, you will have access to a cassette or CD player and will be able to use the *English–No Problem!* audio recording. The recording allows learners to hear a variety of native-speaker and non-native-speaker voices. For teachers who need or prefer to read the audio portions, scripts for listening passages and activities are printed on pages 118–120 of the student book and on pages 118–120 of this book.

In doing listening activities, the following sequence is recommended:
1. Review and model the directions.
2. Play the audio or read the listening script as often as learners want.
3. Play the audio all the way through.

Play it again and stop at transition points (changes in speakers).

Play again and stop for key words.

After learners listen once, check for basic listening comprehension by asking *either/or* questions directly from the passage. (If the passage is long, play short sections and ask learners questions after each.)

Reading Comprehension

The readings in *English—No Problem!* are designed to be as useful as possible to adult English language learners. They are modeled on practical documents that adults want and need to read in everyday life. The reading lessons present the strategies and skills needed to successfully navigate such documents.

Attention Boxes The words in these unlabeled boxes are not active vocabulary, but learners will need them to understand the passage. When possible, demonstrate each word by pointing or miming.

Reading Tips Each tip focuses on a reading strategy, for example, scanning for specific information or predicting content. Help learners apply these strategies to other student book and workbook readings.

In-Class Reading Follow these suggestions when learners read in class:
- Read the passage aloud so that learners can hear correct pronunciation of the words.
- Read it again in comprehensible chunks while learners repeat.

Comprehension Questions (Talk or Write, Speak or Circle, What's Your Opinion?)

- Read the sentences. Have learners repeat. Read the sentences again. For *yes/no* questions, have learners use their *yes/no* cards for responses, especially in the early units.
- Pair learners to answer the questions.
- Make each pair responsible for reporting a question to the class by having one partner read the question and the other answer it.
- Discuss the questions. Answers are provided for all questions except personal ones, for which answers will vary according to learners' experience. When answers are given, learners may use different wording and structures, provided they capture the general concept.
- Listen to learners' responses to any question, whether *yes/no, true/false,* or multiple choice. Then ask the follow-up question "How do you know?" This helps them acquire and practice the skill of supporting their answers. It also naturally slows the pace of instruction and focuses learners' attention on the issues. Learners can point to objects in the photos or words in the readings, the captions, or the speech bubbles. Praise their attempts to support their answers.
- For What's Your Opinion? questions, learners can raise hands to indicate *yes/no* or other answers. Or learners can use their *yes/no* cards to indicate a response. This assures that you can see how well each learner is responding. Another option is to assign an answer (e.g., *always, sometimes, never*) to a particular area in the room and tell learners to go to the area that matches their response. This gives a good visual representation of class opinions.

Vocabulary Practice

Spend plenty of time on each set of words introduced in the Picture Dictionary and Vocabulary boxes.

Introducing Vocabulary These steps will help learners comprehend the words:

- Point to the words or pictures as you read them.
- Read the words in random order and have learners point to the words or the pictures.
- Say each word again and have learners repeat.
- Write the words on the board or an overhead transparency. Point to the letters and have learners spell the words aloud.
- Act out any action words.
- Elicit definitions and sample sentences for vocabulary words that learners already know. Write their ideas on the board. Have learners write their own definitions in pairs.

- Collect the definitions or ask volunteers to write one of their definitions on the board.
- If there is a line for "your word," have learners write another word that is new to them. If there is no line, have learners write new words in their notebooks. List the new words on the board or an overhead transparency. Introduce these words and their meanings as you did the Picture Dictionary and Vocabulary words, using the steps above.
- Have learners act out their words.

Using Vocabulary Cards Use the Vocabulary Card Masters and your own card stock to make vocabulary cards for all Picture Dictionary and Vocabulary words. Consider duplicating the Vocabulary Card Masters in different sizes to accommodate various activities, e.g., a set of larger, laminated cards for whole-group activities or individual sets for each learner. If you have a class set of scissors, have learners cut out their own cards.

Give learners plastic self-closing bags to keep their cards in, or use a hole punch and have learners put the cards on key rings or binder rings in their notebooks.

The sets of words and pictures can be used for a variety of activities like matching, alphabetizing, sorting, and categorizing.

Reinforcing Vocabulary Picture Dictionary and Vocabulary words are used often in the student book and the workbook. These activities use Vocabulary Card Masters to provide further reinforcement:

- Hold up a picture card. At first, ask *yes/no* questions (e.g., Is this an apple? Is this an orange?). Later ask questions demanding more verbal skills (e.g., What is this?).
- Hold up a word card and say, "Read this word."
- After you have practiced the new words, a more advanced learner may take your place showing the cards and asking questions. Or pass around the cards and have each learner ask the question "What is this?"
- Use vocabulary cards throughout the unit to review meaning, pronunciation, and form. Distribute the cards among groups of learners. Ask each group to pronounce the word, give its alternate forms, and create a sentence using the word.
- For assessment purposes, place cards faceup on a table. Then read a word and ask a learner to point to it.
- Use story writing to reinforce both meaning and use of vocabulary. First create a sample story that uses your own set of five words. Write the words on the board or an overhead transparency. Tell learners the

story, or write it on the board too. Then give each group a set of five words and a large piece of paper. Some words may appear in more than one set, or you can include words from previous units. Ask each group to create a story using all of its words. Emphasize that although the story can be silly, it should make sense. It is not necessary to put a vocabulary word in every sentence.

Writing Activities

Don't try to correct every mistake learners make. Help them focus on the intent of the activity. Occasionally ask learners to share their writing with a partner and respond to each other's content. This teaches them to communicate ideas effectively.

Class, Partner, and Group Chats

Follow these steps when introducing a Chat:
- Model the entire conversation as learners listen.
- Explain or mime meanings of unfamiliar words.
- Have learners listen and repeat. Then assign one learner a part to recite with you as a model for other learners.
- Have learners practice in pairs. Pair fluent learners with learners who have more difficulty.
- While learners are conversing in pairs or groups, circulate; join as many conversations as possible.

Role-Plays

Going beyond dialogue practice to role-playing reinforces the speaking skills developed in the conversation practice, but to be successful, learners at this level need to be given carefully structured and limited situations. Follow these steps:
- Describe a situation.
- Assign roles to specific learners.
- Have them act out the dialogue.

Encourage learners to think about the beginning and end of the conversation. Put commonly used phrases on the board so that learners can use them for greeting, introducing, thanking, and saying good-bye. After learners finish, ask volunteers to perform role-plays for the class.

Grammar

The student book deliberately uses only essential grammatical terminology. Each Grammar Talk includes example sentences and questions to help learners arrive at the grammar concept deductively.

Follow these steps to introduce a grammar point:
- Read the sentences to learners.

- Ask learners to repeat.
- Discuss the questions as a class. (Suggested answers are included in the teacher notes.)
- Elicit more example sentences and write them on the board or an overhead transparency.
- Discuss any specific issues related to the grammar point and answer learners' questions.

Pronunciation

Many adult ESL series give scant attention to pronunciation, but *English—No Problem!* gives it proper emphasis within an array of integrated skills. Level 1 gives special emphasis to word and sentence stress, which are so vital for good English pronunciation, as well as to long and short vowel sounds.

Numeracy Skills

Give learners the opportunity to practice numeracy skills by having them count the number of like responses for a given question whenever possible.

Dictations

Tell learners to listen three times, the first time for meaning, the second for specific words, and the third to check their work. Have partners check each other's work. Then check together, putting answers on the board.

Customizable Graphic Organizers

The teacher notes indicate when to use one of the Customizable Graphic Organizers in the reproducible masters. Gather Your Thoughts in the unit opener and the Class/Group/Partner Chats usually are done using one of these forms. Use the following procedure to customize these masters:
- Make one copy of the Customizable Graphic Organizer master (chart, idea map, etc.) appropriate for the activity you are doing.
- Fill in the heads as shown in the student book.
- Duplicate enough copies for each learner or group, and distribute them.

After learners complete their graphic organizers, follow these steps:
- Draw a copy of the chart or idea map on the board or an overhead transparency.
- Fill in the appropriate headings.
- Ask learners to read the answers they recorded from their sheets.
- Write the answers on the chart.

Tried-and-True Techniques and Games for Low Beginning Learners

Total Physical Response (TPR)

TPR is a method for teaching language based on the premise that if we physically act out what we are trying to learn we are more likely to remember it than if we only read or hear about it. To adapt TPR to developing literacy skills using *English—No Problem!*, try the following procedure:

- When teaching Picture Dictionary or Vocabulary words, identify words that can be acted out (e.g., *point, write, sign, walk*).
- Demonstrate each word by acting it out as you say it aloud.
- Have learners say the word as you act it out, then as they act it out.
- Use the Vocabulary Card Masters or write the words on flash cards. Show the cards to learners while saying the words. Ask learners to read each card and perform the action.
- Show the cards to learners first in order and then out of order while learners mime their meaning. Speaking is optional.
- Give learners vocabulary cards. As you act out each word, have learners hold up the corresponding card.
- Ask learners to copy the words from the vocabulary cards.

Spelling Dictations

Begin a learning session by doing a spelling dictation of vocabulary from the previous one:

- Select five to seven words for the dictation.
- Number the words and write a short line for each letter in the word on the board or on learners' papers (e.g., 1. _ _ _). Then spell the word (A-S-K) while learners write it on the lines (1. a s k).
- Repeat the spelling as many times as necessary.
- Have learners exchange papers to correct each other's work.
- Review by saying a word and having learners spell it as you or a volunteer writes it on the board. Then ask learners to read the words aloud together.

Jigsaw Reading

Jigsaws help learners practice all language skills and require real communication. This type of activity can be done with any piece of text that can be divided into four sections. Choose text with previously learned vocabulary. You may also want to use an illustration or photo for each section of text. Jigsaws work best when completed in one session. You may also find that they work best when used at the end of a unit.

Follow these steps:

- Prepare questions or a task that requires learners to synthesize information from all sections of the text (e.g., read about four people and decide which you would hire, read about four apartments and decide which you would rent, read about someone's life and identify the most important, happiest, and saddest events).
- Model a jigsaw for learners, walking them through each step.
- Put one section of the text in each corner of the room. Put learners in groups of four. Each person from a group goes to a different corner of the room to read the information there. (If your class does not divide evenly into groups of four, put five learners in some groups. Have two learners look at the same information in those groups.)
- Have each person learn the information in his or her corner. Then have learners return to their original groups to share the information. Learners should not take notes until they are back in their groups.
- Once learners return to their groups, they can complete the task or answer the questions together. Allow them time to read the task or questions and to practice telling their part of the story to one another.

Concentration

Make vocabulary cards for the unit vocabulary words with the definition on one card and the word on another. Model the steps below:

- Keeping words and definitions separate, learners arrange the cards in rows, facedown on the table.
- Taking turns, learners turn over one word card and one definition card.
- If the cards do not match, the learner turns them facedown again in the same place. A learner who finds a matching pair keeps the cards.

When all cards are matched, the learner with the most matches wins.

Twenty Questions

Give one learner a word card and have the others ask *yes/no* questions about the word. As the cardholder answers the questions, the other learners try to guess the word on the card. If after 20 questions no one has guessed correctly, the cardholder reveals the word, and play begins again with another learner holding a second word card. An easier variation of this game focuses on a particular beginning letter. After giving a learner a card, tell the class which letter the word begins with. Then play the guessing game with 20 questions.

Bingo

Use the generic bingo card (Master 1 in the reproducible masters) to review vocabulary for a unit. Duplicate the master and distribute one copy to each learner. Write unit vocabulary words on the board or an overhead transparency. (You will need 25 words.) Ask learners to choose words randomly and write a word in each square. Circulate to be sure they understand that they should write the words in random order.

Give each learner a pile of markers—dried beans, paper clips, pennies, or small squares of card stock. Then call out the words in random order and have learners place a marker on the word if it appears on their bingo card. The first learner to mark a row of five words down, across, or diagonally calls "Bingo!" and wins. Ask winners to read out the words they have marked and tell you the meanings.

Once learners understand the game well, have learners take turns calling out the words.

Warm-Up Unit: Are You Ready? www

Materials for the Unit

- Overhead transparency or photo-copy enlargement of a school registration form
- Monthly calendar
- Weather section of newspaper
- Large clock with movable hands
- Small teaching clocks
- Unlined paper or card stock
- Customizable Master 2
- Generic Assessment Master 6
- Unit Masters 11–15
- Vocabulary Card Masters for the Warm-Up Unit

Are You Ready?

Follow the suggestions on p. 5 for talking about the title.

- Review the four groups of unit goals listed below the title.
- Explain that in this unit learners will focus on registering for an ESL class, dealing with issues of new students, and succeeding as a learner.

Question

Read the question below the arrow.

- Ask learners to look at the infor-mation on their registration papers.
- Using a transparency or enlargement of a school regis-tration form, point to and name key pieces of information it asks for (e.g., name, address, phone number).

Photo

Follow the suggestions on p. 4 for talking about the photo. Ask learn-ers these questions:

- What is Tomas doing?
- Does he have all the information?
- How do you know?

One Step Up

- Ask learners, "What information is missing?"
- Rephrase the question. Ask, "What information does Tomas *not* have?" Shake your head to indicate the negative.

Caption

Read the sentences under the pic-ture. Have learners repeat them.

Ask learners *either/or* and *yes/no* questions like these:

- Is Tomas at school or at work?
- Does the clerk need money?
- Does the clerk need information?

Attention Box

Say the words and point to the cor-responding items in the photo or on the form. This vocabulary should be understood, but learners should not be expected to produce the words at this point.

Think and Talk

Read the questions. Have learners answer aloud together. Write their responses on the board.

Answers

1. Answers will vary.
2. Tomas needs information (to register for class). He doesn't have the information.
3. Follow up *yes* answers by ask-ing, "Where?"

Picture Dictionary

Read the words in the student book. Follow the suggestions on p. 6 for introducing and reinforcing vocabulary.

Follow the suggestions on p. 6 for using vocabulary cards. Use the cards for the words in the Picture Dictionary.

To introduce the days of the week, use a monthly classroom calendar.

- Ask what day it is. Ask what month it is. Repeat these questions every day until learners can answer without hesitation.
- Looking at the calendar, call out a specific date (e.g., August 14) and ask learners to tell you what day of the week it is. Continue doing this until learners can answer without hesitation.
- You can also practice days and dates with the calendar on p. 125.

One Step Down
Practice the numbers 1–30 before doing the calendar activity.

To demonstrate the meaning of *information*, do the following:
- Say, "My *address* is ___." or "My *state* is ___." Write this *information* on the board.
- Ask learners to look at the form on the previous page and tell you Tomas Chacon's address.
- Have learners ask each other information questions (e.g., What is your name? What is your address?).
- Tell learners to be careful about giving Social Security numbers. Do not have them practice giving these numbers to one another.
- To demonstrate *supplies,* put a notebook, pencil, and book on your desk. Tell learners you have your *supplies.* Tell them you are *ready* for school.

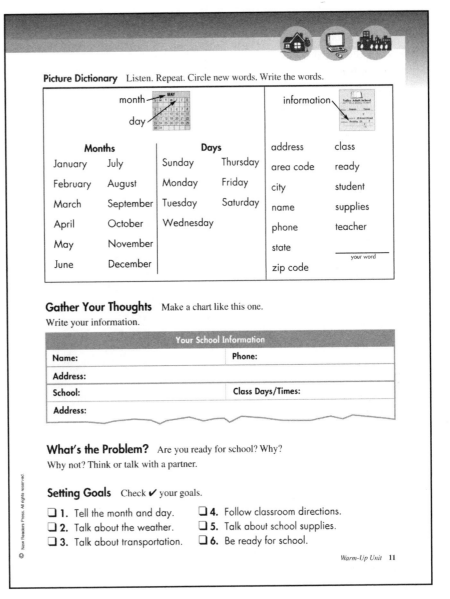

Gather Your Thoughts
Since learners may be unfamiliar with filling in charts, it is best to do this activity as a group.
- Copy the chart on the board or an overhead transparency and demonstrate how to use it.
- Ask one learner for the information for the first blank.
- Continue in the same way, asking a different learner for the information needed for each of the other blanks.

What's the Problem?
Follow the suggestions on p. 5 for identifying and analyzing problems.

- Ask learners if they are ready for school.
- Ask those who say *no* what they need to be ready.

Setting Goals
Follow the suggestions on p. 5 for setting goals. Explain to learners that the listed goals are things to do in English class.

One Step Up
Ask learners with accelerated writing skills to copy the goals they checked into their notebooks. Encourage orally proficient learners to share their goals with the large group.

Lesson 1: I'm Lost! I'm Late! www

- Follow the suggestions on p. 5 for talking about the title. Then point out the lesson objectives listed below it.
- Tell learners this lesson is about *weather, transportation,* and *going to school.* Draw pictures or mime to convey the meaning of these terms.

Attention Box/Idiom Watch

- Write the time the class begins on the board or an overhead transparency (e.g., 7:00 P.M.). Next to it, write *on time.*
- Write a time just before the class begins (e.g., 6:45 P.M.). Next to it, write *early.*
- Write a time shortly after the class begins (e.g., 7:15 P.M.). Next to it, write *late.*
- Point or mime to convey the meaning of *glasses, lost, need, rainy,* and *get up on time.*

This vocabulary should be understood, but learners should not be expected to produce the words at this point.

Reading Tip

Tell learners that pictures will help them understand what they read. Then read the tip aloud.

Photos

Follow the suggestions on p. 4 for talking about the photos. Ask these questions about the left-hand photo:

- Where is Tomas? (Encourage learners to point. Ask *Here?* while pointing to different objects.)
- What is Tomas saying? (Point to his speech bubble.)
- What time is it? (Point to the clocks with the photo.)
- What day is it? (Point to the caption.)
- What's the problem? (Point again to the speech bubble.)

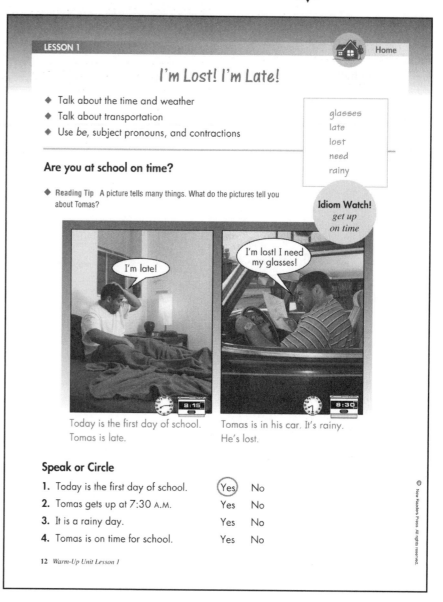

Ask these questions about the right-hand photo:

- Is Tomas in bed or in his car? (Point to Tomas.)
- Is it 8:30 or 12:50? (Point to the clocks with the photo.)
- Is Tomas lost? (Point to the speech bubble.)
- What does he need? (Point to the speech bubble and his face.)
- How is the weather? (Point to the caption.)
- Is Tomas early or late for school? (Point to the clocks with the photo and the speech bubble with the left-hand photo.)

Speak or Circle

This exercise helps learners draw conclusions from what they read.

Follow the suggestions on p. 6 for answering comprehension questions.

<u>Answers</u>
2. No   3. Yes   4. No

<u>One Step Up</u>
After each answer, ask learners, "How do you know?" Commend their attempts to support their answers.

Picture Dictionary

Read the words in the student book. Follow the suggestions on p. 6 for introducing and reinforcing vocabulary.

Follow the suggestions on p. 6 for using vocabulary cards. Use the cards for the words in the Picture Dictionary.

Follow these steps to talk about *weather:*

- Bring in the weather page from a newspaper. Give a copy to each group of learners.
- Point to the weather icons and the weather forecast. Ask learners what days this week will be sunny, rainy, or cloudy.

Follow these steps to talk about *time:*

- Direct learners' attention to the times on the clocks in the book. Explain that we usually say the hour first and then the number of minutes after the hour (e.g., 12:20 = twelve-twenty).
- To practice, use a clock with movable hands. Change the hands and ask learners to tell you the different times using the hour/minutes format.
- Small teaching clocks can also be used. If possible, make these available to each learner or group of learners. Have learners show you each time you call out.
- Continue practicing for several days or until all learners seem comfortable telling time.
- Explain that we use the letters A.M. to show times between midnight and noon and P.M. to show times between noon and midnight.

To talk about *transportation,* tell learners how you get to work. Use one of the expressions from the Picture Dictionary (e.g., I *drive a car* to work.).

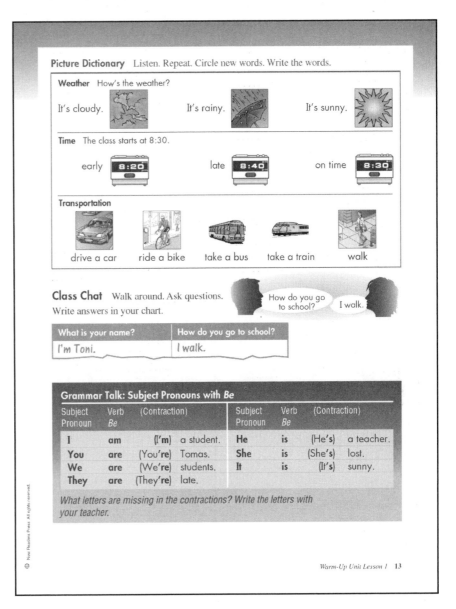

One Step Up

Have individual learners act out words that can be mimed (e.g., *ride a bike, it's rainy*). Have other learners guess the words.

Class Chat

Use Customizable Master 2 (2-Column Chart). Follow the suggestions on p. 7 for customizing and duplicating the master. Make a copy for each learner.

Follow the suggestions on p. 7 for conducting Class Chats.

- Model the questions for learners.
- Model answers by calling on more advanced learners and asking them the questions.

Grammar Talk

Follow the suggestions on p. 7 for introducing the grammar point. Then do the following:

- Point to learners or yourself and make statements, first using a proper noun, then using the appropriate pronoun (e.g., *Maria* is a student. *She* is a student.).
- Focus on the letters that are dropped to make a contraction. For example, write *she is* on the board. Then cross out the *i* and replace it with an apostrophe.

Assign Workbook pp. 4–5, Exercises A–C, now or at any time during the rest of Lesson 1.

Activity A

Before learners do the activity, talk about the picture. Ask learners the questions below and write their answers on the board or an overhead transparency:

- What do you see?
- Is this Raul or a teacher?
- How's the weather?
- What time is it?
- Is he going to school or to work?
- What time is class?
- Is he early?
- Is he on time?
- Is he late?

Answers
2. It is <u>rainy</u>.
3. <u>It</u> is 9:00.
4. Raul is <u>late</u> for school.

One Step Up

If learners write in their books, have them put a check before each word in the box after they use it in a sentence. Point out the check before *is*.

Activity B

Follow the same procedure as in Activity A.

Answers
2. It is <u>sunny</u>.
3. <u>It's</u> 8:20.
4. Raul is <u>early</u> for school.

One Step Up

When learners finish the activity, ask them what is the *same* and what is *different* about the two pictures. These words have not been formally introduced, so model the activity by writing the column heads *Same* and *Different* on the board or an overhead transparency.

Activity C

Model the activity for learners by drawing a picture of yourself going to school. Fill in information about your journey on four blank lines (e.g., *I take a bus. It is sunny.*).

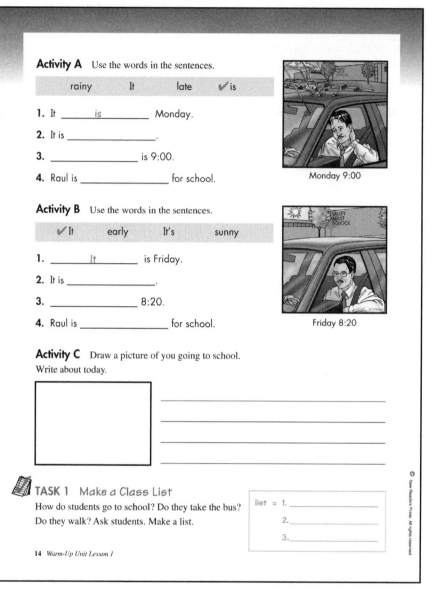

Activity A Use the words in the sentences.

rainy	It	late	✔ is

1. It _____is_____ Monday.
2. It is _____.
3. _____ is 9:00.
4. Raul is _____ for school.

Monday 9:00

Activity B Use the words in the sentences.

✔ It	early	It's	sunny

1. _____It_____ is Friday.
2. It is _____.
3. _____ 8:20.
4. Raul is _____ for school.

Friday 8:20

Activity C Draw a picture of you going to school. Write about today.

TASK 1 Make a Class List
How do students go to school? Do they take the bus? Do they walk? Ask students. Make a list.

list = 1. _____
2. _____
3. _____

14 *Warm-Up Unit Lesson 1*

 Use Unit Master 11 (Grammar: Going to Class) now or at any time during the rest of the unit.

Task 1

On the board or an overhead transparency, list ways learners can get to school (e.g., walk, bike, bus, car, train).

- Ask each learner how he or she goes to school. Tell them to write their names or initials by the relevant word in the list.
- Have learners use the information to create a class list on a large piece of paper.

- Talk about the information on the list. Ask how many learners walk, drive a car, etc.

Assign Workbook p. 5, Exercises D–E.

Lesson 2: Welcome!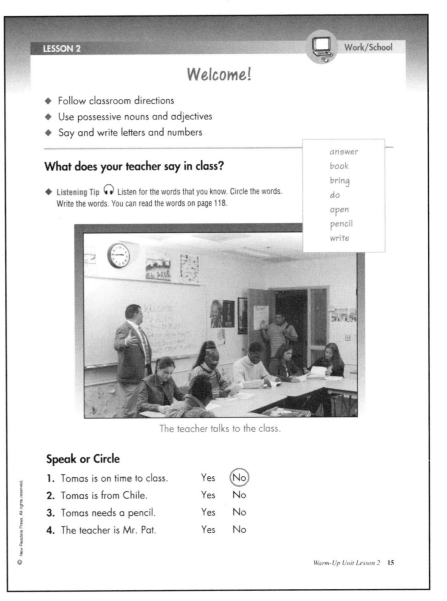

Follow the suggestions on p. 5 for talking about the title. Then point out the lesson objectives listed below it.

- Tell learners that in this lesson they will learn English words for classroom directions.
- They will also learn words to show ownership (*possessive adjectives*) and to say and write the letters of their names in English.

Welcome!

- Ask a learner to leave the room and come back in. As he or she enters, give the learner a big smile and say, "Welcome!"
- Write on the board *welcome = come in.*
- Have several learners go out and re-enter. Each time, say "Welcome" and the learner's name.
- Ask learners, "Does *welcome* mean *hello* or *goodbye?*"

Attention Box

Read the words to learners, pointing or miming to convey meaning. This vocabulary should be understood, but learners should not be expected to produce the words at this point.

Question

Read the question slowly three times. Ask learners for words used often in the classroom (e.g., *welcome, hello, good morning, good-bye,* as well as the direction words in the attention box). Write the words on the board.

Photo

Ask these questions:
- Is it 8:00 or 8:45? *(8:45)*
- Is this Tomas or the teacher? *(Tomas)*
- Is the class at 8:30 or 11:30? *(8:30)*
- Is Tomas late? *(yes)*

LESSON 2

Work/School

Welcome!

- ◆ Follow classroom directions
- ◆ Use possessive nouns and adjectives
- ◆ Say and write letters and numbers

What does your teacher say in class?

- ◆ Listening Tip 🎧 Listen for the words that you know. Circle the words. Write the words. You can read the words on page 118.

answer
book
bring
do
open
pencil
write

The teacher talks to the class.

Speak or Circle

1. Tomas is on time to class.   Yes   (No)
2. Tomas is from Chile.   Yes   No
3. Tomas needs a pencil.   Yes   No
4. The teacher is Mr. Pat.   Yes   No

Listening Tip

Read the tip aloud. Have learners look at the listening script on p. 118.

- Ask learners to circle the words they know or write them in notebooks.
- Have learners say the words they circled. Encourage them to mime the words or otherwise provide meanings.
- Write the words on the board or an overhead transparency.

🎧 Play the audio or read the listening script on p. 118. Follow the suggestions on p. 5 for listening comprehension. Then ask these questions:

- Is the teacher Mr. Tomas or Mr. Allen? *(Mr. Allen)*
- Does Tomas need a pencil or a book? *(a pencil)*
- Does the class do exercise A or exercise B? *(exercise A)*

Speak or Circle

This exercise helps learners understand classroom directions.

Follow the suggestions on p. 6 for comprehension questions.

Answers
2. Yes   3. Yes   4. No

Picture Dictionary

Read the words in the student book. Follow the suggestions on p. 6 for introducing and reinforcing vocabulary.

Follow the suggestions on p. 6 for using vocabulary cards. Use the cards for the words in the Picture Dictionary.

Class Chat

Practice the alphabet by printing learners' first and last names on the board or an overhead transparency.

- Say and then spell each first name several times.
- Ask all learners together to say and spell each name after you.
- Have each learner say and spell his or her own first name.
- Follow the same procedure with learners' last names.

Use Customizable Master 2 (2-Column Chart). Follow the suggestions on p. 7 for customizing the master. Make a copy for each learner.

Follow the suggestions on p. 7 for conducting Class Chats.

Grammar Talk

Follow the suggestions on p. 7 for introducing the grammar point.

Answer
An 's is added to the end of each word.

- Write learners' names in a column on the board.
- To the right of each name, draw a blank line and then write *teacher is (your name)*. Fill in the parentheses with your name. Your sentences may look like this:
  Maria___ teacher is Mr. Allen.
  Tomas___ teacher is Mr. Allen.
- Add 's to the first name in the column. Then have each learner add the 's to his or her name. Read the sentence.
- Read each sentence again. This time, substitute *his* or *her* for

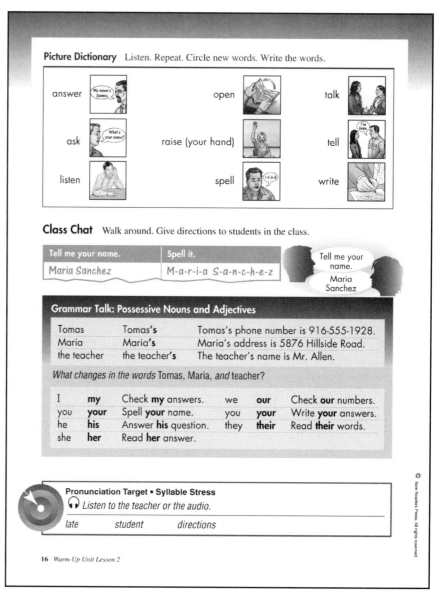

each learner's name and point to the appropriate learner.
- Say the first two names on the list. Have them stand. Say, "*Their* names are ___ and ___." Ask, "What are *their* names?"
- Ask a learner, "What is *your* name?"
- Have volunteers ask the class, "What is *my* name?"
- Have pairs of volunteers ask, "What are *our* names?"

Pronunciation Target

Play the audio or read the words in the student book. Have learners repeat the words.

- Write the words in syllables, underlining the stressed syllable (late, student, directions).
- Clap your hands for each syllable, but clap louder on the stressed syllable. Explain that one part of every word is louder.

Use Unit Master 12 (Phonics: Syllable Stress) now.

Activity A

Before learners begin, point to each card and ask *either/or* and *yes/no* questions like the ones below. Use questions with possessive nouns and pronouns and include the information asked for in the activity.

- Is this a driver's license or a state ID?
- Is this Ramon's card?

<u>Answers</u>
2. Gary's, His
3. Angel's, Her
4. Angel's, Her

One Step Up

Have learners write their partner's information. Ask them to tell you the information about their partners.

Use Unit Master 13 (Grammar: Information Gap) now or at any time during the rest of the unit.

In the US

Tell learners these rules are "good things to do in school in the US."

<u>Extension</u>
Explain that some people like to be called by their first name, while others prefer their last name with the appropriate title (*Miss, Ms., Mrs., Mr., Dr.,* etc.). Tell learners your preference and ask them theirs.

Compare Cultures

Use the world map on pp. 122–123 of the student book to demonstrate the meaning of the word *country.*

Task 2

Give each learner an $8\frac{1}{2} \times 11$ in. piece of unlined paper or card stock. Then ask them to do the following:

- Fold the paper in half crosswise to create a stand-up name card.
- With the paper still folded, write their names beneath the fold on one side of the card.
- Unfold the paper, turn it over, and write their personal information on the back.

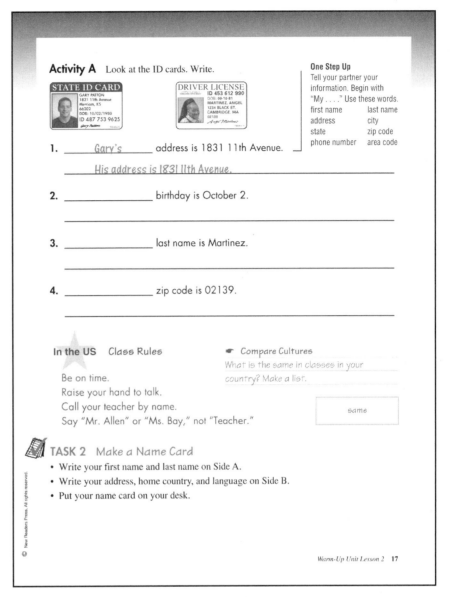

Activity A Look at the ID cards. Write.

STATE ID CARD
GARY PATTON
1831 11th Avenue
Merriam, KS
66202
DOB: 10/02/1980
ID 487 753 9625
Gary Patton

DRIVER LICENSE
ID 453 612 990
DOB: 09-19-81
MARTINEZ, ANGEL
1234 BLACK ST.
CAMBRIDGE MA
02139
Angel Martinez

One Step Up
Tell your partner your information. Begin with "My . . . ." Use these words.
first name   last name
address   city
state   zip code
phone number   area code

1. _____Gary's_____ address is 1831 11th Avenue.
   His address is 1831 11th Avenue.

2. _____ birthday is October 2.
   _____

3. _____ last name is Martinez.
   _____

4. _____ zip code is 02139.
   _____

In the US   Class Rules

Be on time.
Raise your hand to talk.
Call your teacher by name.
Say "Mr. Allen" or "Ms. Bay," not "Teacher."

☛ Compare Cultures
What is the same in classes in your country? Make a list.

| same |

 TASK 2   *Make a Name Card*
- Write your first name and last name on Side A.
- Write your address, home country, and language on Side B.
- Put your name card on your desk.

- Stand the folded cards on their desks with the name facing out.

Ask learners to put the name cards on their desks at the beginning of each learning session. The personal information will be on the inside of the card and will remain private.

<u>One Step Up</u>
Have learners create a class poster showing class rules.

- Write the class rules from the student book on the board or an overhead transparency.
- Have learners suggest additional rules. Add them to the list.
- Model the activity by showing a picture of at least one class rule.

Then pass out magazines to groups of learners and have them find pictures to illustrate the remaining rules.

- Have learners take turns writing the rules and mounting the pictures on a large sheet of paper.

Assign Workbook pp. 6–7, Exercises A–E.

Lesson 3: Money for School! 🌐

Read the title and point out the lesson objectives below it.

- In this lesson, learners will count money.
- They will also make a list of supplies they need at school.

Money for School!

Ask learners why they might need money for school. Model their answers with a situation of your own (e.g., At school, I need money for coffee.).

Attention Box

- Read the words and ask learners to repeat them.
- Use each word in a sentence. Write the sentences on the board.

This vocabulary should be understood, but learners should not be expected to produce the words at this point.

Question

Read the introductory question aloud and write learner responses on the board or an overhead transparency. Be aware that learners may have very limited vocabulary and may not be able to add significantly to the list.

- Circulate, looking at learners' desks for supplies. As you find them, hold up the supplies and ask, "What's this?"
- If no learner can identify a particular supply, say the word yourself and write it on the board.

Photo

Ask these *either/or* and very simple *wh-* questions about the photo:

- What do you see? (Encourage learners to identify as many things as they can.)
- Is this a school or a store?
- Who is this? (Point to Tomas.)
- Who is this? (Point to the clerk, but be aware that learners may have limited vocabulary to answer this question.)

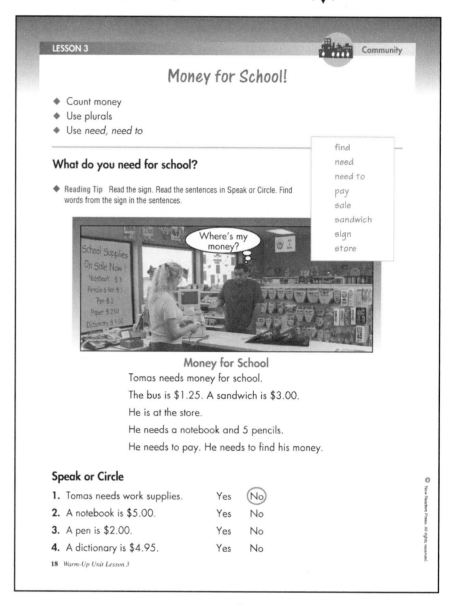

Reading Tip

Read the tip aloud. Then read the Speak or Circle sentences and have learners follow along. Explain that this is the information they need to look for in the picture and text. Follow the suggestions on p. 5 for in-class reading.

- Ask questions about the information on the sign.
- Explain that *on sale* may mean items cost less than they usually do.

Speak or Circle

This exercise helps learners scan for information on a store sign.

- Follow the suggestions on p. 6 for comprehension questions.
- Ask learners to underline or say the sentence or words in the sign that give the correct answer.

Answers
2. No   3. Yes   4. No

Picture Dictionary

Read the words in the student book. Follow the suggestions on p. 6 for introducing and reinforcing vocabulary.

Follow the suggestions on p. 6 for using vocabulary cards. Use the cards for the words in the Picture Dictionary.

To demonstrate the words for various school supplies, find the supplies in the classroom and ask *either/or* questions like these:
- Is this a book or a pencil?
- Is this Tony's dictionary, or is it Shilpa's?

Follow these steps to talk about *money:*
- Model asking the price of something. Hold up various school supplies and ask, "How much?" and "How much is/are ___?"
- Model expressing amounts of money (e.g., two dollars, three ninety-five). Direct learners' attention to the Picture Dictionary box.
- Practice reading the money amounts.

Class Chat

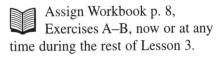 Use Customizable Master 2 2-Column Chart). Follow the suggestions on p. 7 for customizing and duplicating the master. Make a copy for each learner.

Follow the suggestions on p. 7 for conducting Class Chats.

Grammar Talk

Follow the suggestions on p. 7 for introducing the grammar point.
- Write the singular form of some nouns with *regular* plurals on the board or an overhead transparency.
- Explain that most of these words add an *s* when there is more than one.
- Write an *s* on the end of the words you wrote on the board.

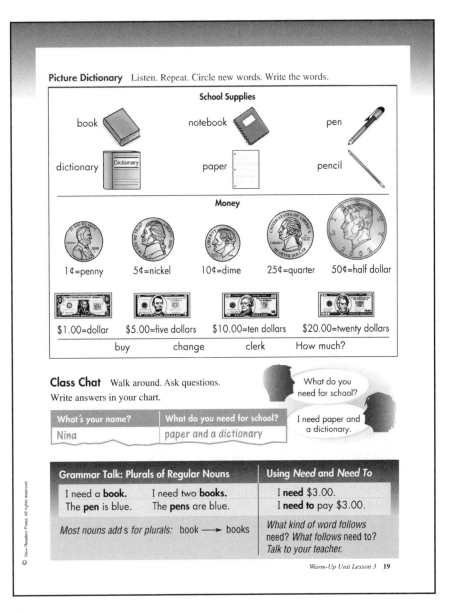

Picture Dictionary   Listen. Repeat. Circle new words. Write the words.

School Supplies

book   notebook   pen
dictionary   paper   pencil

Money

1¢=penny   5¢=nickel   10¢=dime   25¢=quarter   50¢=half dollar

$1.00=dollar $5.00=five dollars $10.00=ten dollars $20.00=twenty dollars

buy   change   clerk   How much?

Class Chat   Walk around. Ask questions. Write answers in your chart.

What do you need for school?

I need paper and a dictionary.

What's your name?	What do you need for school?
Nina	paper and a dictionary

Grammar Talk: Plurals of Regular Nouns		Using *Need* and *Need To*
I need a **book**.	I need two **books**.	I **need** $3.00.
The **pen** is blue.	The **pens** are blue.	I **need to** pay $3.00.
Most nouns add s *for plurals:* book ⟶ books		*What kind of word follows* need? *What follows* need to? *Talk to your teacher.*

Answers

Nouns (words for people, places, and things) follow *need.*

Verbs (action words) follow *need to.*

Extension

Model the verbs in the grammar box by using them in sentences.

Ask learners the questions below. Write their responses on the board or an overhead transparency.
- What do you need?
- What do you need to do?

Assign Workbook p. 8, Exercises A–B, now or at any time during the rest of Lesson 3.

Activity A

 Play the audio or read the listening script below. After learners check their answers, have them call out the answers. Write the answers on the board or an overhead transparency.

Listening Script/Answers
Write the numbers.
1. How much are two notebooks? Two notebooks are $6.00.
2. How much are four pens? Four pens are $8.00.
3. How much are 10 pencils? Ten pencils are $2.00.
4. How much is the paper? The paper is $2.50.

Activity B

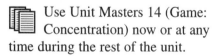 Play the audio or read the listening script below.

Listening Script
Tomas: I need to buy school supplies.
Clerk: What supplies do you need?
Tomas: I need a notebook and a dictionary.
Clerk: English or Spanish-English?
Tomas: Spanish-English, please.
Clerk: That's $8.45.
Tomas: OK. Here's $10.00.
Clerk: And $1.55 in change.

Answers
Column 1 (Tomas): 7, 3, 1, 5
Column 2 (Clerk): 8, 4, 2, 6

Use Unit Masters 14 (Game: Concentration) now or at any time during the rest of the unit.

Assign Workbook p. 9, Exercises C–D, now or at any time during the rest of Lesson 3.

Task 3

Ask pairs of learners to do the following:
- Write school supplies they have.
- Write school supplies they need.
- Tell each other what they have.
- Tell each other what they need.

Activity A Listen to your teacher or the audio. Write the numbers.

1. How much are two notebooks?   Two notebooks are _____.

2. How much are four pens?   Four pens are _____.

3. How much are 10 pencils?   Ten pencils are _____.

4. How much is the paper?   The paper is _____.

Check your answers with your partner. Read the questions and answers with your partner.

One Step Up
Partner A reads the question from Activity A. Partner B reads the answer. Use a pronoun.
A: How much are two notebooks?
B: They are $6.00.

Remember?
$ dollar
¢ cents
$2.00 = two dollars
$3.95 = three ninety-five

Activity B Tomas is at the store. He talks to a clerk. Listen to Tomas and the clerk. Put the conversation in order.

_____ OK. Here's $10.00.
_____ I need a notebook and a dictionary.
__1__ I need to buy school supplies.
_____ Spanish-English, please.

_____ And $1.55 in change.
_____ English or Spanish-English?
__2__ What supplies do you need?
_____ That's $8.45.

Read the conversation with your partner. Check your work.

TASK 3 *Get Ready to Buy School Supplies*
Think about supplies you need for school. What do you have? What do you need? Make a list. Talk to your partner. How are your lists the same? How are they different?

different = not the same

- Circle the items on their own *Have* and *Need* lists that are also on their partner's lists.

On the board or an overhead transparency, write the headings *Have* and *Need*.
- Have learners call out things they have and things they need.
- Ask each learner to write the items he or she calls out on the group list.

Review Unit Skills
Follow the suggestions on p. 8 for games and activities to review the vocabulary and grammar in this unit.

Warm-Up Unit Project

Learners plan a new student booklet.

Get Ready

Tell learners they are going to make a booklet for new learners. Divide the class into four groups and assign the work:
- Group 1: School Information
- Group 2: Parking Information (if applicable)
- Group 3: Classroom Directions
- Group 4: Supplies for School

Do the Work

Tell Group 1 to write this information about their school:
- School name
- School address
- School phone number
- Teacher's name

Tell Group 2 to find and write the following information:
- Places to park
- Street names
- Cost of parking
- How many hours cars can remain there

Tell Group 3 to do the following:
- Write classroom directions. (Have learners refer to the Picture Dictionary on p. 16.)
- Write the directions on a separate sheet of paper and make or find a picture to illustrate them.

Tell Group 4 to write the following:
- School supplies they will need for class
- The name of a store where they can buy the supplies
- The store's address

Present Your Project

When groups present their information to the class, encourage active listening by asking learners questions about the presentations.

Assessment

Use Generic Assessment Master 6 (Oral Communication Rubric) to evaluate the presentations.

WARM-UP Unit Project

Make a New Student Booklet

Do these things to plan a New Student Booklet.

Get Ready

Work in four groups.
- **Group 1:** Find the information about the school. What is the name of the school, the address, phone number, teacher's name, room number? What are the days and hours of the class? What are the school holidays?
- **Group 2:** Is there parking at the school? On the street? How long can you park there?
- **Group 3:** What does a new student need to know in class? Write classroom directions. Use pictures and words.
- **Group 4:** List supplies. What do new students need? Where can students get the supplies? List stores and addresses.

> holiday
> parking
> store

Do the Work

Use the paper from your teacher.
- **Group 1:** Write the name, address, phone number, and other information about your school.
- **Group 2:** Write the places to park at the school. Write the streets where you can park.
- **Group 3:** Write classroom directions for new students.
- **Group 4:** List the supplies that students need to buy.

Present Your Project

Talk to the class about your information. Make copies of the New Student Booklet.

Technology Extra
Make a cover for your booklet on the computer.

Warm-Up Unit Project **21**

Technology Extra

Ask learners to type the title *New Student Information* on the cover page. If possible, have them add a graphic.

Extension

Have learners make copies of the booklet for new students who enter the class throughout the year.

Assign Workbook p. 10 (Check Your Progress). Go over the self-assessment with learners. Be sure they understand how to complete it, especially the first part.
- Explain that the numbers represent a rating scale, with *1* being the lowest score and *5* being the highest.
- If learners have difficulty using the scale, explain that a *2* rating means "not very well, but improving" and that a *4* rating means "fairly well."

Use Unit Master 15 (Unit Checkup/Review) whenever you complete this unit.

Unit 1: My Life Is Changing! 🌐

Materials for the Unit

- A pair of pictures that shows change (e.g., in a child, a pet, a house, a town)
- A photo of you and your family
- Wall map of the world (optional)
- Classroom calendar
- A sample job application form
- Customizable Masters 3 and 4
- Generic Assessment Masters 6, 8, and 9
- Unit Masters 16–22
- Vocabulary Card Masters for Unit 1

Self-Assessment

Give each learner a copy of the Speaking and Listening Self-Check and the Writing and Reading Self-Check (Generic Assessment Masters 8–9). Go over the assessment together. The completed form will become part of each learner's portfolio.

My Life Is Changing!

Follow the suggestions on p. 5 for talking about the title. Then read the four groups of unit goals below the title.

- Tell learners that this unit is about finding a place to live as well as looking for a job.
- To demonstrate the concept of *change,* show learners a pair of pictures that represent change (e.g., in a child, a pet, a house, a town).

Question

Read the question below the arrow.

- Define *relatives* for learners by pointing to Nassim and saying, "Her name is Nassim." Point to the other people in the photo and say, "They are her relatives."
- Display a photo of you and your family. Say, "This is my family. They are my *relatives.*"

Photo

Follow the suggestions on p. 4

for talking about the photo. Then ask these questions:

- How many people are in Nassim's family?
- Is the house big or small?
- What is Nassim saying?
- Is Nassim reading a book or a letter?

Attention Box

- Call attention to the definition of *parents.* Tell learners, "My mother is ___ (name). My father is ___. My parents are ___ and ___."
- Then ask several volunteers these questions:
  Who is your mother?

Who is your father?
Then say, "Your parents are ___ and ___."

This vocabulary should be understood, but learners should not be expected to produce the words at this point.

Think and Talk

Answers
1. Answers will vary. Write learners' responses on the board.
2. A possible answer: Nassim's parents want to live with her. Her home is small.
3. Answers will vary.
4. Answers will vary.

Picture Dictionary

Read the words in the student book. Follow the suggestions on p. 6 for introducing and reinforcing vocabulary.

Act out the words that can be mimed. Have learners guess the words.

Follow the suggestions on p. 6 for using vocabulary cards. Use the cards for the words in the Picture Dictionary.

- Focus learners' attention on the words *home* and *country*. Tell them that their *home country* is the country they came from.
- Reinforce this by saying, "My *home country* is ____."

<u>Extension</u>

- Ask each learner, "What is your home country?" Repeat the one-word answer by saying, "____'s home country is ____."
- Direct learner's attention to a world map, either a large one on the wall or the one on pp. 122–123 of the student book, to help explain the concept *home country*.

Gather Your Thoughts

Make a copy of Customizable Master 3 (3-Column Chart). Follow the suggestions on p. 7 for customizing and duplicating the master. Make a copy for each learner. Make a class chart on the board or an overhead transparency.

Model the activity by asking these questions:

- Do you live in an apartment or a house?
- In your home country, did you live in an apartment or a house?

Before having learners complete their charts, record one learner's answers to these questions on the class chart.

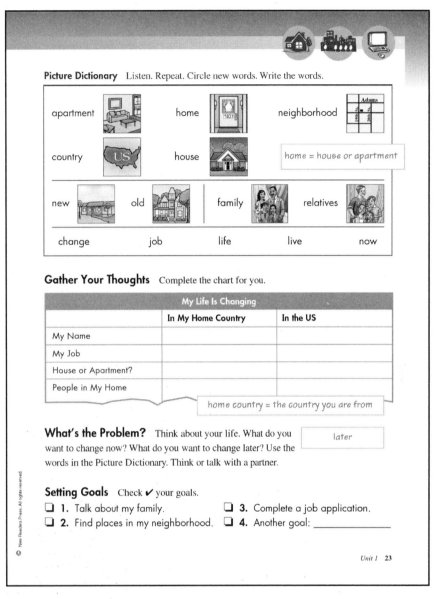

<u>Extension</u>

Tally the results of the question, "Do you live in a house or an apartment?" on the board. Count aloud as you tally. Read out the totals. Tally whenever possible during these early units to provide practice with number words.

What's the Problem?

Follow the suggestions on p. 5 for identifying and analyzing problems.

After reviewing the words in the Picture Dictionary, have learners look at their completed charts. Ask:

- What do you want to change now?
- What do you want to change later?

- If you live in an apartment, do you (someday) want to live in a house?
- Does anyone want to change names? Jobs?

Setting Goals

Follow the suggestions on p. 5 for setting goals.

Lesson 1: A Family Problem www

Read the title and point out the lesson objectives below it.

- Tell learners that in this lesson they will talk about their families.
- Follow the suggestions on p. 5 for talking about titles.

Question

- Write the introductory question on the board or an overhead transparency. Give a few examples from your own life of how you help your family.
- Ask learners the question. Write some of their answers on the board or an overhead transparency.

Keep in mind that learners can formulate only the most basic answers in English at this point. Commend them for their efforts.

Reading Tip

- Remind learners that Reading Tips tell them how to be good readers in English.
- Read the tip aloud. Tell learners that you will read the story aloud and they will listen. Then have them read the story again by themselves.

Follow these steps to complete the reading exercise:

- Have learners put their pencils down and their dictionaries away.
- Ask learners to look at the photo. Ask what they see. *(Nassim is thinking about her apartment.)*
- Read the story aloud slowly. Have learners focus on listening.
- Read the *true/false* statements in the Speak or Circle exercise aloud; do not give the answers. Pause for learners to think about each answer and look for it in the story, but do not ask them to say the answer aloud.
- Read the story and the statements again, as learners read along silently.

- Have learners read aloud with you the third time.

Speak or Circle

This exercise focuses learners on finding the main idea in a reading.

After completing the reading activity above, review the *true/false* statements together one more time. Call on volunteers to respond.

<u>Answers</u>
1. False
2. False
3. True

Picture Dictionary

Read the words in the student book. Follow the suggestions on p. 6 for introducing and reinforcing vocabulary.

Follow the suggestions on p. 6 for using vocabulary cards. Use the cards for the words in the Picture Dictionary.

Assign Workbook p. 11, Exercise A, now or at any time during the rest of Lesson 1.

Class Chat

Use Customizable Master 4 (4-Column Chart). Follow the suggestions on p. 7 for customizing and duplicating the master. Make a copy for each learner.

Follow the suggestions on p. 7 for conducting Class Chats.

Assign Workbook p. 11, Exercises B–C, now or at any time during the rest of Lesson 1.

Grammar Talk

Follow the suggestions on p. 7 for introducing the grammar point.

Using sentence strips, follow these steps:

- Write *I am not his brother.* on a sentence strip.
- Cut the strip apart after the word *I* and between the *a* and *m* in *am.*
- Tape the sentence pieces to the board in order and read the sentence aloud.
- Write an apostrophe on a blank piece of sentence strip.
- Remove the *a* from the sentence and insert the apostrophe. Read the sentence again and have learners repeat.
- Take the apostrophe out, put the *a* back in, and ask a learner to read it aloud.
- Take the *a* out, put the apostrophe back in, and have the same learner read it.
- Ask a learner, "What letter is missing?" *(a)*

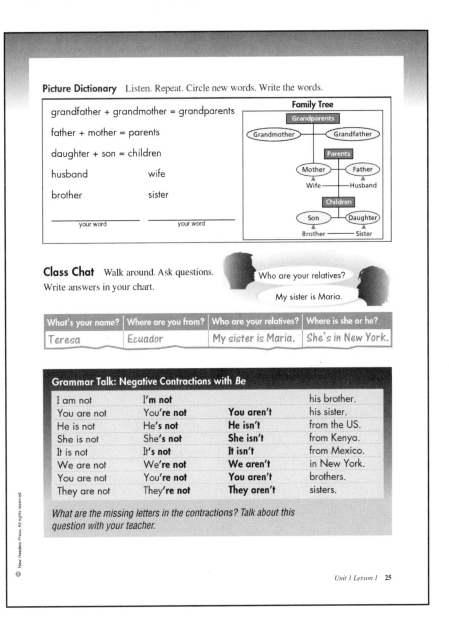

Repeat this procedure with all the sentences.

Answers

I'm	*a*	We're	*a*
You're	*a*	They're	*a*
He's	*i*	aren't	*o*
She's	*i*	isn't	*o*
It's	*i*		

Extension

- Write five short sentences with forms of the verb *be* on the board or an overhead transparency.
- Have learners change the long forms to contractions, first saying the sentence aloud and then writing it next to the corresponding original sentence.

Activity A

- Ask learners to look at the photos.
- Ask, "Who are these people?" To check for understanding, ask questions about the individuals pictured (e.g., How old are they? Are they sons or daughters?).
- Have learners work in pairs to answer the questions. Review as a class.

Answers

1. No 4. Yes
2. Yes 5. Yes
3. No

One Step Up

- Have learners change the Activity A questions to statements.
- Ask a learner to read his or her new sentence while another learner writes it on the board.
- Check for legibility and correct capitalization and punctuation.

Activity B

Model how to complete the chart for the learners. Then do the following:

- Have learners tell who they are in their families (e.g., I am a son and a husband.).
- Ask them to write in their charts all of the information that group members provide orally.
- Point out the speech bubble in the student book and say, "Talk with people in your group."
- Have learners use their charts to tell their groups two things about another group member—what he or she *isn't* (e.g., *Julie isn't a grandmother.*) and what he or she *is* (e.g., *She's a mother.*).

Extension

When everyone has had a turn in his or her group, call on volunteers to give the same responses for all learners.

📖 Assign Workbook p. 12, Exercises D–E, now or at any time during the rest of Lesson 1.

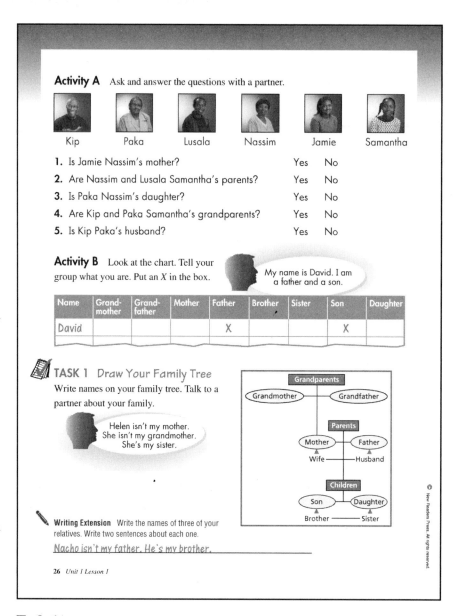

Task 1

Refer learners to the family tree in the Picture Dictionary on p. 25.

- Using the tree as an example, have learners create their own family tree on a piece of paper or in their notebooks.
- Model the activity by drawing your family tree on the board or an overhead transparency. Point out to learners that their trees probably will look different from the tree in the book.

Writing Extension

Have learners select three people from their family tree. Ask them to write two sentences about each.

Lesson 2: The Neighborhood 🌐

Read the title aloud. Then point out the lesson objectives listed below it.

- Explain that in this lesson learners will learn where people live.
- They will also draw a map of the area where they live.

The Neighborhood

To convey the meaning of *neighborhood,* do the following:

- Draw a house on the board or an overhead transparency. Say, "This is my house." Then draw other houses, a store, and a school. Circle everything and say, "This is my *neighborhood.*"
- Draw several circles near the previous one. In each, write *neighborhood* or the names of actual neighborhoods near your school. Then draw a large circle around all the *neighborhood* circles and say, "This is ____ (name of town or city)."

Question

Read the introductory question aloud. Then do the following:

- Write *worry = feel bad* on the board.
- Tell learners something you worry about (e.g., "I worry about my family.").
- Ask learners, "What do you worry about?" Record their answers on an idea map.

Attention Box

Say each word and have the learners repeat it.

- Draw or show a picture for *bedroom.*
- To convey the meaning of *expensive,* show two things with different values (e.g., a pencil and a TV). Circle the TV and say *expensive.* Circle the pencil and say *not expensive.*
- Explain *part-time* in the context of work or study (e.g., "I work two hours a day. I work part-time.").

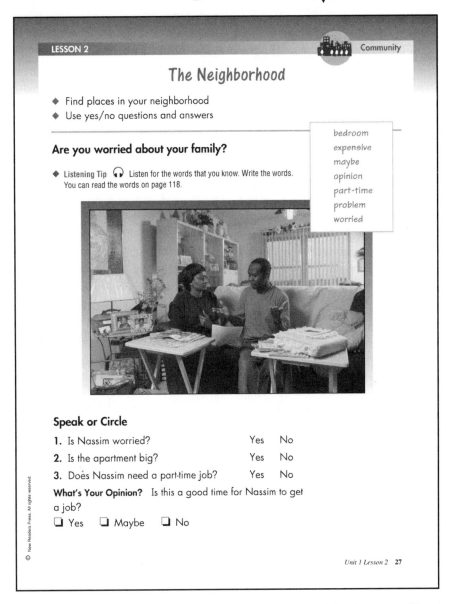

- Dramatize *problem* and *worried* (e.g., furrowed brow, frown).

This vocabulary should be understood, but learners should not be expected to produce the words at this point.

Photo

Point out that the apartment is small for four people (Nassim, her husband, and two children), and very small for six people (Nassim's family and her parents).

Listening Tip

Tell learners to listen and raise their hands when they hear a word they know. Explain that you will write the word when you see hands raised.

🎧 Play the audio or read the listening script on p. 118. Follow the suggestions on p. 5 for listening comprehension.

Speak or Circle

This exercise helps learners listen for the main idea.

Answers
1. Yes   2. No   3. Yes

Picture Dictionary

Read the words in the student book. Follow the suggestions on p. 6 for introducing and reinforcing vocabulary.

Follow the suggestions on p. 6 for using vocabulary cards. Use the cards for the words in the Picture Dictionary.

- Ask learners to read the questions below the Picture Dictionary box.
- Tell learners that with street names alone, they use *on,* but when house numbers are present, they use *at.* Write a few examples on the board (e.g., *on Main Street, at 253 Main Street*).

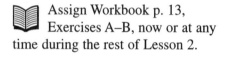 Assign Workbook p. 13, Exercises A–B, now or at any time during the rest of Lesson 2.

Partner Chat

Use Customizable Master 4 (4-Column Chart). Follow the suggestions on p. 7 for customizing and duplicating the master. Make a copy for each learner.

<u>One Step Down</u>

- Have learners provide only one- or two-word answers rather than complete sentences.
- Omit the fourth column in the chart and focus only on names and street addresses.

Grammar Talk

Follow the suggestions on p. 7 for introducing the grammar point. Then ask learners to look at the picture on p. 22 of their books.

- Tell learners, "Nassim is in her apartment." Then ask, "Is Nassim in her apartment?" Learners will answer, "Yes." Reinforce the grammar point by saying, "Yes, she is."
- Write the statement and question on the board; read them again.
- Using arrows, show learners that in the question *is* changes position and stands in front of *Nassim.*

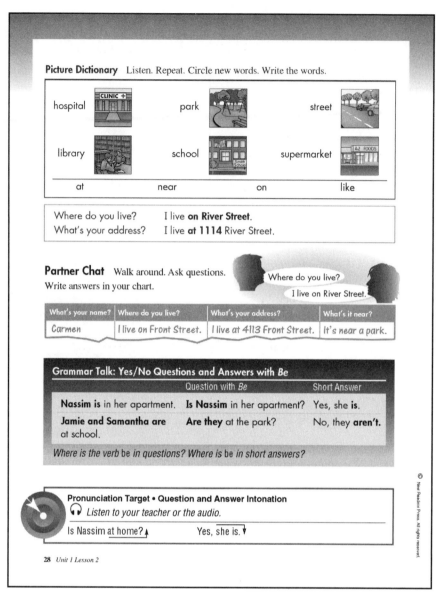

Picture Dictionary   Listen. Repeat. Circle new words. Write the words.

hospital / park / street
library / school / supermarket

at   near   on   like

Where do you live?   I live **on River Street**.
What's your address?   I live **at 1114** River Street.

Partner Chat   Walk around. Ask questions. Write answers in your chart.

Where do you live?
I live on River Street.

What's your name?	Where do you live?	What's your address?	What's it near?
Carmen	I live on Front Street.	I live at 4113 Front Street.	It's near a park.

Grammar Talk: Yes/No Questions and Answers with *Be*

	Question with *Be*	Short Answer
Nassim is in her apartment.	**Is Nassim** in her apartment?	Yes, she **is**.
Jamie and Samantha are at school.	**Are they** at the park?	No, they **aren't**.

Where is the verb be *in questions? Where is* be *in short answers?*

Pronunciation Target • Question and Answer Intonation

🎧 *Listen to your teacher or the audio.*

Is Nassim at home? ↗   Yes, she is. ↘

28   *Unit 1 Lesson 2*

Follow this procedure with the other statement and question.

<u>Answers</u>

- In questions, the verb *be* is at or near the beginning of the question.
- In short answers, the verb *be* is at the end of the sentence.

Pronunciation Target

🎧 Play the audio or read the sentences. Then follow these steps:

- Repeat the question and write it on the board.
- Draw a curved arrow over the question so that the arrow points

up to demonstrate the rising intonation of the question. Have learners repeat the question.

- Repeat this procedure with the answer. This time, draw an arrow pointing down.
- Practice the intonation pattern with other *yes/no* questions using *be.*

Use Unit Masters 16 (Game: Guess the Sentence) and 17 (Pronunciation: Questions and Answers) now or at any time during the rest of the unit.

Activity A

- Model asking *yes/no* questions and providing short answers.
- After learners ask and answer with a partner, have volunteers write some of their questions and answers on the board.

Activity B

Ask learners these questions:
- Where do you see flyers?
- What kinds of information do you find on flyers?

Read the flyer aloud. Then follow these steps:
- Review the word *expensive*.
- Refer to the last sentence of the conversation and explain the meaning of *I don't know*.
- Write the first sentence on the board, leaving a blank line for *apartment*. Ask learners, "What word goes here?" Write *apartment* on the blank line.

Answers
2. neighborhood 5. near
3. park 6. expensive
4. school

One Step Up

Have partners exchange notebooks to check their work.

Use Unit Master 18 (Grammar: The Neighborhood) now or at any time during the rest of the unit.

Assign Workbook p. 14, Exercise C, now or at any time during the rest of Lesson 2.

Attention Box

The words *map* and *building* should be understood, but learners should not be expected to produce them at this point.
- Refer learners to the US and world maps on pp. 121–123 in their books.
- Ask learners, "Do you use maps?" Have them hold up their

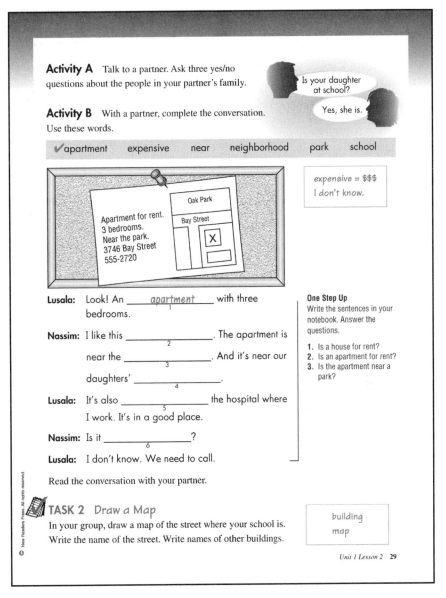

Activity A Talk to a partner. Ask three yes/no questions about the people in your partner's family.

Is your daughter at school?

Yes, she is.

Activity B With a partner, complete the conversation. Use these words.

✓apartment   expensive   near   neighborhood   park   school

expensive = $$$
I don't know.

Apartment for rent.
3 bedrooms.
Near the park.
3746 Bay Street
555-2720

Oak Park
Bay Street
X

Lusala: Look! An ____apartment____ with three bedrooms.
                                          1

Nassim: I like this _____. The apartment is
                                    2
              near the _____. And it's near our
                                  3
              daughters' _____.
                                    4

Lusala: It's also _____ the hospital where
                                  5
              I work. It's in a good place.

Nassim: Is it _____?
                          6

Lusala: I don't know. We need to call.

Read the conversation with your partner.

One Step Up
Write the sentences in your notebook. Answer the questions.

1. Is a house for rent?
2. Is an apartment for rent?
3. Is the apartment near a park?

TASK 2 Draw a Map
In your group, draw a map of the street where your school is. Write the name of the street. Write names of other buildings.

building
map

yes/no cards (see p. 4). Ask, "When?"

Task 2

On the board, draw a simple picture of the school or building where you hold class. Draw a line for the street nearest the school and label it.
- Have learners draw a map of the same street, adding as much information as possible (e.g., houses, stores, street signs, bus stops).
- When they finish, review the maps together. Circulate; suggest what places should be labeled on the maps and where they should be placed.

Extension

- Have each learner draw a map of his or her neighborhood.
- Provide a short list of words for neighborhood places (e.g., *gas station, store*) so that learners can label these on their maps.

One Step Up

Using a large sheet of paper, have learners work together to create a class map of the street where their school is. Tell them to talk together to be sure they have put the buildings on the map correctly.

 Assign Workbook p. 14, Exercise D.

Lesson 3: Jobs, Jobs, Jobs!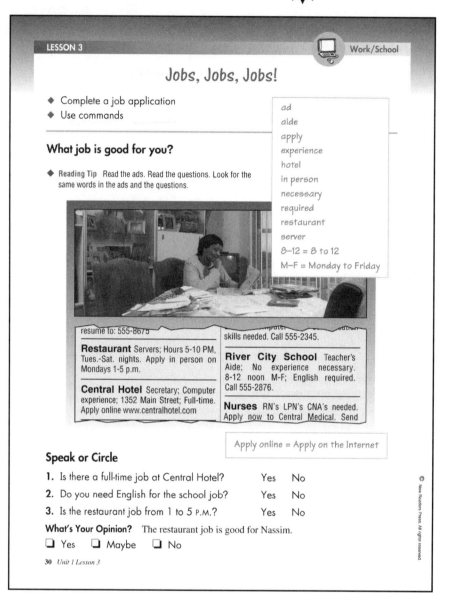

Read the title and point out the lesson objectives below it.
- Ask learners these questions:
  Do you have a job?
  Do you know how to find a job?
- Tell learners that in this lesson they will learn about finding a job. They also will write a name on a job application form.

Question

Read the introductory question above the photo aloud.

Photo

Ask these questions about the photo:
- What do you see?
- Is Nassim reading a book or a newspaper?
- What is she looking for?

Reading Tip

Read the tip aloud; then do the following:
- Read the questions at the bottom of the page aloud, but don't have learners answer.
- Ask learners to underline or write in their notebooks key words in the questions (*job, hotel, full-time, English, school, restaurant, 1 to 5 P.M.*)

Direct learners' attention to the ads. Ask these questions:
- Which ad is from a *hotel?* (Have learners circle it or point to it as you circulate).
- Do you see the word *job* in the ad? (No, but they may be able to identify *secretary* as a job. Have them circle that word.)
- Do you see the word *full-time?* (Have learners circle or point. To help them with comprehension, tell them *full-time* usually means *35–40 hours each week.*)

Ask them to answer the first question. Then repeat this procedure for questions 2 and 3.

LESSON 3 · Work/School

Jobs, Jobs, Jobs!

◆ Complete a job application
◆ Use commands

ad
aide
apply
experience
hotel
in person
necessary
required
restaurant
server
8–12 = 8 to 12
M–F = Monday to Friday

What job is good for you?

◆ Reading Tip   Read the ads. Read the questions. Look for the same words in the ads and the questions.

resume to: 555-8675 ... skills needed. Call 555-2345.

Restaurant Servers; Hours 5-10 PM, Tues.-Sat. nights. Apply in person on Mondays 1-5 p.m.

River City School Teacher's Aide; No experience necessary. 8-12 noon M-F; English required. Call 555-2876.

Central Hotel Secretary; Computer experience; 1352 Main Street; Full-time. Apply online www.centralhotel.com

Nurses RN's LPN's CNA's needed. Apply now to Central Medical. Send

Apply online = Apply on the Internet

Speak or Circle

1. Is there a full-time job at Central Hotel?   Yes   No
2. Do you need English for the school job?   Yes   No
3. Is the restaurant job from 1 to 5 P.M.?   Yes   No

What's Your Opinion?   The restaurant job is good for Nassim.
☐ Yes   ☐ Maybe   ☐ No

Speak or Circle

This exercise helps learners scan job ads for information in English.
- Have volunteers read the questions and answers.
- Refer to the ads again to show where the information was found.

Answers
1. Yes
2. Yes
3. No (You apply from 1 to 5 P.M. on Monday, but the job is from 5 to 10 P.M.)

What's Your Opinion?

Follow the suggestions on p. 6 for comprehension questions.

- Read the three options aloud.
- Ask learners to express their opinions by raising their hands when they hear the option they agree with.

One Step Up

Ask learners to tell why their answer is correct (e.g., *No. Night work.*).

Vocabulary

Read the words in the student book. Follow the suggestions on p. 6 for introducing and reinforcing vocabulary.

Follow the suggestions on p. 6 for using vocabulary cards. Use the cards for the words in the Vocabulary box.

- To convey the meaning of *ad,* refer to the ads on the previous page of the student book.
- For *application,* show learners a simple job application. Point out *experience* and *education* on the application. Then write these definitions on the board
  experience = your jobs
  education = your classes/schools
- Mime a job interview.
- Demonstrate the words *call, circle, print,* and *sign.*
- Point out the blank line at the bottom of the vocabulary box. Brainstorm related new words together (e.g., *job, work, write, talk, phone, apply, online*).

Class Chat

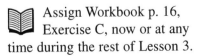 Use Customizable Master 3 (3-Column Chart). Follow the suggestions on p. 7 for customizing and duplicating the master.

Follow suggestions on p. 7 for conducting Class Chats.

- Before learners begin, introduce the word *homemaker* so they can use it in their answers.
- Explain the verb phrase *learn about.* Use the example of a newspaper as one place where people can *learn about* different things (e.g., jobs, world news, prices of clothing and food).

Assign Workbook p. 15, Exercises A–B, now or at any time during the rest of Lesson 3.

Grammar Talk

Follow the suggestions on p. 7 for introducing the grammar point.

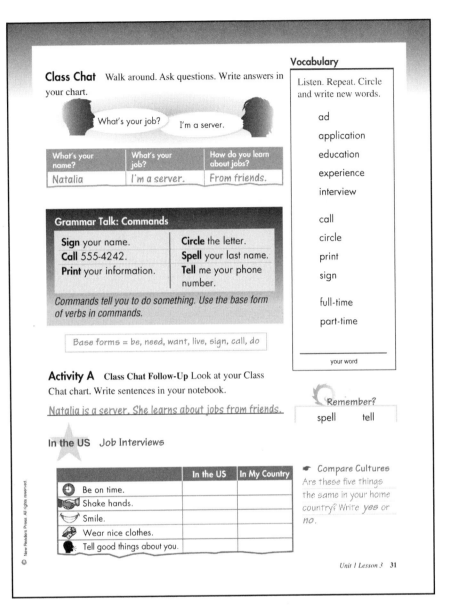

- Read the first sentence aloud. Then sign your name.
- Repeat this procedure for the remaining sentences, each time either performing the command or miming it.

Use Unit Master 19 (Grammar: Commands) now or at any time during the rest of the unit.

Assign Workbook p. 16, Exercise C, now or at any time during the rest of Lesson 3.

In the US

- Read the first column of the chart. Have learners repeat each line after you.

- Ask *yes/no* questions about some of the items (e.g., Are you *on time* for an interview?).
- Model the last item by saying two good things about yourself (e.g., I am a good worker. I am always on time.). Then call on a few learners to do the same.

Compare Cultures

Have learners compare the items in the chart with customs in their home countries. Ask them to indicate whether customs are the same by writing *yes* or *no* in their charts.

Assign Workbook p. 16, Exercises D–E, now or at any time during the rest of Lesson 3.

Activity B

- Go over each section of the application with learners in detail.
- If learners have difficulty completing the activity, ask them to review the Grammar Talk on the previous page.

Answers
2. Circle
3. Sign
4. List

One Step Up

- Have learners write five questions in their notebooks about Nassim's job application.
- Ask learners to exchange notebooks and write answers to their partners' questions.
- Have partners check each other's work.

Task 3

Tell learners to look at the information in Activity B if they need help with this task.

- Model the task with a volunteer who takes the part of Nassim.
- Ask partners to interview each other using commands. During the interview, they should write the information about their partner in their notebooks.
- Have learners exchange papers, check each other's work, and make corrections as needed. Tell them they will use this information to complete the Unit Project.

 Use Unit Master 20 (Thinking Skill: Solving Problems).

Review Unit Skills
See p. 8 for suggestions on games and activities to review the unit vocabulary and grammar.

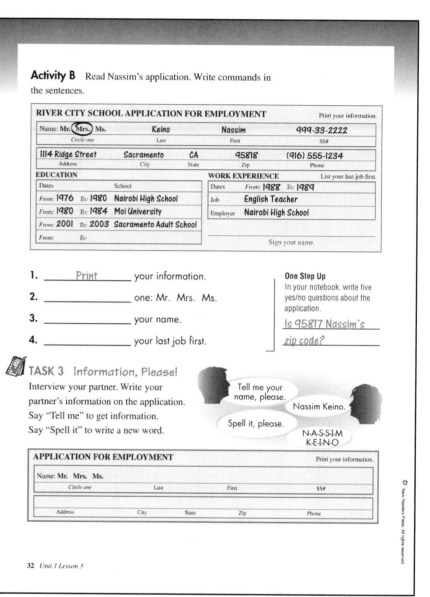

Activity B Read Nassim's application. Write commands in the sentences.

RIVER CITY SCHOOL APPLICATION FOR EMPLOYMENT   Print your information.

| Name: Mr. (Mrs.) Ms. | Keino | Nassim | 999-33-2222 |
| Circle one | Last | First | SS# |

| 1114 Ridge Street | Sacramento | CA | 95818 | (916) 555-1234 |
| Address | City | State | Zip | Phone |

EDUCATION

Dates	School
From: 1976 To: 1980	Nairobi High School
From: 1980 To: 1984	Moi University
From: 2001 To: 2003	Sacramento Adult School
From: To:	

WORK EXPERIENCE   List your last job first.

Dates	From: 1988 To: 1989
Job	English Teacher
Employer	Nairobi High School

Sign your name.

1. ____Print____ your information.

2. _____ one: Mr. Mrs. Ms.

3. _____ your name.

4. _____ your last job first.

One Step Up
In your notebook, write five yes/no questions about the application.

Is 95817 Nassim's
zip code?

TASK 3 Information, Please!
Interview your partner. Write your partner's information on the application. Say "Tell me" to get information. Say "Spell it" to write a new word.

Tell me your name, please.

Nassim Keino.

Spell it, please.

N-A-S-S-I-M
K-E-I-N-O

APPLICATION FOR EMPLOYMENT   Print your information.

Name: Mr. Mrs. Ms.			
Circle one	Last	First	SS#
Address	City	State	Zip	Phone

Unit 1 Project

Learners will make a personal information sheet to use for schools where they want to study and jobs they want to apply for.

Get Ready

Use Unit Master 21 (Unit 1 Project: Writing Personal Information). Distribute a copy to each learner.

Ask learners to do the following:
- Think about their education and work experience.
- Bring information to class about their current job, any past jobs, and their education.

Encourage learners to also think about the skills they use at home and at school.
- Homemakers do many things that are important for jobs outside the home (e.g., manage time and money, plan, make schedules, help other people learn).
- Students do many things that are important for jobs outside of school (e.g., write, work in teams, speak to groups).

Brainstorm other skills learners might have.

Do the Work
- Have learners complete their Personal Information Sheets individually.
- For help with dates, have them refer to a classroom calendar or p. 125.
- If they do not remember the exact dates of a job or school enrollment, have them write just the month and year.

Present Your Project
- Divide learners into small groups. Ask them to practice their presentations in front of their groups before presenting to the whole class.
- When learners present for the larger group, model active listening by asking questions.

- Encourage learners to ask one another questions as well.

Assessment

Use Generic Assessment Master 6 (Oral Communication Rubric) to evaluate the presentations.

One Step Up

If learners are unable to acquire their own sample job applications, obtain one and make copies. Encourage learners to bring the completed copies to class so you can check their work.

Writing Extension

Have volunteers write sentences on the board. Review the sentences with all learners.

Technology Extra

Help learners with photocopying their information sheets.

Assign Workbook p. 17 (Check Your Progress).

Use Unit Master 22 (Unit Checkup/Review) whenever you complete this unit.

UNIT 1 PROJECT

Writing Personal Information

Plan, write, and present your Personal Information Sheet.

Get Ready

What do you need? Driver's license? Passport? Social Security card? Find your information.

Do the Work

Complete the Personal Information Sheet from your teacher. Check your work. Is it correct?

Personal Information Sheet
Name:
Address:
Phone:
What country are you from?
What languages do you speak?
Education
Work Experience

 business
 keep

Present Your Project

Talk to your group or the class about your Personal Information Sheet.
- Where do you live?
- What country are you from?
- What work experience do you have?

One Step Up
Go to a business. Ask for an application. Complete the application. Use your Personal Information Sheet. Give the application to your teacher to check your work.

✏️ **Writing Extension** Use your Personal Information Sheet. Write five sentences.
My name is Julia Gutierrez. I live at 1036 East Street. I live in Washington. I am from Mexico. I speak Spanish and English.

💾🖥 **Technology Extra**
Photocopy your Personal Information Sheet. Keep one copy with you. Keep one copy at home.

Unit 1 Project **33**

Unit 2: I Need to Plan a Party

Materials for the Unit
- Wall calendar of the current year
- Picture of a business meeting
- Customizable Masters 3–5
- Unit Masters 23–30
- Vocabulary Card Masters for Unit 2

I Need to Plan a Party
Review the four groups of unit goals listed below the title.
- Explain that in this unit learners will focus on planning activities, getting advice, and making work schedules.
- Tell learners this unit is about a father and mother planning a birthday party for their son.

Question
Read the question below the arrow; then ask learners the questions below. Model at least one answer for each question. Use examples from your own experience or ask an accelerated learner to answer the question.
- Do you have parties for people in your family?
- Who do you have parties for?
- Why do you have parties?
- Who helps with the parties?

Photo
Follow the suggestions on p. 4 for talking about the photo. Then ask these questions:
- Who do you see in the picture?
- Where are they?
- What does Pavel want?
- What do Pavel's parents think?

Think and Talk
Answers
1. Answers will vary. Write learners' responses on the board.
2. Pavel's father has to work on Pavel's birthday. Pavel's mother needs help planning the party.
3. Answers will vary. Write learners' responses on the board.

What's Your Opinion?
Follow the suggestions on p. 6 for asking comprehension questions.

As learners respond, tally their opinions. Then ask these questions:
- Why or why not invite all Pavel's friends?
- What is a good number of children to have at a party?

Picture Dictionary

Read the words in the student book. Follow the suggestions on p. 6 for introducing and reinforcing vocabulary.

Follow the suggestions on p. 6 for using vocabulary cards. Use the cards for the words in the Picture Dictionary.

- Explain that an *activity* is someone *doing something* or people *doing something* together. The *activity* in this story is a birthday party, but there are many other kinds of *activities.*
- Point out the *Activity* heads in their book. Explain that learners *do something* in each *activity.*
- Ask learners what *activities* they *plan* with their families or friends. Point to the picture for *plan,* which shows a notepad with three things to do.
- Ask learners what other things they do when *planning.* Explain how *planning* leads to two other words—*calendar* and *schedule.*
- Ask if they have a *calendar* at home to write on. Ask, "Does anyone have a *calendar* with them?" If possible, point to a *calendar* on the wall.
- Ask a learner who works what his or her work *schedule* is. Write the schedule on the board or an overhead transparency.
- The rest of the words can also be part of a planning process. To convey their meaning, point to the word *invite* on the list in the illustration for *plan.* Then add the remaining words to the list (e.g., send *invitations,* buy *presents*).

Gather Your Thoughts

Use Customizable Master 5 (Idea Map). Follow the suggestions on p. 7 for customizing and duplicating the master. Make a copy for each learner.

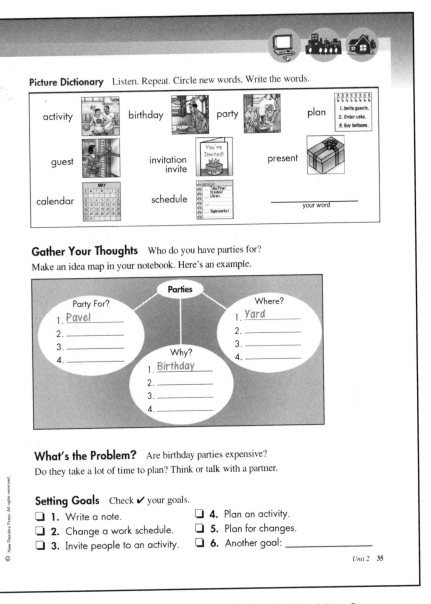

Ask learners the following:
- Who do you have parties for?
- Why do you have parties?
- Where do you have parties? Do you have parties at your house? What other places are good for parties?

Using the idea map in the student book as a model, draw a class idea map on the board or an overhead transparency.
- Write volunteers' responses on the class idea map to give other learners ideas.
- Have learners complete their own idea maps.

What's the Problem?

Follow the suggestions on p. 5 for identifying and analyzing problems. Then ask these questions:
- Are parties expensive?
- If yes, what makes them expensive? (e.g., food, presents)
- How can you save money on parties? (e.g., make food at home—do not buy it at a restaurant; use your own dishes instead of buying paperware)

Write learners' responses on the board or an overhead transparency.

Setting Goals

Follow the suggestions on p. 5 for setting goals.

Lesson 1: I Need a Favor! 🌐

Read the title aloud and point out the lesson objectives below it.

- Tell learners that in this lesson they will read a schedule and write a note (a short letter).
- Follow the suggestions on p. 5 for talking about titles.

Attention Box

Write the words on the board or an overhead transparency. Read the words aloud. Then do the following:

- Tell learners Pavel's father, Boris, works at a *bakery,* where he makes bread, cakes, cookies, and pies.
- Explain that Boris needs help—a *favor*—from another worker. Boris does not want to work on Pavel's birthday. He wants another worker to work for him that day. Have learners talk about *favors* they do for other people. Write their examples on the board or transparency.
- Demonstrate *trade* by exchanging books with a learner. Say, "I *trade* the book." When people *trade,* each one gets something.

This vocabulary should be understood, but learners should not be expected to produce the words at this point.

Question

Read the introductory question aloud. Then do the following:

- Using the work schedule in the student book as a model, write the days of the week horizontally across the board or an overhead transparency.
- Ask if any learners are taking classes besides yours. Have those who answer *yes* tell you their school schedules. Write their names under *Name.*
- For each learner, first write the hours of your class under the days that it meets. Then write the hours for other classes each learner is taking.

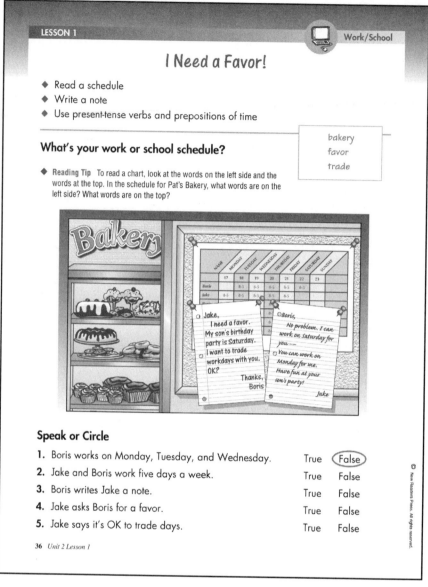

Follow this procedure for showing work schedules. Ask *yes/no* and *either/or* questions about the schedules.

Reading Tip

Read the tip aloud. Then refer to the school and work schedules just completed and ask:

- What words are on the left side?
- What words are at the top?

Talk about the notes in the illustration. Ask questions like these:

- Is this Boris's note or Jake's note? (Point to each note.)
- Who needs a favor? Why?
- How does Jake say OK?
- What days do Boris and Jake trade?

Speak or Circle

Ask learners to indicate *True* or *False* nonverbally (cards or thumbs up/down).

Answers
2. True   4. False
3. True   5. True

Vocabulary

Read the words in the student book. Follow the suggestions on p. 6 for introducing and reinforcing vocabulary.

Follow the suggestions on p. 6 for using vocabulary cards. Use the cards for the words in the Vocabulary box.

Assign Workbook p. 18, Exercises A–B, now or at any time during the rest of Lesson 1.

Partner Chat

Use Customizable Master 3 (3-Column Chart). Follow the suggestions on p. 7 for customizing and duplicating the master. Make a copy for each learner.

Draw the chart in the student book on the board or an overhead transparency. Then ask learners these questions:

- Do you have a job?
- What time do you start work? What time do you end work?
- Do you have other classes?
- What time does your ____ class start? When does it end?

As learners answer, write their information in the chart. Follow the suggestions on p. 7 for Partner Chats.

Grammar Talk

Follow the suggestions on p. 7 for introducing the grammar point.

- Explain that the *present tense* tells about things that are happening now or that happen all the time.
- Point out where the tense form is the same or different (*he, she, it* take *s; I, you, we, they* do not).

Point out the irregular verbs *have* and *go* at the bottom of the box.

- Write *have* and *has* on the board. Say, "I have a book. ____ has a book."
- Use the same procedure to demonstrate *do* and *go*.

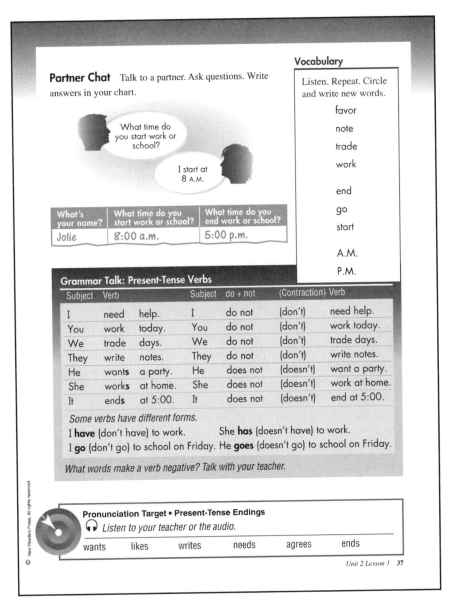

Partner Chat Talk to a partner. Ask questions. Write answers in your chart.

What time do you start work or school?

I start at 8 A.M.

What's your name?	What time do you start work or school?	What time do you end work or school?
Jolie	8:00 a.m.	5:00 p.m.

Vocabulary

Listen. Repeat. Circle and write new words.

favor
note
trade
work
end
go
start
A.M.
P.M.

Grammar Talk: Present-Tense Verbs

Subject	Verb		Subject	do + not	(Contraction)	Verb
I	need	help.	I	do not	(don't)	need help.
You	work	today.	You	do not	(don't)	work today.
We	trade	days.	We	do not	(don't)	trade days.
They	write	notes.	They	do not	(don't)	write notes.
He	wants	a party.	He	does not	(doesn't)	want a party.
She	works	at home.	She	does not	(doesn't)	work at home.
It	ends	at 5:00.	It	does not	(doesn't)	end at 5:00.

Some verbs have different forms.
I **have** (don't have) to work.   She **has** (doesn't have) to work.
I **go** (don't go) to school on Friday. He **goes** (doesn't go) to school on Friday.

What words make a verb negative? Talk with your teacher.

Pronunciation Target • Present-Tense Endings
Listen to your teacher or the audio.

wants   likes   writes   needs   agrees   ends

Unit 2 Lesson 1 37

Extension

- Ask a learner at what time she or he starts class. Write, "I start class at ____ (e.g., 7:00)." on the board or an overhead transparency.
- Ask another learner to repeat the information given about the previous learner (e.g., "She starts class at 7:00."). Write the response on the board; underline the *s* at the end of the verb.
- Ask a learner, "What do you need?" Then ask a different learner to repeat the information given about the previous learner (e.g. "He needs a pencil.").
- Continue calling on learners until all have used both first- and third-person forms.

Answer

Do not and *don't* make a verb negative.

Pronunciation Target

Play the audio or read the words in the student book, emphasizing the *s* endings. Then do the following:

- Write the words on the board.
- Read the words and ask learners what sound they hear at the end of each, /s/ or /z/.
- Write an *s* or *z* after each word to indicate the last sound (*wants, likes,* and *writes* end in /s/; *needs, agrees,* and *ends* end in /z/).

Unit 2 *Lesson 1* **37**

Activity A

Have learners work in pairs. Model the activity using the example in the student book.

One Step Up

Have learners write complete sentences from the answers to their questions.

Attention Box

Read the sentences aloud, pointing out the prepositions *on, at,* and *from.* Ask learners *Wh-* questions to practice using the prepositions (e.g., When is the party?).

Activity B

Extension

Have learners work in pairs to ask and answer questions like the questions in Activity B (e.g., Who gets up at *7 A.M.?* Who lives near a *park?*) Write words on the board or a transparency that learners can use to make new questions (e.g., *7 A.M.* and *park*).

Use Unit Master 23 (Grammar: A Birthday Party) now or at any time during the rest of the unit.

Assign Workbook p. 19, Exercises C–D, now or at any time during the rest of Lesson 1.

Task 1

Before learners begin the task, do the following:

- Remind the class about the favor that Boris needed from Jake.
- Ask learners which favors they need. Tell them to use the examples in the student book or to think of one on their own.
- Have them use the words, "I need help with ___."

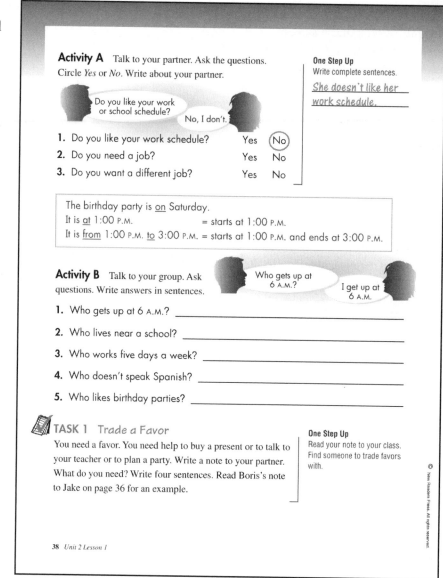

Activity A Talk to your partner. Ask the questions. Circle *Yes* or *No*. Write about your partner.

Do you like your work or school schedule?

No, I don't.

One Step Up
Write complete sentences.

She doesn't like her work schedule.

1. Do you like your work schedule? Yes No
2. Do you need a job? Yes No
3. Do you want a different job? Yes No

The birthday party is <u>on</u> Saturday.
It is <u>at</u> 1:00 P.M. = starts at 1:00 P.M.
It is <u>from</u> 1:00 P.M. <u>to</u> 3:00 P.M. = starts at 1:00 P.M. and ends at 3:00 P.M.

Activity B Talk to your group. Ask questions. Write answers in sentences.

Who gets up at 6 A.M.?

I get up at 6 A.M.

1. Who gets up at 6 A.M.? _____
2. Who lives near a school? _____
3. Who works five days a week? _____
4. Who doesn't speak Spanish? _____
5. Who likes birthday parties? _____

TASK 1 Trade a Favor

You need a favor. You need help to buy a present or to talk to your teacher or to plan a party. Write a note to your partner. What do you need? Write four sentences. Read Boris's note to Jake on page 36 for an example.

One Step Up
Read your note to your class. Find someone to trade favors with.

38 *Unit 2 Lesson 1*

One Step Up

Tell learners to listen to other learners' notes for a favor they are able to do. When they hear one, they can raise their hands and say, "I can ___ for you. Can you ___ for me?"

Lesson 2: Planning the Party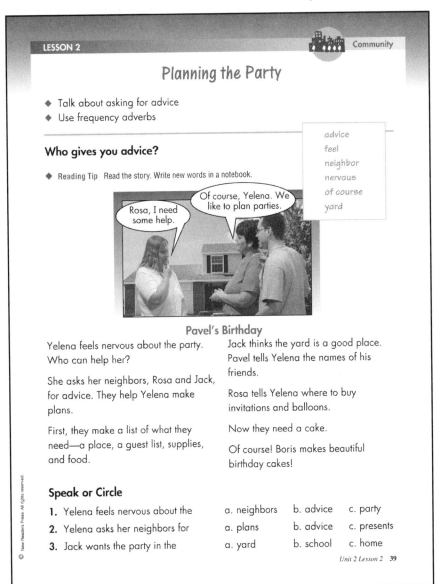

Read the title and point out the lesson objectives below it.

- Tell learners that in this lesson they will think about asking people for ideas, or *advice*.
- Follow the suggestions on p. 5 for talking about the title.

Attention Box

- To convey the meaning of *feel*, tell how you *feel* today with very simple words (e.g., *good, bad, happy, sad, worried*).
- Ask if anyone feels *nervous*. Mime that word.
- Explain that *of course* means *yes* or *certainly*.

This vocabulary should be understood, but learners should not be expected to produce the words at this point.

Question

Read the introductory question aloud. Then ask learners these questions:

- Who has parties? What help or *advice* do you need?
- Are there other times you need *advice?*

Write responses on the board or an overhead transparency.

Photo

Before learners read, ask these questions:

- What do you see?
- Who are these people? (Learners should be able to identify Pavel's mother. Tell them her name is Yelena. Encourage them to identify the other woman and the man as Yelena and Boris's *neighbors*. Recall the word *neighborhood* for them.)
- Who needs help?
- How does Yelena feel? How do you know? *(She looks nervous and worried.)*
- Who can help her?

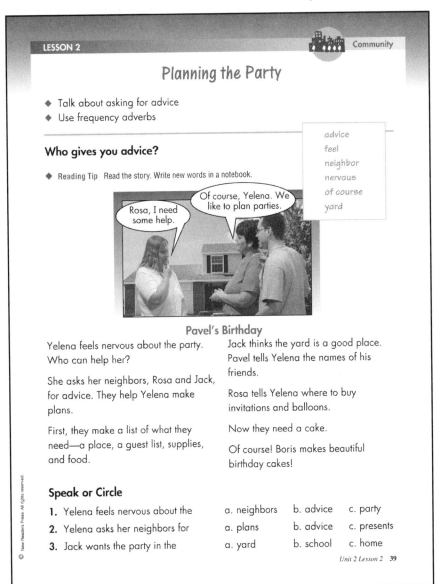

LESSON 2 Community

Planning the Party

- ◆ Talk about asking for advice
- ◆ Use frequency adverbs

Who gives you advice?

advice
feel
neighbor
nervous
of course
yard

- ◆ Reading Tip   Read the story. Write new words in a notebook.

Rosa, I need some help.

Of course, Yelena. We like to plan parties.

Pavel's Birthday

Yelena feels nervous about the party. Who can help her?

She asks her neighbors, Rosa and Jack, for advice. They help Yelena make plans.

First, they make a list of what they need—a place, a guest list, supplies, and food.

Jack thinks the yard is a good place. Pavel tells Yelena the names of his friends.

Rosa tells Yelena where to buy invitations and balloons.

Now they need a cake.

Of course! Boris makes beautiful birthday cakes!

Speak or Circle

1. Yelena feels nervous about the   a. neighbors   b. advice   c. party
2. Yelena asks her neighbors for   a. plans   b. advice   c. presents
3. Jack wants the party in the   a. yard   b. school   c. home

Unit 2 Lesson 2 **39**

Reading Tip

Read the tip aloud. Then follow the suggestions for in-class reading on p. 5.

Speak or Circle

This exercise helps learners become skilled at reading for details.

- Tell learners to circle the *letter* of the correct answer.
- Have volunteers read their answers.
- Have other learners hold up their *yes/no* cards to show agreement or disagreement (see p. 4).
- Ask individual learners to read aloud the sentences in the story that answer each question.

Answers
1. c   2. b   3. a

Vocabulary

Read the words in the student book. Follow the suggestions on p. 6 for introducing and reinforcing vocabulary.

Follow the suggestions on p. 6 for using vocabulary cards. Use the cards for the words in the Vocabulary box.

- Draw illustrations on the board for *balloons* and *cake.*
- For *date,* point to a calendar and say, "The *date* today is ___."
- If possible, bring a picture of a business *meeting.* Say, "I have *meetings* with other teachers." Ask, "Do you have *meetings?*"

Group Chat

Use Customizable Master 3 (3-Column Chart). Follow the suggestions on p. 7 for customizing and duplicating the master. Make a copy for each learner.

Follow the suggestions on p. 7 for conducting Group Chats.

Adverb Chart

- Write the percentages on the board or a transparency.
- Point to each as you say the corresponding adverb. Have learners repeat after you.
- Ask learners what they *always, often, sometimes, rarely,* and *never do* (e.g., Do you *often* go to parties? Which places do you *never* go?).
- Write a sentence using one of the adverbs and the verb *be* (e.g., I am always on time.). Explain that the adverbs follow *be* but precede other verbs.

In the US

- Read the passage twice. The second time, have learners repeat each sentence after you.
- Ask learners to read the passage silently.

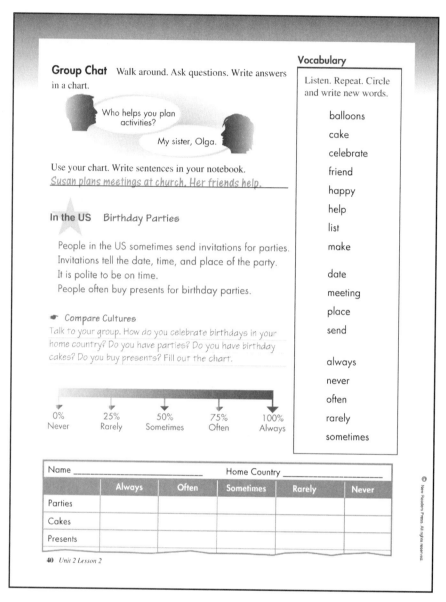

- Ask *yes/no* questions to check comprehension.

One Step Up

Ask learners if in their countries it is *polite* to be on time. Is it *polite* to be early? Is it *polite* to be late? Have learners raise their *yes/no* cards to answer (see p. 4).

Compare Cultures

- Model the activity from your own experience. Use some of the five adverbs of frequency.
- Ask learners to complete the chart for themselves in their books or notebooks.

- Draw a large version of the chart and post it. Have each learner write his or her name and home country in the appropriate place in each row of the group chart.

Use Unit Master 24 (Grammar: Frequency Adverbs) now or at any time during the rest of the unit.

Assign Workbook p. 20, Exercises A–B.

Activity A

Before learners begin the activity, point out that each sentence needs two words.

- Read the example aloud. Point out that *plan* and *from* were chosen from the words above.
- Check comprehension before learners continue.
- When learners finish writing, have them read their sentences to a partner.

<u>Answers</u>

2. Pavel <u>sends</u> invitations <u>on</u> Monday.
3. On Saturday they <u>buy</u> balloons <u>at</u> 9:00 A.M.
4. Boris <u>makes</u> the birthday cake <u>at</u> 11 A.M.

Activity B

- If you do not have a full-year calendar displayed in the room, bring one to show learners.
- Post the calendar, and have each learner check on what day his or her birthday falls.
- Have learners walk around to complete their charts.

One Step Up

On a large sheet of paper, plot a bar graph to show how many class birthdays are on each day of the week. Follow these steps:

- Write the days of the week across the bottom of the graph.
- Put numbers on the left side, with zero at the bottom.
- Place a dot above each day at the level of the corresponding number of learners who have birthdays on that day.
- Draw bars of appropriate heights to complete the graph.

Task 2

 Use Customizable Master 4 (4-Column Chart). Divide the second column in half vertically to make it look like the chart in the

book. Follow the directions on p. 7 for customizing and duplicating the master and distributing the copies. Give one copy to each group.

<u>Extension</u>

Have learners write sentences in their notebooks using information from their charts. Ask learners to use the Writing Checklist on p. 126 of their books to check their sentences.

Assign Workbook p. 21, Exercises C–D.

Activity A Write the correct words in the sentence.

at	buy	✔from	makes	at	sends	on	✔plan

1. Yelena and Rosa _____*plan*_____ the party _____*from*_____ 1:00 P.M. to 3:00 P.M.

2. Pavel _____ invitations _____ Monday.

3. On Saturday they _____ balloons _____ 9:00 A.M.

4. Boris _____ the birthday cake _____ 11 A.M.

Read the sentences to your partner.

Activity B Look at a calendar. Ask people in your class questions. Write in your notebook.

What's your name?	What day is your birthday this year?	What do you want?
Lisa	Tuesday	clothes

One Step Up
With your class, count the birthdays on Monday, Tuesday, and other days. Make a class chart that shows how many birthdays are on each day.

TASK 2 Who Gives You Advice?

In your group, think about an activity you need to plan for your home, school, work, or community. Do you need help? Who can give you advice?

	Name	Activity	What do I need help with?	Who can give me advice?
Work	Josef	Meeting	Bring coffee	Friend at work
School				
Home				
Community				

Unit 2 Lesson 2 41

Lesson 3: Changing Plans! 🌐

Follow the suggestions on p. 5 for talking about the title.
- Point out the lesson objectives listed below it.
- Tell learners this lesson is about having to change plans.

Question

Read the introductory question twice. Then write these sentences on the board or an overhead transparency:
- *Making careful plans is always good.*
- *Changing plans is sometimes good, too.*

Next write this sentence:
- *Buy party supplies on Sunday.*

To convey the meaning of *change plans,* do the following:
- Cross out *Sunday* in the sentence above and write *Monday.*
- Tell learners that you planned to buy party supplies on Sunday, but the party store was closed on Sunday.
- Explain that you will *change* your *plans* and buy party supplies on Monday.

Attention Box

- Read the words in the box and have learners repeat them.
- Write each word in a sentence.
- Read the sentences to learners.

This vocabulary should be understood, but learners should not be expected to produce the words at this point.

Photo

Ask learners these questions:
- What do you see?
- What do you think will happen next?

Listening Tip

Read the tip aloud; then do the following:
- Tell learners they will hear a conversation at a birthday party

Changing Plans!

- Change plans
- Use present tense with *yes/no* questions and answers

porch
run
take

Why do you change plans?

- Listening Tip 🎧 Listen to people talk. Think about how they feel. Are they happy, sad, worried? Listen to your teacher or the audio. What happens at the party? Is Yelena worried? Are the children happy or sad? You can read the words on page 118.

Happy Birthday, Pavel.

Speak or Circle

1. How is the weather?	a. sunny	b. windy	c. rainy
2. Where do they go?	a. home	b. the park	c. the porch
3. Who takes the presents?	a. Pavel	b. Yelena	c. Boris
4. Who has the cake?	a. Pavel	b. Yelena	c. Boris

for Pavel, the son of Boris and Yelena.
- Point to the picture in the student book and ask, "How does Yelena feel?"
- Ask them to listen carefully and think about how Yelena feels.

🎧 Play the audio or read the listening script on p. 118.
Follow the suggestions on p. 5 for listening comprehension.

Speak or Circle

This exercise helps learners listen for details.
- Read the questions and possible answers.

- Ask for nonverbal answers (*yes/no* cards or hand signals).

Answers
1. c   2. c   3. b   4. c

One Step Up
Ask learners to write the correct answers in complete sentences (e.g., The weather is rainy.).

Have them read the sentences to a partner. Are their answers the same or different? Why?

Vocabulary

Read the words in the student book. Follow the suggestions on p. 6 for introducing and reinforcing vocabulary.

Follow the suggestions on p. 6 for using vocabulary cards. Use the cards for the words in the Vocabulary box.

Ask learners these questions:
- What do you say to people who help you? (*thanks, thank you*)
- How do you feel when something good happens? (*glad, great*)

Write on the board or an overhead transparency *glad = happy*. Do the following to convey the meaning of the remaining words:
- Ask volunteers to mime *eat* and *see*.
- Mime *take* by handing a book to a learner and saying, "*Take the book.*"
- Introduce *there* by contrasting it to *here*. Place your book far away and say, "My book is *there*." Then put the book on your desk and say, "My book is *here*."
- Ask learners to practice *there* and *here* using different objects.

Class Chat

Use Customizable Master 3 (3-Column Chart). Follow the suggestions on p. 7 for customizing and duplicating the master. Make a copy for each learner.

Extension
After completing the Class Chat, have volunteers read about other learners. Complete a class chart on large paper and post it.

Grammar Talk

Follow the suggestions on p. 7 for introducing the grammar point. Point out these things:
- The main verb (e.g., *need, like, see, eat*) is always in the base form in these questions.
- The first word in the question (*do* or *does*) is repeated in the short answer.

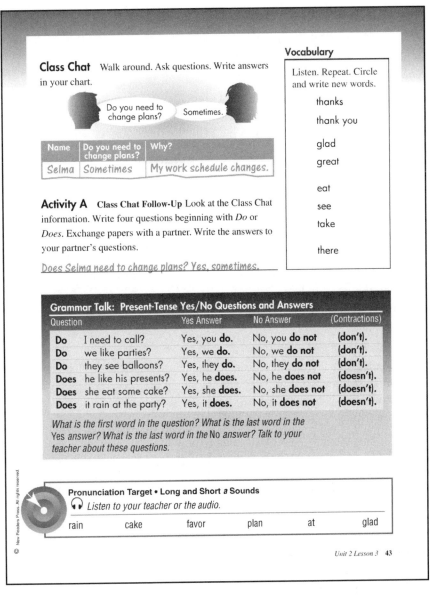

Class Chat Walk around. Ask questions. Write answers in your chart.

Do you need to change plans? Sometimes.

Name	Do you need to change plans?	Why?
Selma	Sometimes	My work schedule changes.

Activity A **Class Chat Follow-Up** Look at the Class Chat information. Write four questions beginning with *Do* or *Does*. Exchange papers with a partner. Write the answers to your partner's questions.

Does Selma need to change plans? Yes, sometimes.

Vocabulary
Listen. Repeat. Circle and write new words.

thanks

thank you

glad

great

eat

see

take

there

Grammar Talk: Present-Tense Yes/No Questions and Answers

Question		Yes Answer	No Answer	(Contractions)
Do	I need to call?	Yes, you **do**.	No, you **do not**	(don't).
Do	we like parties?	Yes, we **do**.	No, we **do not**	(don't).
Do	they see balloons?	Yes, they **do**.	No, they **do not**	(don't).
Does	he like his presents?	Yes, he **does**.	No, he **does not**	(doesn't).
Does	she eat some cake?	Yes, she **does**.	No, she **does not**	(doesn't).
Does	it rain at the party?	Yes, it **does**.	No, it **does not**	(doesn't).

What is the first word in the question? What is the last word in the Yes answer? What is the last word in the No answer? Talk to your teacher about these questions.

Pronunciation Target • Long and Short *a* Sounds
Listen to your teacher or the audio.

| rain | cake | favor | plan | at | glad |

Unit 2 Lesson 3 **43**

Review the negative contractions.

Answers
Do or *does* is the first word in the question. *Do* or *does* is the last word in the *Yes* answer. *Do not* or *does not* are the last words in the *No* answers.

Pronunciation Target
Play the audio or read the words in the book, emphasizing the long and short *a* sounds.

Extension
Make a chart with the heads *long a* and *short a*. Ask for other long or short *a* words (e.g., *train, make, date* and *hat, that, can*). Post the lists for future reference and add to them as new vocabulary is presented.

One Step Up
You may want to introduce these basic English phonics concepts:

VCe (vowel-consonant-silent *e*) = the long vowel sound as in *cake*

CVC (consonant-vowel-consonant) = the short vowel sound as in *can*

ai = long *a* sound as in *rain*

Use Unit Master 25 (Phonics: Sounds of *a* and Present-Tense Endings) now or at any time during the rest of the unit.

Assign Workbook p. 22, Exercises A–B, now or at any time during the rest of Lesson 3.

Unit 2 *Lesson 3* **43**

Attention Box

Show learners a real *backpack*.

Explain that we use the question *really?* to ask if something is true.

This vocabulary should be understood, but learners should not be expected to produce the words at this point.

Activity B

Tell learners that they will hear people talking at the party. Ask them to write numbers to show the order in which they hear the sentences.

🎧 Play the audio or read the listening script below. Then read the sentences as they appear on the student page. Then play or read the conversation again.

Listening Script

Miguel: Hello, Yelena. I am Miguel and this is Sylvia. We are Ben's parents.

Yelena: It's nice to meet you, Miguel and Sylvia. This is my husband, Boris.

Miguel: Hi, Boris. Thank you for inviting Ben to the party.

Boris: It's nice to have Ben here. Pavel, thank Ben for his present.

Pavel: Thanks for the backpack, Ben. It's great!

Ben: I'm glad you like it. Thanks for the cake. Mom, Pavel's dad makes great cakes.

Sylvia: Really? I need to call you, Boris. I need a cake for a church meeting next week.

Answers

5, 6, 3, 1, 2, 4, 7

Extension

After learners write their answers, ask volunteers to role-play the conversation.

One Step Up

Have learners write the conversation in the correct order in their notebooks.

Activity B 🎧 Listen to your teacher or the audio. Write numbers 1 to 7 to put the conversation in the correct order.

_____ **Pavel:** Thanks for the backpack, Ben. It's great!

_____ **Ben:** I'm glad you like it. Thanks for the cake. Mom, Pavel's dad makes great cakes.

_____ **Miguel:** Hi, Boris. Thank you for inviting Ben to the party.

__1__ **Miguel:** Hello, Yelena. I am Miguel and this is Sylvia. We are Ben's parents.

_____ **Yelena:** It's nice to meet you, Miguel and Sylvia. This is my husband, Boris.

_____ **Boris:** It's nice to have Ben here. Pavel, thank Ben for his present.

_____ **Sylvia:** Really? I need to call you, Boris. I need a cake for a church meeting next week.

> backpack
> Really? = True?

One Step Up
Write the conversation in the correct order.

Activity C Read the questions to your partner. Write yes/no answers.

1. Do Ben's parents meet Boris and Yelena? _Yes, they do._

2. Does Miguel thank Pavel for inviting Ben? _____

3. Does Pavel thank Sylvia for his present? _____

4. Does Ben like the cake? _____

📝 **TASK 3** Talk About Changing Plans

You and your partner plan a party for your class. Think about the day of the party:

- Someone forgets the food. What can you do?
- Your party is outside. It rains. What can you do? Where do you go?
- Think about two other problems. What can you do?

44 *Unit 2 Lesson 3*

📑 Use Unit Master 26 (Game: Crossword Puzzle) now or at any time during the rest of the unit.

Activity C

Extension

When partners finish asking and answering the questions, have them check each other's work against the listening script on p. 118 of their books.

📑 Use Unit Master 27 (Grammar: Questions and Answers) at any time during the rest of the unit.

 Assign Workbook p. 23, Exercise C.

Task 3

If learners' speaking skills are rudimentary, have them work in small groups rather than in pairs. Then do the following:

- To help learners plan, read the questions aloud and number them on the board or an overhead transparency.
- Circulate to monitor their progress.
- Have one learner from each group read their plan. Ask them to describe any changes.

Review Unit Skills

See p. 8 for suggestions on games and activities to review the unit vocabulary and grammar.

Unit 2 Project

Learners plan, prepare, and have a party.

Get Ready

 Use Unit Master 28 (Unit 2 Project: Plan a Party!). Distribute a copy to each learner. Display the master as an overhead transparency.

Tell learners they are going to plan a party.

- Determine whom to invite (e.g., friends, family, another class) as well as the maximum number of people to be accommodated.
- Have all learners work together, or assign different steps to different groups.
- Ask learners to think about the headings on the master. Write their ideas on the transparency or the board.
- Discuss learners' ideas until you reach consensus on these points:
  kind of party
  date and time
  food and who brings it
  music and who brings it
  guests (List guests' names or the name of a class.)
  other advice (What other questions do you need to think about? Do you need to get permission from the school before planning? Do you need to check dates with other classes?)

Do the Work

- Help learners make a time line on a large piece of paper to show what needs to be done by when.
- Assign each group one or two tasks.
- Make sure the invitations are delivered well in advance.
- Tell learners to monitor their progress regularly by referring to the time line and checking to see if everyone is on task.

Assessment

 As each group does its work, complete a copy of Unit

Plan a Party!

Do these things to plan, prepare, and have a party.

Get Ready

- What kind of party do you want? A birthday party? A holiday party? Or?
- Make a list of people to invite (teachers, students, friends, relatives).
- What time is the party? How long is it?
- What do you need? Food? Music?
- Do you need advice? Who do you ask?

Make a chart with this information.

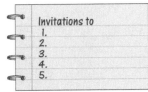

Invitations to
1.
2.
3.
4.
5.

We Need
Food—Olga, Ramon, Sara
Music—Mei and Esteban

Do the Work

- Make invitations with the date, time, and place.
- Send the invitations.

Present Your Project

Have your party! At the party:
- Welcome your guests.
- Thank them for coming.
- Have a good time!

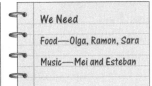

Please Come to Our Party

Date: Friday, December 20
Time: 2:00 to 4:00 p.m
Place: Central Adult School
2543 Main Street, Room 202

🖳 **Technology Extra**
Make your invitation on the computer. Make copies on the copy machine.

Unit 2 Project **45**

Master 29 (Project Assessment Form). Make a copy of the form for each group member's portfolio.

Present Your Project

Have your party!
- Caution learners that they need to be able to change plans quickly and smoothly.
- Assist them in greeting guests with appropriate words and phrases (e.g., *Welcome to our party. Do you want something to eat? Drink? Do you want to sit down?*).
- Say good-bye (e.g., *I'm glad you came. Thanks for coming.*).

Technology Extra

Have learners make a simple flyer or a traditional folded invitation. If skills and resources are available, have them use a word processing or computer graphics program.

 Assign Workbook p. 24 (Check Your Progress).

 Use Unit Master 30 (Unit 2 Checkup/Review) whenever you complete this unit.

Unit 3: How Do You Feel?

Materials for the Unit

- Sample packages and labels for prescription and over-the-counter medicines
- Medicine spoon with (dosage indicated) or teaspoon (measuring spoon)
- Teaspoon (flatware)
- Customizable Masters 3–5
- Generic Assessment Masters 6 and 10
- Unit Masters 31–37
- Vocabulary Card Masters for Unit 3

How Do You Feel?

Follow the suggestions on p. 5 for talking about the title.

- Review the four groups of unit goals listed below the title.
- Explain that in this unit learners will focus on calling in sick to work, making a doctor's appointment, following a doctor's instructions, and reading medicine labels.

Question

Read the question below the arrow.

One Step Down

For lower-level learners, you may want to ask an *either/or* question (e.g., How do you feel today, sick or well?) and have learners raise their hands to answer.

One Step Up

Ask as many individual learners as possible these additional questions:

- How do you feel?
- Are you sick today?
- Do you ever get sick? (Remind learners to use adverbs of frequency in their answer.)

Photo

Follow the suggestions on p. 4 for talking about the photo. Then say the following:

- Sometimes I'm sick. When I'm sick, I don't go to work. I *stay*

home from work. (Write *I'm sick* and *I stay home* on the board or an overhead transparency.)
- Do you *stay home* when you're sick? (Tally on the board how many learners *stay home* and how many do not.)

Caption

Read the caption aloud. Then check for understanding by using these *either/or* and *yes/no* questions:

- Is today Tuesday?
- Does Jim feel sick?
- Does Jim have a big party at work?

Think and Talk

Read the questions. Have learners call out their answers. Write them on the board or an overhead transparency.

Answers

1. Answers will vary.
2. He's sick, but he has to go to work.
3. Answers will vary.

What's Your Opinion?

Follow the suggestions on p. 6 for comprehension questions. Tally learner responses on the board or an overhead transparency.

Picture Dictionary

Read the words in the student book. Follow the suggestions on p. 6 for introducing and reinforcing vocabulary.

Follow the suggestions on p. 6 for using vocabulary cards. Use the cards for the words in the Picture Dictionary.

- Model each word by using it in a sentence (e.g., The doctor asks about my *symptoms*. I say, "I have a *fever* and a *headache*.").
- Elicit the vocabulary by asking learners questions (e.g., How do you *feel* today? Who has a *sore throat*? Who is *well*?).

One Step Up

- Using the words in the Picture Dictionary, write a number of questions on the board (e.g., How do you *feel*? Are you *sick*? Do you have *allergies*?).
- Have learners form two groups or lines.
- A learner from one group asks a member of the other group one of the questions.
- You may want to teach the expression "What's wrong?" and encourage learners to use it in this activity.
- A group gets one point for a correct question and one for a correct answer. Set a time limit to determine which group wins.

Gather Your Thoughts

Make a copy of Customizable Master 5 (Idea Map). Customize it as shown in the student book. Then make a copy for each group. If possible, have learners form groups of four. Ask these questions:

- What do you do when sick?
- Do you call your boss?
- Do you go to bed?
- What else do you do?

Encourage learners to generate their own ideas (e.g., *go to school, go to the doctor, find a baby-sitter.*)

- Have learners work with others in their group to complete the idea map. Have groups add more circles if they have more ideas.
- Divide each group into pairs. One partner asks the question (What do you do when you're sick?), and the other answers. Then they switch roles.
- When all learners are finished, compare the group maps.

What's the Problem?

Follow the suggestions on p. 5 for identifying and analyzing problems. Then say to learners, "When I'm sick, I call the doctor *(mime using the telephone)*. I like my doctor. She is a good doctor. I get good medical

help. What about you? Do you have a doctor? Is your doctor good? Can you get good medical help?"

One Step Up

Elicit further information from learners by asking *why* or *why not* after the last question. Using the same questions, ask learners about medical help in their home countries. Write their responses on the board.

Setting Goals

Follow the suggestions on p. 5 for setting goals. Remind them that the goals are things to do in English.

One Step Up

Have volunteers read their most important personal goal for this unit.

Lesson 1: Sick at Work [www]

Read the lesson title and point out the lesson objectives listed below it.
- Explain that this lesson is about how and when to ask for sick leave from work. Tell learners, "In this lesson, you will tell a boss why you need to leave work or you will tell a teacher why you need to leave school."

Sick at Work

Follow the suggestions on p. 5 for talking about titles.

Attention Box

Read the words to learners, pointing or miming to convey meaning if possible. This vocabulary should be understood, but learners should not be expected to produce the words at this point.
- Write these sentences to convey the meaning of *leave:*
  I come to school at 7:00.
  I go home at 9:00.
  I *leave* school at 9:00.
- Write this definition on the board or an overhead transparency:
  terrible = very bad

Question

Read the question aloud. Clarify the meaning of *stay home* by writing this definition: *stay home = not go out of or leave your home*

Reading Tip

Explain the tip. Ask learners these questions:
- What is the title of this reading?
- What is this story about?
- What does the title tell you about Jim?

Follow the suggestions for reading comprehension on p. 5.
- Mime unfamiliar vocabulary such as *cough, sneeze, stay,* and *aspirin.*
- Review the meaning of *meeting.*

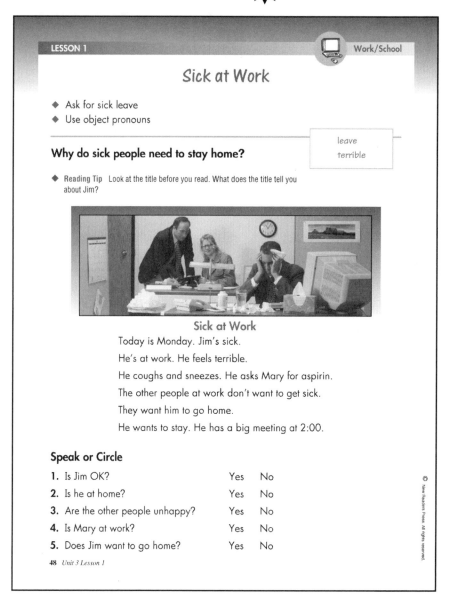

LESSON 1 — Work/School

Sick at Work

- Ask for sick leave
- Use object pronouns

Why do sick people need to stay home?

leave
terrible

◆ **Reading Tip** Look at the title before you read. What does the title tell you about Jim?

Sick at Work

Today is Monday. Jim's sick.
He's at work. He feels terrible.
He coughs and sneezes. He asks Mary for aspirin.
The other people at work don't want to get sick.
They want him to go home.
He wants to stay. He has a big meeting at 2:00.

Speak or Circle

1. Is Jim OK?	Yes	No
2. Is he at home?	Yes	No
3. Are the other people unhappy?	Yes	No
4. Is Mary at work?	Yes	No
5. Does Jim want to go home?	Yes	No

48 *Unit 3 Lesson 1*

Speak or Circle

Follow the suggestions on p. 6 for comprehension questions.
This exercise helps learners locate the main idea in what they read.

<u>Answers</u>
1. No   4. Yes
2. No   5. No
3. Yes

<u>One Step Up</u>
Extend some of the questions by asking *why.*

Vocabulary

Read the words in the student book. Follow the suggestions on p. 6 for introducing and reinforcing vocabulary.

Follow the suggestions on p. 6 for using vocabulary cards. Use the cards for the words in the Vocabulary box.

Assign Workbook p. 25, Exercises A–B, now or at any time during the rest of Lesson 1.

Class Chat

Use Customizable Master 3 (3-Column Chart). Follow the suggestions on p. 7 for customizing and duplicating the master. Make a copy for each learner.

Follow the suggestions on p. 7 for Class Chats.

Then do the following:

- Have learners walk around and ask each other questions using vocabulary from pp. 47 and 49. (e.g., When you have a <u>fever</u>, what are your symptoms? What do you take for it?)
- After learners finish, elicit names of illnesses. Write the names in a two-column chart on the board or an overhead transparency, or ask learners to write them.
- Ask learners to tell you what symptoms they wrote in their charts. Add them to the class chart in the same way.
- Ask other learners to call out the symptoms they wrote for the same illness. Write these below the first list of symptoms.
- Ask the questions below. Encourage learners to respond and to discuss with one another:
  Are the symptoms the same or different?
  What is different?
  Which are correct?

Grammar Talk

Follow the suggestions on p. 7 for

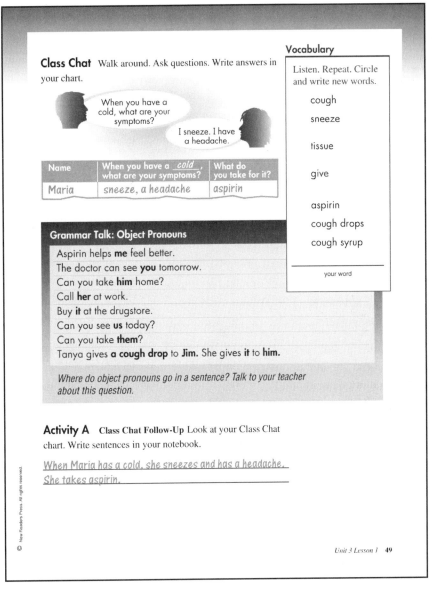

Class Chat Walk around. Ask questions. Write answers in your chart.

When you have a cold, what are your symptoms?

I sneeze. I have a headache.

Name	When you have a _cold_, what are your symptoms?	What do you take for it?
Maria	sneeze, a headache	aspirin

Vocabulary

Listen. Repeat. Circle and write new words.

cough

sneeze

tissue

give

aspirin

cough drops

cough syrup

your word

Grammar Talk: Object Pronouns

Aspirin helps **me** feel better.
The doctor can see **you** tomorrow.
Can you take **him** home?
Call **her** at work.
Buy **it** at the drugstore.
Can you see **us** today?
Can you take **them**?
Tanya gives **a cough drop** to **Jim**. She gives **it** to **him**.

Where do object pronouns go in a sentence? Talk to your teacher about this question.

Activity A **Class Chat Follow-Up** Look at your Class Chat chart. Write sentences in your notebook.

<u>When Maria has a cold, she sneezes and has a headache. She takes aspirin.</u>

Unit 3 Lesson 1 **49**

introducing the grammar point. Explain that an object pronoun is used *in place of* a noun. Then do the following:

- Write each word in the sentences below on a sheet of 8½ × 11 in. paper:
  He feels terrible.
  Can you take him home?
- Post the sheets across the front of the class, but leave out the two pronouns *(He and him).*
- Read the sentences to the class and show learners the two pronoun sheets. Ask where each pronoun goes.
- Read the sentences again and have volunteers place the pro-

nouns in the correct places. Refer to the "subject pronoun *he*" and the "object pronoun *him*" as you proceed.

- Repeat this activity with the Grammar Talk sentences, having learners physically place the pronoun sheets within the sentences.

<u>Answers</u>

Object pronouns in a sentence usually follow the verb. (Explain the corollary: *subject pronouns* usually precede a verb.)

Activity A

Ask learners to use the information in their Class Chat charts to write sentences in their notebooks.

Activity B

Answers

2. her   3. them   4. him

Extension

In pairs, have learners write the sentences on the board and read them aloud.

Activity C

Answers

2. She, him   4. It, him
3. He, them   5. He, her

 Use Unit Master 31 (Grammar: Making Sentences) now or at any time during the rest of the unit.

 Assign Workbook p. 26, Exercise C.

Task 1

Learners can use the completed Exercise C from Workbook p. 26 for this task. Suggest that they copy any sentences from Exercise C that they can use in their conversations.

Ongoing Assessment

While learners do Task 1, circulate. Listen to at least five interactions, involving at least three different groups. Take notes on how well learners perform on the following criteria:

a. General quality of statements
   0 = no statements
   1 = abrupt, halting statements
   2 = smooth, clear statements

b. General quality of language function (making an excuse)
   0 = many problems/not understandable
   1 = some problems with clarity
   2 = clear and appropriate although not perfect

• Which one or two categories were most difficult for learners?

• In the follow-up period, discuss and model appropriate communication for the task before continuing.

Activity B   Change the **word** to an object pronoun. Read the sentence to your partner.

1. Maria takes **aspirin** for a headache.

   Maria takes it for a headache.

2. Michael asks **Susan** for a tissue.

   _____

3. John has **tissues** on his desk.

   _____

4. Please give **John** some cough drops.

   _____

Subject		Object
I	→	me
you	→	you
he	→	him
she	→	her
it	→	it
they	→	them

Activity C   One partner reads the sentence. The other partner reads the sentence with subject and object pronouns. Both partners write the new sentence with pronouns.

1. **Jim** talks to **Mary**.   _He talks to her._____

2. **Mary** tells **Jim** to go home. _____

3. **Jim** has a meeting with **Mr. and Mrs. Mankin**. _____

4. **The meeting** is very important to **Jim**. _____

5. **Jim** writes a note to **Mrs. Ramirez**. _____

 TASK 1   Ask to Leave Early

With a partner, role-play a conversation with your boss or teacher. Tell why you are leaving work or school.

Writing Extension   Write a note. Your note tells why you need to leave work or school. Read your note to your partner.

50   *Unit 3 Lesson 1*

Writing Extension

Use the completed Exercise C from Workbook p. 26 for this extension. Check for salutation, closing, and legibility.

Tell learners to use the Writing Checklist on p. 126 of their books to edit their sentences.

 Assign Workbook p. 26, Exercise D.

Lesson 2: Making a Doctor's Appointment ▓www▓

Read the lesson title and point out the lesson objectives listed below it.
- In this lesson, students learn to make a doctor's appointment and provide medical information.
- Follow the suggestions on p. 5 for talking about the title.

Attention Box

Read the word *receptionist* to learners, pointing to the *receptionist* in the photo. Mime answering phones and taking messages.

Question

- Write on the board: *The receptionist makes appointments for the doctor.*
- Role-play making a doctor's appointment, playing both the receptionist and the caller. Use this sample dialogue:
  Good morning. I need an appointment with Dr. White. Your name, please?
  Patty Kerns.
  When do you want to come in?
  Thursday afternoon is good for me.
  Is 2:00 OK?
  Yes. Thursday at 2:00 is good.
  Fine. See you Thursday, Ms. Kerns.
- Ask learners these questions:
  Do you make appointments?
  How do you make them? Do you call or go to the office?
  Do you make them in English?

Photos

Follow the suggestions on p. 4 for talking about photos. Ask:
- Is Jim talking to the doctor?
- Is the receptionist writing or reading?
- What is Jim saying?

Listening Tip

Read the tip aloud.

Tell learners it is always good to take notes in important phone calls.

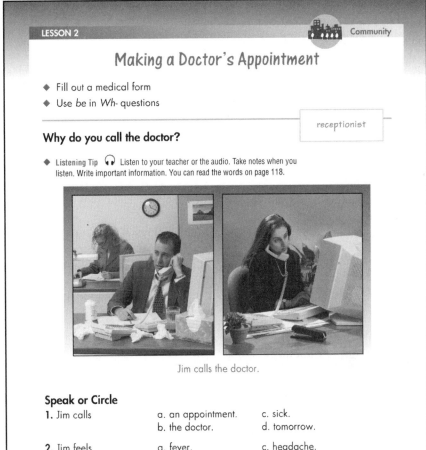

LESSON 2 Community

Making a Doctor's Appointment

◆ Fill out a medical form
◆ Use *be* in *Wh-* questions

receptionist

Why do you call the doctor?

◆ Listening Tip 🎧 Listen to your teacher or the audio. Take notes when you listen. Write important information. You can read the words on page 118.

Jim calls the doctor.

Speak or Circle

1. Jim calls
   a. an appointment.   c. sick.
   b. the doctor.   d. tomorrow.

2. Jim feels
   a. fever.   c. headache.
   b. sick.   d. throat.

3. Jim has
   a. a note.   c. a sore throat.
   b. a stomachache.   d. an aspirin.

4. Jim's appointment is
   a. tomorrow at noon.   c. tomorrow at 3:00.
   b. Sunday at 3:00.   d. today at 4:00.

Unit 3 Lesson 2 **51**

Ask them what things they might want to write (e.g., dates, days, times, names).

🎧 Play the audio or read the listening script on p. 119. Then ask these questions:
- What is the doctor's name? *(Lee)*
- Is Jim's last name Lee or Martin? *(Martin)*
- Does he need an appointment or a stomachache? *(appointment)*
- Is Jim's temperature 101 degrees or 110 degrees? *(101)*

Speak or Circle

Read the first part of each sentence aloud (e.g., *Jim calls, Jim feels*).

Tell learners to listen for these words.

🎧 Play the audio or read the listening script again. As learners listen, have them circle the letter of each correct answer or write it in their notebooks.

Answers
1. b   2. b   3. c   4. c

Vocabulary

Read the words in the student book. Follow the suggestions on p. 6 for introducing and reinforcing vocabulary.

Follow the suggestions on p. 6 for using vocabulary cards. Use the cards for the words in the Vocabulary box.

Class Chat

Follow the suggestions on p. 7 for Class Chats.

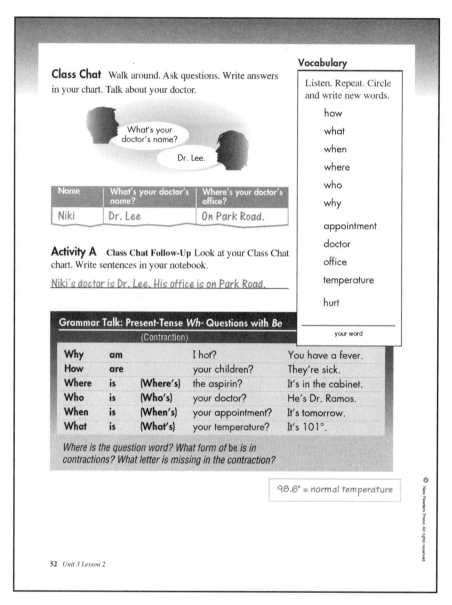

Use Customizable Master 3 (3-Column Chart). Follow the suggestions on p. 7 for customizing and duplicating the master. Make a copy for each learner.

Activity A

Ask learners to use the information in their Class Chat charts to write sentences in their notebooks.

Grammar Talk

Follow the suggestions on p. 7 for introducing the grammar point. Review these *Wh-* question words:

who = person
when = time
where = place

Write these definitions on the board or an overhead transparency. Then do the following:

- Read the questions and answers to learners. Tell them that all these questions ask for information.
- Read the first question. Have learners answer. Elicit a variety of possible responses (e.g., You have a fever. The room is hot. It's a hot day.).
- Continue this way with the remaining questions.

Answers
The *question word* is placed at the *beginning* of the sentence.

The verb *is*.

The letter *i* is missing from the contractions.

Assign Workbook p. 27, Exercises A–B, now or at any time during the rest of Lesson 2.

Activity B

Read the directions for the activity. Explain that many doctors require people with appointments to fill out forms.

Go over the form with learners. Then follow these steps to model the activity:

- Write question 1 on the board just as it appears in the book. Ask, "What is missing? What words do you need to make a question?"
- Write *is, at,* and *the* above question 1 in the places where they belong. Then write the complete sentence for learners.
- After reviewing the entire exercise in this way, have learners complete the activity.

Answers

1. Why <u>is</u> Jim <u>at</u> <u>the</u> doctor's office today? *(sore throat, fever)*
2. Where <u>is</u> Jim's office? *(349 Gray Street, San Francisco, CA 94112)*
3. When <u>is</u> Jim's birthday? *(3/12/75)*
4. What <u>are</u> his allergies? *(penicillin, cats)*
5. What <u>are</u> his phone numbers? *[(415) 555-8437, (415) 555-2334]*
6. What <u>is</u> Jim's last name? *(Martin)*

 Assign Workbook p. 28, Exercises C–D, now or at any time during the rest of Lesson 2.

Use Unit Masters 32 (Grammar: At the Doctor's Office) and 33 (Life Skill: Gathering Information) now or at any time during the rest of the unit.

Task 2

Model the activity with a volunteer in front of the whole group (e.g., **Teacher:** When is your birthday? **Student:** My birthday is ___. **Teacher:** ___'s birthday is ___.).

Activity B Jim is at the doctor's office. He needs to fill out a medical information form. Write the questions.

1. Last Name Martin	First Name James
2. Address 1650 Teal Avenue, San Francisco, CA 94119	3. Date of birth 3-12-75
4. Phone Number: Day (415) 555-8437	Evening (415) 555-2334
5. Employer: Pacific Bank	6. Address: 349 Gray Street, San Francisco, CA 94112
7. Allergies? Medicine: penicillin Other: cats	8. Reason for this visit? sore throat, fever

1. Why/Jim/doctor's office/today? <u>Why is Jim at the doctor's office today?</u>
2. Where/Jim's office? _____
3. When/Jim's birthday? _____
4. What/his allergies? _____
5. What/his/phone numbers? _____
6. What/Jim's/last name? _____

Exchange papers with your partner. Check your partner's work. One partner asks a question. One answers. Write the answers. Check your answers with your partner.

TASK 2 Give Medical Information

Use the form above. Talk to your partner. Give information about you for questions 1 to 4 on the form. Ask your partner questions 1 to 4. Tell the class about your partner.

Unit 3 Lesson 2 53

Peer Assessment

Give each learner a copy of Generic Assessment Master 10 (Peer Assessment Form for Projects and Tasks). Review the assessment form with learners to be sure they know how to use it. Then do the following:

- Have partners rehearse in front of their group.
- Tell group members to use the assessment forms to evaluate the rehearsals.
- Collect the assessment forms and decide the best way to give the feedback to the performers.

During rehearsals, partners should also give each other suggestions for improvement before they make their final presentations.

Assessment

Use Generic Assessment Master 6 (Oral Communication Rubric) to evaluate the presentations.

Lesson 3: Take Your Medicine! 🔳

- Point out the lesson objectives listed below the title.
- Tell learners that in this lesson they will learn how to read medicine labels and talk about medicines.

Attention Box

- Read the words and have learners repeat them.
- Point out the *expiration date* on a prescription medicine bottle. Tell learners that the *expiration date* is when the prescription *expires*. The pharmacy cannot refill the prescription after this date.

This vocabulary should be understood, but learners should not be expected to produce the words at this point.

Question

- Draw a two-column chart on the board or an overhead transparency.
- Write the heads *Prescription Medicines* and *Over-the-Counter Medicines* at the top of the chart. Explain that for *prescription medicines,* people need to have a doctor's prescription, but *over-the-counter medicines* can be purchased without one.
- Read the question aloud. Write learners' responses under the appropriate heading in the chart.

Reading Tip

Read the tip aloud.
- Have learners sit in small groups.
- Give each group some medicine labels and packages.
- Ask learners why some of the words on the labels are in bold print or in color. *(because they contain important information)*

Point to the medicines in the picture.
- Have learners scan the medicine labels for words from the word box. Explain that *Exp* on a medicine label is an abbreviation for *expire* or *expiration.*

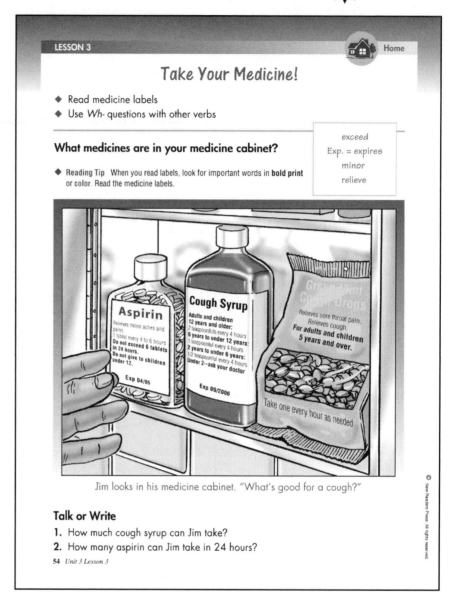

Take Your Medicine!

- ◆ Read medicine labels
- ◆ Use *Wh-* questions with other verbs

What medicines are in your medicine cabinet?

> exceed
> Exp. = expires
> minor
> relieve

- ◆ **Reading Tip** When you read labels, look for important words in **bold print** or color. Read the medicine labels.

Aspirin
Relieves minor aches and pains.
1 tablet every 4 to 6 hours.
Do not exceed 6 tablets in 24 hours.
Do not give to children under 12.
Exp 04/05

Cough Syrup
Adults and children 12 years and older:
2 teaspoonfuls every 4 hours
6 years to under 12 years:
1 teaspoonful every 4 hours
2 years to under 6 years:
1/2 teaspoonful every 4 hours
Under 2--ask your doctor
Exp 09/2006

Green-mint Cough Drops
Relieves sore throat pain.
Relieves cough.
For adults and children 5 years and over.
Take one every hour as needed

Jim looks in his medicine cabinet. "What's good for a cough?"

Talk or Write
1. How much cough syrup can Jim take?
2. How many aspirin can Jim take in 24 hours?

54 *Unit 3 Lesson 3*

- Use a measuring spoon to show the dosage of the cough syrup. Hold up an ordinary teaspoon (tableware) and a teaspoon measure. Explain that some teaspoons for eating are small and some are big. They should not be used as measuring spoons.
- Ask clarification questions for each label (e.g., Can you give cough drops to a baby?).

<u>One Step Up</u>
Ask learners whether they have medicines like these at home. If so, have them compare the labels with those in the picture and report back any differences they see.

Talk or Write

This exercise gives learners practice in scanning for information.

<u>Answers</u>
1. 2 teaspoonfuls every 4 hours
2. 6

Vocabulary

Read the words in the student book. Follow the suggestions on p. 6 for introducing and reinforcing vocabulary.

Follow the suggestions on p. 6 for using vocabulary cards. Use the cards for the words in the Vocabulary box.

Assign Workbook p. 29, Exercise A, now or at any time during the rest of Lesson 3.

Class Chat

Use Customizable Master 3 (3-Column Chart). Follow the suggestions on p. 7 for customizing and duplicating the master. Make a copy for each learner.

Follow the suggestions on p. 7 for Class Chats.

Activity A

Ask learners to use the information in their Class Chat charts to write sentences in their notebooks.

Grammar Talk

Follow the suggestions on p. 7 for introducing the grammar point. Use sentence strips or an overhead transparency to present the sentences. Follow these steps:

- Write the question word in one color and *do/does* in another. Write the rest of the question and the answer in black.
- For the sentence "Where does Dr. Lee work?" point out the *s* in *does* and the *s* at the end of the verb in the answer.
- Refer to *do* and *does* as *helper verbs* that help the main verb make questions.

Answers
The question word is at the beginning of the questions.

Do or *does* (helper verb) follows the question word.

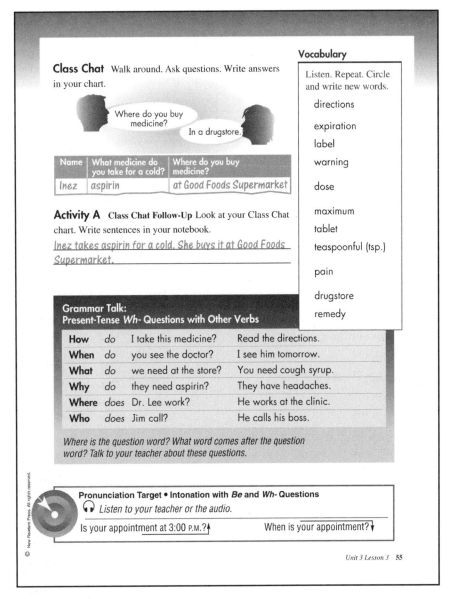

Pronunciation Target

Play the audio or read each question several times. Have learners repeat what they hear.

- Ask learners if *be* questions have rising or falling intonation. *(rising)*
- Ask if *wh-* questions have rising or falling intonation. *(falling)*
- Point to the *wh-* questions in Grammar Talk as additional examples. Read them aloud, stressing their falling intonation.
- Write a brief summary of the rules for intonation in questions on the board or an overhead

transparency (e.g., *Be* questions have *rising* intonation. The voice goes *up* at the end. . . .).

Use Unit Master 34 (Pronunciation: Intonation) now or at any time during the rest of the unit.

Assign Workbook p. 29, Exercise B, now or at any time during the rest of Lesson 3.

Activity B

- Read the words down the side of the chart. Have learners say them aloud after you.
- Ask learners questions about the medicine labels. Elicit as much information as possible (e.g., What is this? What is it for? When do you need it? How much can you take?).
- Have learners complete the chart for medicine labels. Then ask them the follow-up questions in their books.

<u>One Step Up</u>
Have learners create questions from the chart (e.g., What is the dose for aspirin?). Then have them ask and answer the questions in pairs or groups.

Assign Workbook p. 30, Exercise C, now or at any time during the rest of Lesson 3.

Use Unit Master 35 (Grammar: Ask about Medicines) now or at any time during the rest of the unit.

In the US

- First, have learners read the passage silently. Then read it to them aloud and have them repeat each line.
- Ask *yes/no* questions about some of the statements (e.g., Do people always use medicine when they are sick?).
- Ask information questions about the statements (e.g., What remedy do some people use for a sore throat?).

Compare Cultures

Have learners sit in their groups.

- Ask learners to create questions and give answers about home remedies in their home countries. Tell them to follow the model in their books.
- Have individual learners from

each group write questions and answers on the board.
- Lead a class discussion about the remedies.

Task 3

If learners are unable to name medicines, use the medicine labels and packages from earlier in the lesson.

Use Customizable Master 4 (4-Column Chart). Write in the words shown in the first column of the chart in Activity B. Make a copy of the master for each learner.

- Model the task using the chart in Activity B.
- Tell learners to write the names of their three medicines at the top

of the three blank columns in their charts.
- Have learners talk with one another in their groups and complete the charts.
- Compile the information in a class chart on an overhead transparency or on the board. Have learners write their information on the chart.

Assign Workbook p. 30, Exercise D, now.

<u>Review Unit Skills</u>
See p. 8 for suggestions on games and activites to review vocabulary and grammar in this unit.

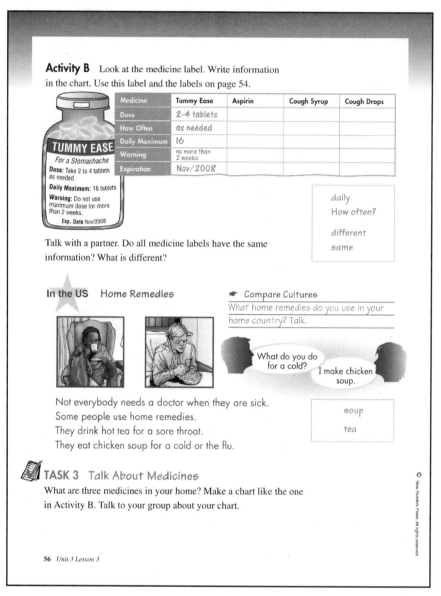

Activity B Look at the medicine label. Write information in the chart. Use this label and the labels on page 54.

Medicine	Tummy Ease	Aspirin	Cough Syrup	Cough Drops
Dose	2-4 tablets			
How Often	as needed			
Daily Maximum	16			
Warning	no more than 2 weeks			
Expiration	Nov/2008			

TUMMY EASE
For a Stomachache
Dose: Take 2 to 4 tablets as needed.
Daily Maximum: 16 tablets
Warning: Do not use maximum dose for more than 2 weeks.
Exp. Date Nov/2008

Talk with a partner. Do all medicine labels have the same information? What is different?

daily
How often?
different
same

In the US Home Remedies

Not everybody needs a doctor when they are sick.
Some people use home remedies.
They drink hot tea for a sore throat.
They eat chicken soup for a cold or the flu.

☞ Compare Cultures
What home remedies do you use in your home country? Talk.

What do you do for a cold?
I make chicken soup.

soup
tea

TASK 3 Talk About Medicines
What are three medicines in your home? Make a chart like the one in Activity B. Talk to your group about your chart.

Unit 3 Project

Learners plan, prepare, and complete a family medical information form.

Get Ready

Have learners bring in the following:

- Their spouse's and children's daytime information, including addresses and phone numbers
- Information about their doctor or other health care provider

 Distribute multiple copies of Unit Master 36 (Unit 3 Project: Family Medical Information Form) to each learner. Each learner will need a copy for each of their family members.

Do the Work

Have learners complete the project masters.

Present Your Project

Have learners practice the conversation with a partner.

Ongoing Assessment

While learners complete the project, circulate. Listen to at least five different interactions involving at least three different pairs. Make notes on how well learners perform on the following criteria:

a. General quality of medical information
  - 0 = lack of statements or incomprehensible
  - 1 = partially formed or partially understood
  - 2 = clear and appropriate although not perfect

b. General quality of legibility
  - 0 = lack of legibility or unreadable
  - 1 = partially legible
  - 2 = clearly written although not perfect

c. Features of language functions (making an appointment)
  - 0 = many problems or not understandable
  - 1 = some problems with clarity
  - 2 = clear and appropriate although not perfect

UNIT 3 Project

Family Medical Information Form

Do these things to complete the Family Medical Information Form.

Get Ready
Do these things:
- Get your medical information and your family's medical information.
- Make a list of the addresses where you and your family are during the day.
- Make a list of the phone numbers.

Do the Work
Use the Family Medical Information Forms from your teacher:
- Complete one form for you.
- Complete forms for people in your family.

Present Your Project
- Make copies of your forms. Keep the forms at home. Give a copy to each family member. Give a copy to your neighbor.
- Practice the phone conversations with a partner.

When you call a doctor: "Hello. This is _____. I need to make an appointment. I have a _____."

When you call your children's school: "Hello. This is _____. My son/daughter, _____, is sick today."

When you call work: "Hello. This is _____. I'm sick today."

Technology Extra
Call and leave a message for the teacher. Say you are sick today.

Unit 3 Project 57

Technology Extra

Explain to your learners what number they need to call and what they need to do to leave you a message.

One Step Up

If 911 emergency service is available in your area, explain that this number is for emergency medical care and other emergency help.

- Tell learners that if they call 911, the operator will ask them for the nearest cross street.
- Work with each learner to formulate appropriate 911 emergency information.
- Make sure learners understand that 911 is only for emergencies.

Review what qualifies as an emergency (e.g., a fire, an injury, etc.).

Extension

Teach learners to request a map on the Internet. Type in an address on a map-finding web site (e.g., www.mapquest.com). Then request and print out a detailed map that shows the cross streets near the address.

Assign Workbook p. 31 (Check Your Progress).

Use Unit Master 37 (Unit 3 Checkup/Review) whenever you complete this unit.

Unit 4: I Need a Budget! 🔆

Materials for the Unit

- Some of your monthly bills
- Picture of people shopping for clothes (optional)
- Articles of clothing to illustrate the adjectives *loose, tight, long,* and *short*
- Customizable Masters 2, 3, and 5
- Generic Assessment Masters 6, 8, 9, and 10
- Unit Masters 38–45
- Vocabulary Card Masters for Unit 4

I Need a Budget!

Follow the suggestions on p. 5 for talking about the title.

- Point out the four groups of unit goals listed below the title.
- Tell learners that this unit will focus on making a budget, saving money, and improving work skills to earn more money.

Attention Box

These words should be understood, but learners should not be expected to produce them at this point.

- Take a book from a learner and say, "I need to *borrow* this book."
- After a few minutes, return the book and say, "Thank you for letting me *borrow* your book."
- Tell learners that to *borrow* something means to take something that you will return.

Question

Read the question under the arrow.

- Show learners some of your bills. Say, "This is my electric bill," "This is my rent bill," etc.
- Ask learners about their bills.
- List different kinds of bills on the board or a transparency.

Photo

Follow the suggestions on p. 4 for talking about the photo. Then ask these *either/or* questions:

- Is Ramon in his car or house?
- Is he at his table or in his bed?
- Is he paying bills or writing bills?

Practice reading numbers by going over amounts in the budget. Call on individual learners to read them.

Caption

Read the caption aloud and have learners repeat after you. Then ask these *yes* or *no* questions:

- Is Ramon from China?
- Does he live in Texas now?
- Does he have much money?
- Does he work?

Think and Talk

Read the questions aloud. Write learners answers on the board or a transparency.

Answers

1. Answers will vary.
2. Ramon has too many bills. He doesn't have much money left at the end of the month.
3. Possible answers: borrowing from relatives or friends, buying less, working more, not paying bills now, paying only a little now.

What's Your Opinion?

Tally learners' opinions on the board or an overhead transparency.

Picture Dictionary

Read the words in the student book. Follow the suggestions on p. 6 for introducing and reinforcing vocabulary.

Follow the suggestions on p. 6 for using vocabulary cards. Use the cards for the words in the Picture Dictionary.

- Explain that a *budget* is a plan to save and spend money.
- Ask learners how they can pay *bills* (e.g., paper money, *credit card, check*).
- Talk about the concept of *opposites* (e.g., big/small, cheap/expensive, spend/save).

Gather Your Thoughts

Use Customizable Master 5 (Idea Map). Follow the suggestions on p. 7 for customizing and duplicating the master. Make a copy for each learner.

Discuss ways to save money with learners; then have them fill in the other circles in their idea maps. Ask these questions:

- Do you buy things on sale? Where?
- Do you make your clothes?
- Do you grow your own food?

One Step Down

If learners do not have the vocabulary to tell how they save money, ask them to mime their answer. Alternatively, have them draw pictures on the board or an overhead transparency.

What's the Problem?

Follow the suggestions on p. 5 for identifying and analyzing problems.

Setting Goals

Follow the suggestions on p. 5 for setting goals. Reinforce the idea that goals 2–4 are things they want to do using English language.

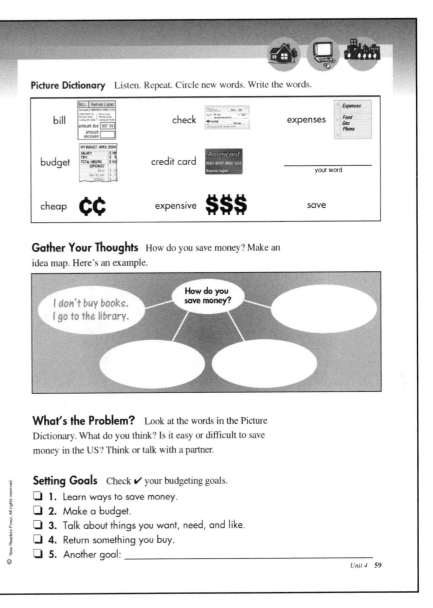

Extension

Ask learners how many of these things they do in English. Read each goal and have learners who do that activity raise their hands.

Lesson 1: Thinking about Saving Money

- Follow the suggestions on p. 5 for talking about titles; then point out the lesson objectives listed below it.
- Tell learners that this lesson is about saving money.

Question

Read the question aloud. List learners' responses on the board or an overhead transparency. If learners have difficulty, tell them to look again at Ramon's budget on p. 58.

Attention Box

- Write these definitions on the board or a transparency:
  quit = stop
  rent = money you pay for an apartment
  journal = a book for writing
- Read the words and use each in a sentence.

This vocabulary should be understood, but learners should not be expected to produce the words at this point.

Photo

Follow the suggestions on p. 4 for talking about photos.

- Ask learners what they see in the photo. Ask, "What's happening?" Write their responses on the board.
- Explain that a *journal* is used to write your own thoughts.
- Ask learners why they think Ramon writes his journal in English. (Possible answer: to practice English for his class.)

Reading Tip

Read the tip aloud.

- Tell learners they do not need to know every word in a reading to understand it. Explain that many readers guess the meaning of a new word from how it is used.
- Tell learners to look at any pictures before they read and to look at other words near the new

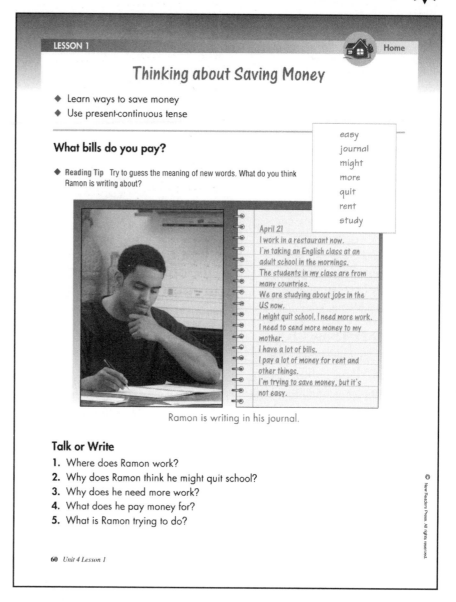

Thinking about Saving Money

- Learn ways to save money
- Use present-continuous tense

What bills do you pay?

- Reading Tip Try to guess the meaning of new words. What do you think Ramon is writing about?

easy
journal
might
more
quit
rent
study

April 21
I work in a restaurant now.
I'm taking an English class at an adult school in the mornings.
The students in my class are from many countries.
We are studying about jobs in the US now.
I might quit school. I need more work.
I need to send more money to my mother.
I have a lot of bills.
I pay a lot of money for rent and other things.
I'm trying to save money, but it's not easy.

Ramon is writing in his journal.

Talk or Write

1. Where does Ramon work?
2. Why does Ramon think he might quit school?
3. Why does he need more work?
4. What does he pay money for?
5. What is Ramon trying to do?

word. Pictures and other words can help them make good guesses about meaning.

Follow the suggestions for reading comprehension on p. 5. Then ask *yes/no* questions like these:
- Does Ramon go to school?
- Is he taking a class at night?
- Does he have a job?

Talk or Write

This exercise improves skill in discerning cause and effect.

Ask learners to answer the questions aloud; then have them write the answers. Ask where learners found answers.

Answers
1. He works at a restaurant.
2. He needs more work.
3. He needs money.
4. He pays for rent and other things.
5. He's trying to save money.

Vocabulary

Read the words in the student book. Follow the suggestions on p. 6 for introducing and reinforcing vocabulary.

Follow the suggestions on p. 6 for using vocabulary cards. Use the cards for the words in the Vocabulary box.

Attention Box

This phrase should be understood, but learners should not be expected to produce it at this point.

- Write these two sentences on the board or an overhead transparency:
  I use e-mail a lot.
  He sends a lot of e-mails.
- Write these two definitions:
  a lot = often, many times
  a lot of = much, many
- Explain that in the first sentence *a lot* is at the end of the sentence. Ask learners what they do *a lot* (e.g., Do you read *a lot?* Do you watch television *a lot?*). Write their responses on the board.
- In the second sentence, point out that *a lot of* is not at the end of the sentence. It comes before a noun. Ask learners what they do *a lot of*. Elicit examples such as, "I watch *a lot of* television."

Class Chat

Use Customizable Master 5 (Idea Map). Follow the suggestions on p. 7 for customizing and duplicating the master. Make one copy for each learner.

Follow the suggestions on p. 7 for Class Chats.

Extension

Choose one sentence from each circle in the idea map, and write it on the board. Then tell learners to write six sentences in their notebooks, two from each circle. Have volunteers read their sentences aloud.

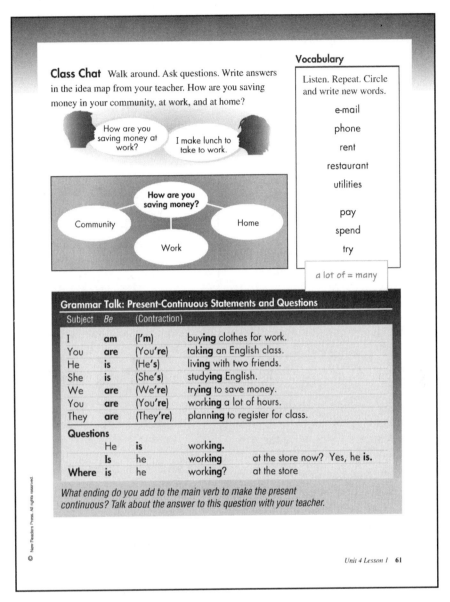

Unit 4 Lesson 1 **61**

Grammar Talk

Follow the suggestions on p. 7 for introducing the grammar point.

Tell learners the present-continuous tense tells about something happening *now*. Then do the following:
- Read the first sentence using the long form of the verb.
- Write the verb on the board or an overhead transparency.
- Circle *am* and *-ing* in the verb to show the difference between this form and the present tense.

Review contractions with *be*. Then write the following formula for the present continuous on the board or an overhead transparency:
Subject + *be* + verb + *ing*
- Write the first two sentences underneath the formula.
- Ask, "What ending do you add to the main verb to form the present continuous?"
- Ask learners questions with the present continuous (e.g., What are you studying?).

Assign Workbook p. 32, Exercises A–C, now or at any time during the rest of Lesson 1.

Activity A

- Read learners the directions. Then model the activity using the first picture.
- Have learners look at the second picture. Ask a learner to read a sentence. Write it on the board or an overhead transparency.
- After learners have written the sentences in their notebook, have volunteers read their sentences aloud. Write them on the board.

Answers
1. She is e-mailing her mother.
2. They are paying their bill.
3. I am saving five dollars.
4. She is renting a video.

Activity B

- First ask questions about the pictures (e.g., *Picture 1:* Where is Ken? How much is the gas? *Picture 2:* Where is Hector? What is he doing?).
- After learners write, have them read their sentences aloud.
- Ask how Ken can save money (e.g., What kind of gas is he using? Can he use another kind? Is there a less expensive way to get to work?). Encourage learners to discuss these questions based on their experiences.

Possible Answers
1. Ken is buying (expensive or premium) gas.
2. Hector is taking the bus.
3. Ken is eating in a restaurant (buying lunch).
4. Hector is eating his lunch from home (a sandwich).

 Use Unit Master 38 (Grammar: Interview) now or at any time during the rest of the unit.

Assign Workbook p. 33, Exercises D–E, now or at any time during the rest of Lesson 1.

Task 1

- After learners work with their partners, have them report to the

---

Activity A Choose one word from each column. Write sentences about the pictures in your notebook.

She	am	renting	her mother.
He	is	e-mailing	the bill.
They	are	saving	five dollars.
I		paying	a video.

Read the sentences to your partner. Exchange papers with your partner. Check your partner's work.

Activity B Who is saving money today? Look at the pictures of Hector and his friend, Ken. Write sentences in your notebook. What are Hector and Ken doing?

1. Ken 2. Hector 3. Ken 4. Hector

How can Ken save money? Talk with the students in your class.

TASK 1 I'm Spending a Lot of Money
Work with a partner. Share information. What are you spending a lot of money on? Tell your partner how you can save money. Make a list.
I'm calling Russia a lot. To save money, I can use e-mail.

Make a poster of how to save money. Put it on the wall in your classroom.

62 *Unit 4 Lesson 1*

---

class about the different ways they can save money.
- Have learners write their ideas on a large sheet of poster paper and post it in the classroom.

Extension
Have learners vote on the 10 best ideas for saving money.
- As learners report their ideas, ask listeners to write down the best ideas they hear.
- Have learners read out the ideas they liked best.
- List the ideas on the board or an overhead transparency.
- Take a hand vote and tally the responses. Use these ideas on the poster.

Lesson 2: Improving Your Job Skills 🪟

- Read the title aloud; then point out the lesson objectives listed below it.
- Tell learners that in this lesson they will talk about ways to earn more money at work.

Improving Your Job Skills

To convey the meaning of *improve,* do the following:

- Make a very rough drawing of a face on the board or an overhead transparency. Say, "It is bad."
- Redraw the poorly rendered elements as you say, "I am *improving* it."

Explain that one way to make more money is to *improve* your job skills.

Attention Box

Read the words to learners, pointing or miming when possible. Use each word in a sentence. This vocabulary should be understood, but learners should not be expected to produce the words at this point.

Tell learners these things about *tips:*

- A *tip* at a restaurant is extra money for good service.
- Servers usually expect a *tip.*
- In the US, 15 to 20 percent of the bill is a good *tip.*

Question

- Explain that *service* has many meanings. Here it means help, especially from waiters.
- Read the question aloud. Write learners' responses on the board (e.g., fast service, friendly service, the right order).

Photo

Remind learners that looking at the details in a picture can help them better understand what they read. Then ask these questions:

- What is Ramon's job?
- Who is Mr. Martin?
- Is Ramon Mr. Martin's boss?
- Is Ramon well dressed?

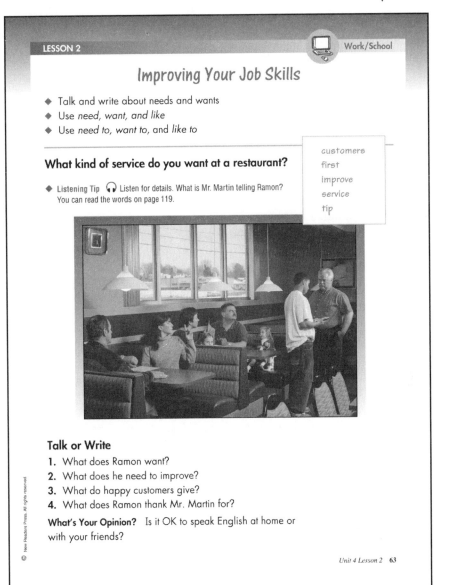

LESSON 2   Work/School

Improving Your Job Skills

- ◆ Talk and write about needs and wants
- ◆ Use *need, want,* and *like*
- ◆ Use *need to, want to,* and *like to*

What kind of service do you want at a restaurant?

- ◆ Listening Tip 🎧 Listen for details. What is Mr. Martin telling Ramon? You can read the words on page 119.

customers
first
improve
service
tip

Talk or Write
1. What does Ramon want?
2. What does he need to improve?
3. What do happy customers give?
4. What does Ramon thank Mr. Martin for?

What's Your Opinion? Is it OK to speak English at home or with your friends?

Unit 4 Lesson 2 **63**

- Who are the other people? Are they happy? Why or why not?
- What is Mr. Martin saying?

Listening Tip

 Play the audio or read the listening script on p. 119.

Follow the suggestions on p. 5 for listening comprehension. Then ask these questions:

- Is Mr. Martin asking Ramon to work more hours?
- What languages does Ramon speak?
- Does Ramon want to improve?

Talk or Write

This exercise helps learners become skilled at listening to conversations.

Answers
1. more hours at work
2. his service, his clothes, and his English
3. good tips
4. his advice

What's Your Opinion?

Tally learners' opinions on the board or an overhead transparency.

Vocabulary

Read the words in the student book. Follow the suggestions on p. 6 for introducing and reinforcing vocabulary.

Follow the suggestions on p. 6 for using vocabulary cards. Use the cards for the words in the Vocabulary box.

Class Chat

Use Customizable Master 3 (3-Column Chart). Follow the suggestions on p. 7 for customizing and duplicating the master. Make a copy for each learner.

Follow the suggestions on p. 7 for Class Chats. Ask learners to be as specific as possible in their answers.

Grammar Talk

Follow the suggestions on p. 7 for introducing the grammar point.

- Tell learners that this is a review of the verbs *want* and *need* (taught in the Warm-Up Unit) and that they will now learn the new verb *like*.
- Review the simple present. Write these sentences on the board, circling the *s* on *likes*:
  I like my job.
  Ramon likes his job.
- Ask each learner questions using the verb forms in the grammar box (e.g., What foods do you *like*? What activities you *like* to do?).
- Write learners' responses on the board or an overhead transparency.

Answers

Adjectives and nouns follow *want, need,* and *like.* The base forms of verbs (e.g., *study, work, sleep*) follow *want to, need to,* and *like to.*

One Step Up

- Ask learners with whom they *need* to speak English and with whom they *like* to speak English.
- Ask with whom they *need* or *like* to speak their native language.

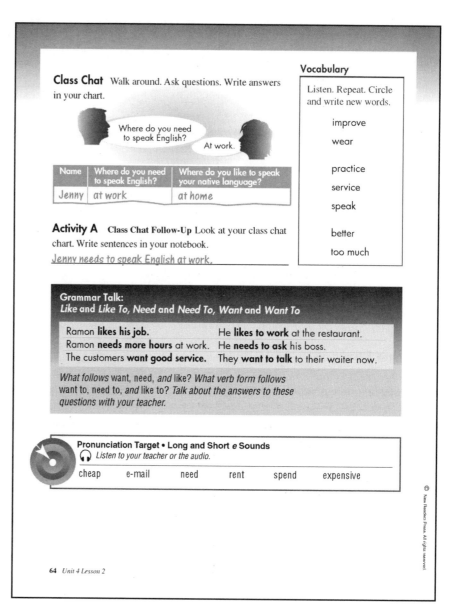

- Encourage them to tell why (e.g., "I *need* to speak English with my boss at work. He doesn't speak Spanish." "I *like* to speak Farsi with my daughter. She needs to speak two languages.").

Pronunciation Target

- Remind learners that they have already learned the two sounds of the letter *a*, long *a (cake)* and short *a (cap).*
- Explain that the letter *e* also has two sounds, long *(read)* and short *(send).* Ask them to listen for these sounds.

 Play the audio or read the words in the student book.

- Have learners repeat the words.
- Use each word in a sentence.
- Write the heads *Long e* and *Short e* on the board.
- Say each word again and ask learners where to write it.

Answers

Long e: cheap, e-mail, need
Short e: rent, spend, expensive

Extension

Point out the words *better* and *speak* in the Vocabulary box. Ask learners in which column to put those words.

Assign Workbook p. 34, Exercises A–B, now or at any time during the rest of Lesson 2.

Activity B

Read the sample sentences. Ask learners for other examples. Have partners check each other's sentences.

Activity C

<u>Extension</u>
- Have learners read their sentences aloud.
- As they read, make a class list of things learners like and like to do. Write the list on the board or an overhead transparency.
- Sort the list into groups of related items (e.g., items about working with people, items about technology, items about money, etc.).
- Form groups of learners who like similar things. Have them discuss what they like or like to do at work or school.

<u>One Step Up</u>
Have each group make a list of other jobs they would like to do or classes they would like to take.

 Assign Workbook p. 35, Exercises C–D, now.

Use Unit Master 39 (Grammar: Likes, Wants and Needs) now or at any time during the rest of the unit.

Task 2

Use Customizable Master 3 (3-Column Chart). Follow the suggestions on p. 7 for customizing and duplicating the master. Make a copy for each learner.

Respect learners' needs for privacy in this exercise. Some learners may not want to share information about the changes they want to make in their lives. Ask learners how many want to share their responses before posting any of their lists.

<u>Assessment</u>
Use Generic Assessment Master 6 (Oral Communication Rubric) to evaluate learner performance.

Activity B What do you want at school or work? What do you want to do? Write two answers for *want* and two answers for *want to* in your notebook.

Want	Want to
1. <u>I want better tips.</u>	<u>I want to use the computer.</u>

Read your sentences to your partner. Listen to your partner's sentences. Tell another person in your group about your partner.

<u>He wants better tips.</u>

Activity C What do you like at school or work? What do you like to do? Write two answers for *like* and two answers for *like to* in your notebook.

Like	Like to
1. <u>I like the people.</u>	<u>I like to talk to the customers.</u>

Read your sentences to your partner. Listen to your partner's sentences. Tell another person in your group about your partner.

<u>Ken likes to talk to the customers.</u>

TASK 2 Make a Change

What do you want to change? With a partner, ask and answer questions about things that you want to change. Write your partner's answers in the chart. Then tell your partner what to do. Write your advice.

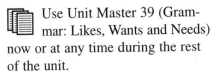

What do you want to change?

I want to get a better job.

You need to improve your English.

Name	What do you want to change?	You need to _____.
Sonali	job	improve your English

Lesson 3: Shopping for Clothes

Follow the suggestions on p. 5 for talking about the title.

- Make sure that learners understand the meanings of *shopping* and *clothes*. If possible, show a picture of people shopping for clothes.
- Point out the lesson objectives listed below the title.
- Tell learners that this lesson is about reading shopping ads and shopping for clothes.

Attention Box

Read the words to learners, pointing or miming to convey meaning when possible. Use them in a sentence. This vocabulary should be understood, but learners should not be expected to produce the words at this point.

- Tell learners that the clothing sizes small, medium, and large are often written as letters *(S, M, L)*. Many people use three other sizes, extra small *(XS)*, extra large *(XL)*, and extra extra large *(XXL)*. Explain that *extra* means *very*.
- Remind learners that sometimes sizes are numbers (e.g., 8, 38).
- Explain that *clothes = clothing*.

Question

Read the question and write volunteers' answers on the board.

Extension

Tally the answers, asking learners to help you count. Post a list of the stores and the number of learners that buy clothes there. Include store addresses so other learners can visit them.

One Step Up

Ask these questions:

- Do you like to shop for clothes? Why or why not?
- Do you always shop for clothes in the same store?

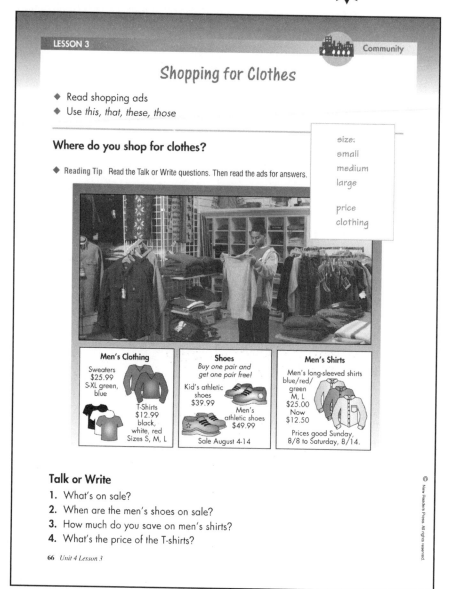

Photo

Follow the suggestions on p. 4 for talking about the photo. Ask:

- Who is this? *(Ramon)*
- What do you see? *(clothes on sale in a store)*
- What's happening? *(Answers will vary.)*

Reading Tip

Tell learners that reading the questions first will help them look for the important information.

- Read the questions beneath the ads.
- Ask what information they will look for.

- Ask learners to tell you the price of different items in the ads.

Talk or Write

This exercise helps learners become skilled at scanning for information.

Answers

1. sweaters, T-shirts, athletic shoes, long-sleeved shirts
2. August 4 to 14
3. 50%, or $12.50
4. $12.99

One Step Down

If learners have difficulty answering the questions, convert them to *either/or* and *yes/no* questions.

Vocabulary

Read the words in the student book. Follow the suggestions on p. 6 for introducing and reinforcing vocabulary.

Follow the suggestions on p. 6 for using vocabulary cards. Use the cards for the words in the Vocabulary box.

Ask learners these questions:
- What clothes do you buy?
- Do you try them on in the store?
- What problems (e.g., *loose, tight, long, short*) do some clothes have? Illustrate each adjective with clothes brought from home.

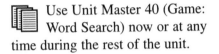 Use Unit Master 40 (Game: Word Search) now or at any time during the rest of the unit.

Remember?

Practice colors and clothing with learners. Ask, "What color is ___ wearing?" "Who is wearing red?"

<u>One Step Up</u>
Have learners ask each other the questions.

Class Chat

Use Customizable Master 2 (2-Column Chart). Follow the suggestions on p. 7 for customizing and duplicating the master. Make a copy for each learner.

Follow the suggestions on p. 7 for Class Chats.
- Model the activity before learners do it on their own.
- Draw two columns on the board or an overhead transparency. Write in the heads *This* and *These*. Under each head, write appropriate clothing words (e.g., *This:* shirt, sweater, T-shirt; *These:* pants, clothes, shoes).
- In doing the activity, learners should point to an article of clothing they are wearing and ask questions like these:
  What color is *that* sweater?
  What color are *those* pants?

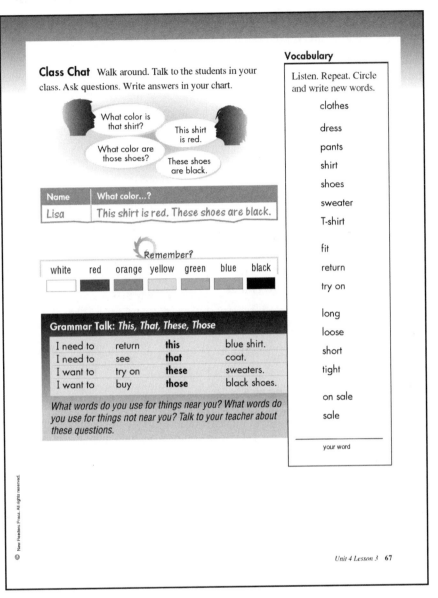

Grammar Talk

Follow the suggestions on p. 7 for introducing the grammar point. Repeat *this* and *these* several times to differentiate between the vowel sounds. Then do the following:
- Ask a learner near you to stand. Point to his or her shirt and ask, "What color is *this* shirt?"
- Ask another learner farther away to stand. Point to that learner and ask, "What color is *that* sweater?"
- Repeat the same activity with *these* and *those,* using two more learners.
- Finally, alternate between *this, that, these,* and *those* with other learners.

Answers

Use *this* and *these* for things that are near. Use *that* and *those* for things that are not near.

Assign Workbook p. 36, Exercises A–B, now or at any time during the rest of Lesson 3.

Use Unit Masters 41 (Grammar: *This, That, These, Those*) and 42 (Phonics: Sounds of *e*) now or at any time during the rest of the unit.

Activity A

 Play the audio or read the listening script below.

- Tell learners to use the words in the box to complete the conversation.
- Have partners check each other's work.
- Read the sentences aloud. Ask learners to call out the answers.
- Write the answers on the board.

Listening Script/Answers

Ramon: I <u>need to</u> return <u>these</u> shirts.
Salesperson: What's the problem?
Ramon: They don't fit well. Is that <u>shirt</u> on sale?
Salesperson: No, it isn't. <u>This</u> shirt is on sale.
Ramon: Good! I need a medium in <u>black</u>.
Salesperson: OK. Anything else?
Ramon: No, thanks. That's it for today.

One Step Up

Have two volunteers role-play the conversation in front of the class.

Activity B

Model the role-play. Begin with sentences like these:
Customer: *I am returning . . .*
Salesperson: *What's the problem?*

Tell learners to use the clothing words on p. 67.

One Step Up

Have learners write the role-plays.

In the US

Tell learners that the phrase "The customer is always right!" is a well-known saying in the US.

Compare Cultures

Tally learners' responses on the board or an overhead transparency. Ask three learners to count the votes for the different options.

One Step Up

Have learners who answered *yes* or *no* in the Compare Cultures activity

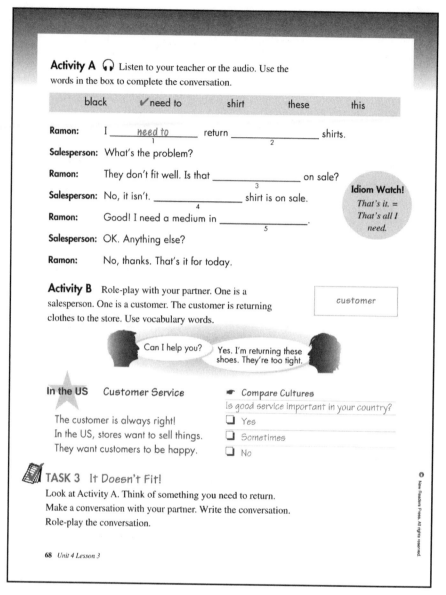

Activity A Listen to your teacher or the audio. Use the words in the box to complete the conversation.

| black | ✔ need to | shirt | these | this |

Ramon: I ____need to____ return _____ shirts.

Salesperson: What's the problem?

Ramon: They don't fit well. Is that _____ on sale?

Salesperson: No, it isn't. _____ shirt is on sale.

Ramon: Good! I need a medium in _____.

Salesperson: OK. Anything else?

Ramon: No, thanks. That's it for today.

Idiom Watch!
That's it. = That's all I need.

Activity B Role-play with your partner. One is a salesperson. One is a customer. The customer is returning clothes to the store. Use vocabulary words.

customer

Can I help you?
Yes. I'm returning these shoes. They're too tight.

In the US Customer Service

The customer is always right!
In the US, stores want to sell things. They want customers to be happy.

☛ **Compare Cultures**
Is good service important in your country?
❑ Yes
❑ Sometimes
❑ No

TASK 3 It Doesn't Fit!
Look at Activity A. Think of something you need to return.
Make a conversation with your partner. Write the conversation.
Role-play the conversation.

tell which countries they are from. Write the countries on the board. What can learners say about the answers?

 Assign Workbook p. 37, Exercises C–D, now.

Task 3

- Tell learners that stores in the US usually allow people to return things, as long as they have their sales receipts.
- List reasons why people return things. Then do the role-play.

Peer Assessment

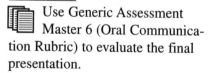 Distribute Generic Assessment Master 10 (Peer

Assessment Form). Have each pair rehearse in front of a small group. Learners can use the form to give each other suggestions on how to improve their conversations.

Assessment

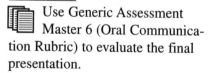 Use Generic Assessment Master 6 (Oral Communication Rubric) to evaluate the final presentation.

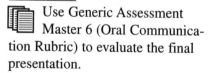 Use Unit Master 43 (Life Skill: Saving Money) now.

Review Unit Skills

See p. 8 for suggestions on games and activities to review the unit vocabulary and grammar.

Unit 4 Project

Get Ready

Learners plan, make, and present a budget.

Tell learners to look at Ramon's budget. Explain that Ramon has made some changes to his old budget (p. 58).

Ask learners these questions:
- What is the change in Ramon's salary?
- What is the change in his tips?
- What is the change in his total income?

Have learners think about how Ramon can make more money and increase his savings. Write their suggestions on the board or an overhead transparency.

Do the Work

Distribute a copy of Unit Master 44 (Unit 4 Project: Preparing a Budget) to each learner.

Extension

After learners complete the form, have them write their ideas for making money (e.g., working more hours, getting a better job, using special talents, etc.).

Present Your Project

Ask a volunteer from each group to write on the board one of the group's ideas for saving money.

Extension

Have groups write their ideas on a large sheet of paper and post them.

Technology Extra

- On a large sheet of paper, make a list of things that learners want to buy.
- After each item, write the name of the learner who wants the item.
- Post the list.
- Find several web sites that sell at least some of those items.
- Have each learner find the best price for the thing he or she wants to buy and write it after that item.

UNIT 4 Project

Make a Budget

Do these things to plan, make, and present a budget.

Get Ready

With your partner, do these things:
- Look at Ramon's old budget on page 58. Look at Ramon's new budget.
- Ken is living with Ramon now. They are sharing expenses.
- How is Ramon saving money now?
- How can he save more money?

June 2004		How Ramon is saving money	How Ramon is making more money	How can Ramon save more money?
Salary	$1500			
Tips	$300		better service	
Total Income	$1800			
Expenses				
Rent	$275	getting a roommate		
Gas for car	$100			
Utilities	$37.50	getting a roommate		
Phone	$130			
Car Insurance	$45			
Food	$160			
Credit card	$50			
For Mother	$150			
Total Expenses	$947.50			
$$ Remaining	$852.50			

Do the Work

Think about your budget.
Use the budget form from your teacher.
- Complete the budget form for you.
- How are you saving money now?
- How can you save more money?

Present Your Project

With your group, talk about your budget.
- Ask your group, "How can I save more money?"
- Write on the board one way your group says you can save money.

Technology Extra
Do you need to buy something? Ask your teacher for a web site. Find the price. Talk with your partner.

Unit 4 Project **69**

Extension
- If another learner finds a better price for a posted item, have the learner add the price to the list.
- Talk together about the prices. Are they better than prices in stores?

 Assign Workbook p. 38 (Check Your Progress).

 Use Unit Master 45 (Unit Checkup/Review) whenever you complete this unit.

Self-Assessment

 Give each learner a copy of Generic Assessment Masters 8 (Speaking and Listening Self-Check) and 9 (Writing and Reading Self-Check). Go over the items together. The completed forms will become part of each learner's portfolio.

Materials for the Unit

- Magazines and newspapers with food coupons, food ads, and pictures of food
- Supermarket flyers
- Candy bar and apple
- Count and noncount items (pencils, pens, books, bottle of water, bag of flour, loaf of bread)
- Pictures of hamburgers and of french fries (optional)
- Local phone books (optional)
- Customizable Masters 1–5
- Generic Assessment Masters 6, 7
- Unit Masters 46–52
- Vocabulary Card Masters for Unit 5

What's for Dinner?

Follow the suggestions on p. 5 for talking about the title.

- Review the four groups of unit goals listed below the title.
- Tell learners that this unit will focus on buying food at a variety of stores, saving money on groceries, and thinking about eating habits.

Photo

Read the question below the arrow. Then ask learners these questions:

- Are you hungry?
- What kind of food are you thinking about?
- What do you like to eat for dinner?
- What do other people in your family like for dinner?

Follow the suggestions on p. 4 for talking about the photo; then ask these questions:

- How many people are in the picture?
- What are they thinking?

Write responses on the board.

To develop the idea of *eating out* versus *eating at home*, do the following:

UNIT 5

What's for Dinner?

Choosing Good Food

Community 1 Home 2 Work/School 3

- ◆ **Vocabulary** Foods • Coupons
- ◆ **Language** Count and noncount nouns • *There is* and *there are* • Questions and answers with *or*
- ◆ **Pronunciation** Intonation with words in a list
- ◆ **Culture** Fast food

Let's eat. Anything! Anywhere!

Do all the people in your family like the same food?

Miyako and her family are hungry. They want different things to eat.

Think and Talk

1. What do you see?
2. What's the problem?
3. What do you like to eat for dinner?

70 *Unit 5*

- Say "I eat at home most days, but on ____ (name of day) I like to eat out."
- Draw a one-week calendar on the board or an overhead transparency. Write *at home* on each day of the week except the day you eat out. On that day, write the name of a well-known local restaurant where you eat.
- Ask learners where they like to go when they eat out, and write the names of the places on the board

Think and Talk

Possible Answers

1. Learners will have a variety of answers. Write them on the board or an overhead transparency.
2. Everybody wants something different for dinner. The husband is tired and wants to eat now.
3. Learners will have a variety of answers. Write them on the board or an overhead transparency.

Picture Dictionary

Read the words in the student book. Follow the suggestions on p. 6 for introducing and reinforcing vocabulary.

Follow the suggestions on p. 6 for using vocabulary cards. Use the cards for the words in the Picture Dictionary.

Gather Your Thoughts

Use Customizable Master 5 (Idea Map). Follow the suggestions on p. 7 for customizing and duplicating the master. Make a copy for each group.

Ask learners these questions:
- What kind of fruit do you like?
- What kind of vegetables do you like?

Write their answers on the board. Then ask questions like these:
- Who eats fruit for breakfast?
- Who eats fruit for lunch?
- Who eats vegetables for breakfast? For lunch?

Repeat this procedure with other foods from the Picture Dictionary. Then do the following:
- Ask learners to work with their groups to fill in the idea map.
- After the maps are completed, have each learner ask the next group member a question based on the map (e.g., When do you eat ___?).
- All learners should have a chance to ask and answer a question.
- When everyone is finished, compare the group maps.

What's the Problem?

Follow the suggestions on p. 5 for identifying and analyzing problems. Then do the following:
- Explain that *healthy* means "good for you."
- Hold up a candy bar. Ask, "Is this *healthy* or *unhealthy?*"
- Hold up an apple. Ask, "Is this *healthy* or *unhealthy?*"

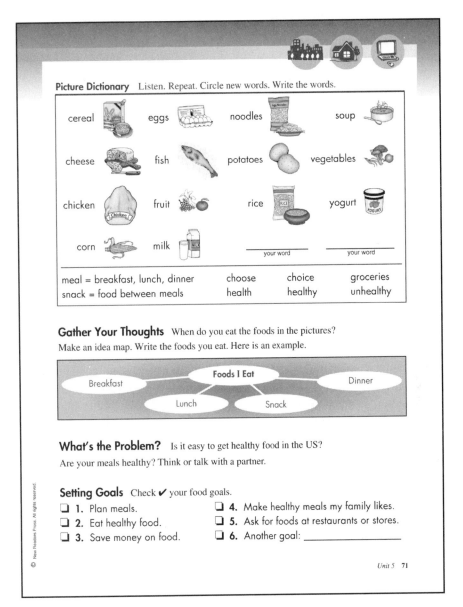

Picture Dictionary Listen. Repeat. Circle new words. Write the words.

cereal · eggs · noodles · soup
cheese · fish · potatoes · vegetables
chicken · fruit · rice · yogurt
corn · milk · your word · your word

meal = breakfast, lunch, dinner · choose · choice · groceries
snack = food between meals · health · healthy · unhealthy

Gather Your Thoughts When do you eat the foods in the pictures?
Make an idea map. Write the foods you eat. Here is an example.

Breakfast · Foods I Eat · Dinner · Lunch · Snack

What's the Problem? Is it easy to get healthy food in the US?
Are your meals healthy? Think or talk with a partner.

Setting Goals Check ✔ your food goals.
- ❏ 1. Plan meals.
- ❏ 2. Eat healthy food.
- ❏ 3. Save money on food.
- ❏ 4. Make healthy meals my family likes.
- ❏ 5. Ask for foods at restaurants or stores.
- ❏ 6. Another goal: _____

- Ask learners to suggest other foods that are *healthy*. Write the food names on the board.
- Ask for *unhealthy* foods. Write their names on the board.
- Ask learners, "Which foods are easy to find? Which are hard to find?"

Read and discuss the questions in the student book. Elicit more information by asking *why* or *why not*. Then ask these follow-up questions:
- Do you buy food because it tastes good? Because it is inexpensive? Healthy? Easy or fast to prepare?
- Who in your family makes the decisions about which foods to buy?

- Who in your family shops for food?

Setting Goals

Follow the suggestions on p. 5 for setting goals.

Lesson 1: At the Supermarket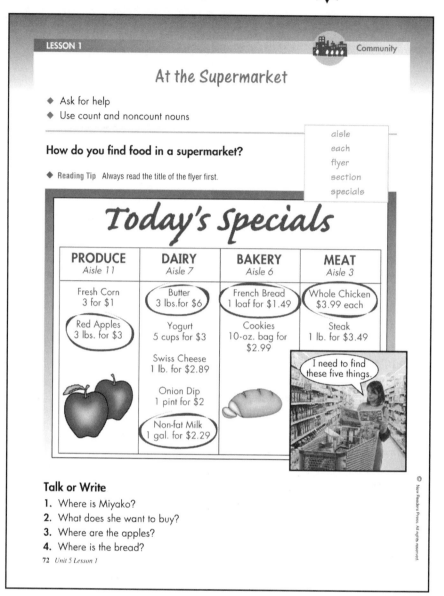

Follow the suggestions on p. 5 for talking about the title. Then point out the lesson objectives listed below it.

- This lesson is about getting help in a supermarket and finding different kinds of foods.
- Learners will also write a grocery list.

Attention Box

- Write *aisle* on the board or an overhead transparency.
- Cross out *a*, *s*, and *e*. Tell learners those letters are *silent*, i.e., you do not say or hear them.
- Explain that an *aisle* is a space between rows. In a supermarket, an *aisle* is where you walk between rows of shelves.
- Look at the small picture of Miyako and point to the *aisle* behind her in the store. Ask "Where else do you see an *aisle?*" *(theater, church, bus)*
- Write *special* on the board. Circle *ci* and say *sh*. Have learners repeat the sound, then the word. Explain that *specials* are items sold at reduced prices.

This vocabulary should be understood, but learners should not be expected to produce the words at this point.

Reading Tip

Read the tip aloud. Explain that reading the title of a flyer tells you what it is about. Ask:
- What does the title say?
- What is this flyer about?

Tell learners *flyers* are types of advertisements. Ask:
- Where do you see flyers? *(mail, bulletin boards, kiosks, stores)*
- Where is this flyer from? *(the supermarket where Miyako is shopping)*

Talk or Write

This exercise helps learners become skilled at reading charts.

- Bring in other supermarket flyers or ads and ask *wh-* and *either/or* questions about them.
- If learners have difficulty with question 2, point out the items circled on the flyer.

<u>Answers</u>
1. Miyako is at the supermarket.
2. She wants to buy apples, butter, milk, bread, and chicken.
3. The apples are in the produce section in aisle 11.
4. The bread is in the bakery section in aisle 6.

<u>One Step Up</u>
Explain that foods are sold in certain quantities or in containers of certain sizes. These quantities and sizes are often referred to in advertising.

- Using the items on the flyer, write on the board how each is measured and sold [e.g., *pounds (lb.), cups, pints (pt.), gallons (gal.),* and *ounces (oz.)*].
- Point out that the abbreviations for *pound* and *ounce* are not directly formed from the words.

<u>One Step Down</u>
Ask learners to look in magazines for pictures of foods they like. Have them talk about the foods in their groups.

Picture Dictionary

Read the words in the student book. Follow the suggestions on p. 6 for introducing and reinforcing vocabulary.

Follow the suggestions on p. 6 for using vocabulary cards. Use the cards for the words in the Picture Dictionary. Have learners organize the cards into categories (e.g., healthy/unhealthy, fruit/vegetable, count/noncount).

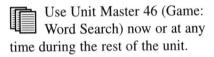 Use Unit Master 46 (Game: Word Search) now or at any time during the rest of the unit.

Partner Chat

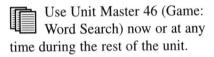 Use Customizable Master 3 (3-Column Chart). Follow the suggestions on p. 7 for customizing and duplicating the master. Make copies for each learner.

Follow the suggestions on p. 7 for Partner Chats.

Have volunteers model asking and answering questions.

Grammar Talk

Follow the suggestions on p. 7 for introducing the grammar point.

- Explain that a noun names a person, place, or thing. List several nouns on the board.
- Tell learners that *count nouns* name things you can count. They can be singular or plural. Demonstrate *count nouns* by counting out pencils, pens, and books.
- Explain that *noncount nouns* name things you cannot count. They cannot be made plural unless we qualify them. Show these items to demonstrate *noncount nouns:*
  water – bottle of water
  flour – bag of flour
  bread – loaf or slice of bread
- Ask learners to name other *count* and *noncount* nouns.

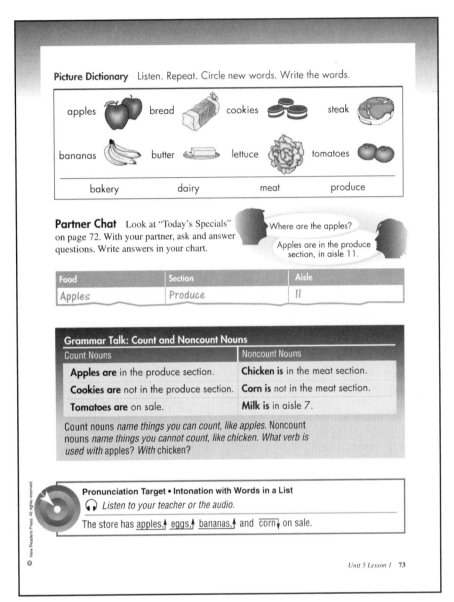

- Point to the *count-noun* sentences in the grammar box. Ask learners, "Is the noun singular or plural?" "Is the verb singular or plural?" Repeat for the *noncount* sentences.

Answers

The plural verb *are* is used with *apples.*

The singular verb *is* is used with *chicken.*

Pronunciation Target

🎧 Play the audio or read the sentence in the student book. Have learners repeat the sentence.

- Exaggerate the intonation slightly so that learners hear the voice rise on the first three items and then pause before the last phrase, which has a falling intonation.
- Ask learners to list three foods they like and three they do not like. Have them practice saying the foods in a sentence with the right intonation (e.g., "I like cookies, apples, and bread.").

📖 Assign Workbook p. 39, Exercises A–B, now or at any time during the rest of Lesson 1.

Activity A

Review the difference between count and noncount nouns.

- On the board or an overhead transparency, draw a three-column chart. Write the heads *Count* and *Noncount* above the second and third columns.
- In the first column, list the foods from the ad in Activity A: *carrots, lettuce, potatoes, mushrooms, strawberries,* and *bananas.*
- Ask learners which words are *count* nouns and which are *noncount.* Write the words in the appropriate column.
- Write *is* above the *noncount* noun *(lettuce)* and *are* above the remaining *(count)* nouns.
- Have partners ask each other questions about the cost of the items in the ad.

<u>Extension</u>
- Tell learners to copy signs they see at stores and bring the information to class.
- Have learners write four questions about the signs.
- Write the questions on the board.

Activity B

Ask learners to complete the sentences. Then refer to the flyer on p. 72 in the student book to do the following:

- Check learners' answers as a group.
- Model the dialogue by role-playing with the class. First, read Miyako's part and have learners read the clerk's part together. Then exchange roles.
- Have partners read the dialogue to each other several times. Be sure each partner gets practice saying each part.

<u>Answers</u>
1. are
2. produce
3. is
4. bakery
5. Is
6. sale

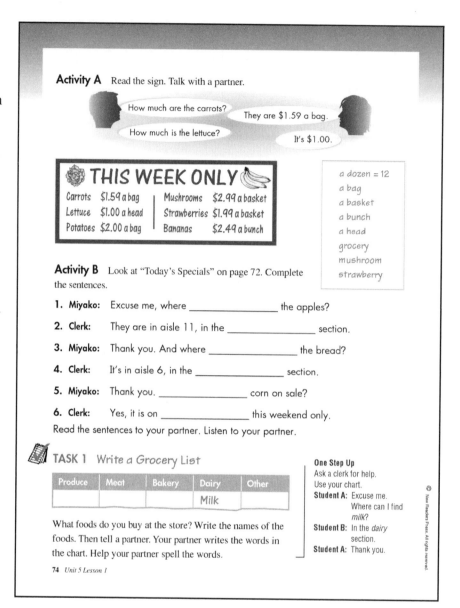

Activity A Read the sign. Talk with a partner.

How much are the carrots?
They are $1.59 a bag.
How much is the lettuce?
It's $1.00.

THIS WEEK ONLY

Carrots	$1.59 a bag	Mushrooms	$2.99 a basket
Lettuce	$1.00 a head	Strawberries	$1.99 a basket
Potatoes	$2.00 a bag	Bananas	$2.49 a bunch

a dozen = 12
a bag
a basket
a bunch
a head
grocery
mushroom
strawberry

Activity B Look at "Today's Specials" on page 72. Complete the sentences.

1. **Miyako:** Excuse me, where _____ the apples?
2. **Clerk:** They are in aisle 11, in the _____ section.
3. **Miyako:** Thank you. And where _____ the bread?
4. **Clerk:** It's in aisle 6, in the _____ section.
5. **Miyako:** Thank you. _____ corn on sale?
6. **Clerk:** Yes, it is on _____ this weekend only.

Read the sentences to your partner. Listen to your partner.

 TASK 1 Write a Grocery List

Produce	Meat	Bakery	Dairy	Other
			Milk	

What foods do you buy at the store? Write the names of the foods. Then tell a partner. Your partner writes the words in the chart. Help your partner spell the words.

74 *Unit 5 Lesson 1*

One Step Up
Ask a clerk for help.
Use your chart.
Student A: Excuse me. Where can I find *milk?*
Student B: In the *dairy* section.
Student A: Thank you.

Assign Workbook p. 40, Exercises C–D, now.

Task 1

Use Customizable Master 4 (4-Column Chart). Divide one column vertically to make a 5-column chart. Follow the suggestions on p. 7 for customizing and duplicating the master. Make a copy for each set of partners.

- Read the question "What foods do you buy at the store?" aloud. Let learners respond informally.
- Have learners work with their partners to fill out the charts.

- Tell partners to discuss which foods go into each column so items are not duplicated.
- Have each pair make an overhead transparency of their chart to share with the class. Discuss which foods are the most and least popular among the whole group.

One Step Up

Have partners practice the conversation using other food vocabulary words.

Lesson 2: Saving Money on Food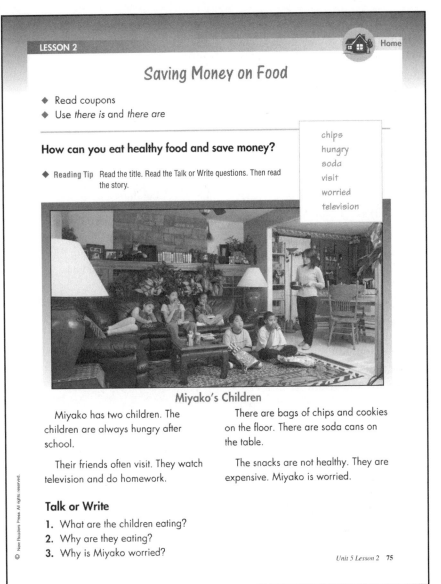

Read the title. Then point out the lesson objectives below it.
- Tell learners that this lesson is about using coupons and saving money.
- Follow the suggestions on p. 5 for talking about titles.

Question
- Read the introductory question aloud.
- Record learners' answers on an idea map drawn on the board or an overhead transparency.
- Encourage discussion by asking these follow-up questions:
  Do you look for sales?
  Do you look for coupons?
  Do you look for healthy food?
  Is healthy food inexpensive or expensive?

Attention Box
Read the words to learners, pointing or miming to convey meaning. Point to the *chips* and *soda* in the photo.

This vocabulary should be understood, but learners should not be expected to produce the words at this point.

Reading Tip
Read the tip aloud. Tell learners that by reading the questions first, they will know what information to look for, and that reading the title will tell them what the story is about.

Have learners read the title aloud. Then ask the following questions:
- Who is the story about? *(Miyako's children)*
- What are they doing? *(eating and watching TV)*

Have learners read the Talk or Write questions aloud. Tell them the story will answer these questions. Then do the following to introduce the reading:
- Tell learners Miyako's children are home from school.

LESSON 2 — Home

Saving Money on Food

- Read coupons
- Use *there is* and *there are*

How can you eat healthy food and save money?

- **Reading Tip** Read the title. Read the Talk or Write questions. Then read the story.

chips
hungry
soda
visit
worried
television

Miyako's Children

Miyako has two children. The children are always hungry after school.

Their friends often visit. They watch television and do homework.

There are bags of chips and cookies on the floor. There are soda cans on the table.

The snacks are not healthy. They are expensive. Miyako is worried.

Talk or Write
1. What are the children eating?
2. Why are they eating?
3. Why is Miyako worried?

Unit 5 Lesson 2 **75**

- Ask learners, "What do children do after school?" Write their responses on the board or a transparency.
- Say, "Let's find out what Miyako's children do after school."

Talk or Write
This exercise helps learners make inferences from what they read.

Tell learners to ask and answer the questions with their partner. Then have learners read aloud the sentences in the story that answer each question.

Answers
1. The children are eating chips, cookies, and soda.
2. They're hungry.
3. The snacks aren't healthy, and they are expensive.

Vocabulary

Read the words in the student book. Follow the suggestions on p. 6 for introducing and reinforcing vocabulary. Show learners real coupons, magazines, and newspapers.

Follow the suggestions on p. 6 for using vocabulary cards. Use the cards for the words in the Vocabulary box.

Class Chat

Use Customizable Master 2 (2-Column Chart). Follow the suggestions on p. 7 for customizing and duplicating the master. Make a copy for each learner. Follow the suggestions on p. 7 for Class Chats.

Grammar Talk

Follow the suggestions on p. 7 for introducing the grammar point.

- Hold up a sample flyer or super-market ad. Have learners read aloud the first statement in their book (*There is a special today.*).
- Hold up a magazine and say, "There is a food coupon in the magazine." Have learners repeat. Read and repeat the other statements in the same manner.
- Write *there is* on the board. Draw an arrow from *is* to show how it moves in front of *there* to make a question.
- Remind learners to use *is* with singular and noncount nouns and *are* with plural count nouns.
- Practice using short answers (e.g., *Yes, there is. No, there aren't.*) by asking questions about the flyer on p. 72 (e.g., "Is there a special on butter?").

Use Unit Masters 47 (Grammar: Questions) and 48 (Grammar: Statements) now or at any time during the rest of the unit.

Activity A

Tell learners this is a conversation that is out of order. Their task is to

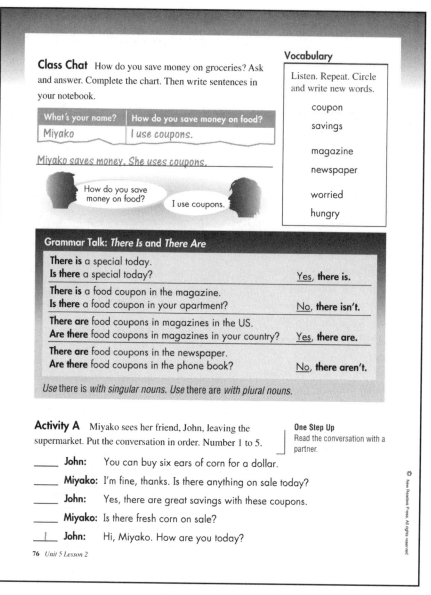

put it in the right order. Model the task in this way:

- Read the sentences aloud; have learners repeat after you.
- Remind learners that in a conversation the speakers alternate. Explain that if John says something first, Miyako is going to say something next.
- Point out the *1* written before the last line in the activity. Tell learners to put the conversation in order by numbering the remaining sentences.

Check answers as a class. Have partners role-play the dialogue in the correct order.

Answers
5, 2, 3, 4, 1

Extension
Have learners write the conversation in the correct order.

Assign Workbook p. 41, Exercises A–B, now or at any time during the rest of Lesson 2.

Extension
Use vocabulary cards and Unit Masters 47 (Grammar: Questions) and 48 (Grammar: Statements) for further practice with *there is/there are*. Have learners work together to make questions (using Master 47) and statements (using Master 48) with the vocabulary words from this unit.

Attention Box

- Point to the first coupon. Explain that *Expires 5-19-05* means that May 19, 2005, is the *expiration date* and that you cannot use the coupon after that date.
- Refer to the second coupon. Read, "*Limit* one coupon per purchase." Ask, "How many cans of tomatoes can you buy for the sale price?"
- Explain that *limit* means "no more than." You can use only one coupon to buy tomatoes at the special price.

This vocabulary should be understood, but learners should not be expected to produce the words at this point.

Activity B

- Ask, "What are food coupons for?" Write the answer *(to save money)* on the board.
- Read the activity directions with learners.
- Point to the first ad. Read the information *(yogurt, 32 ounces)* and ask these questions:
  What is on sale? *(yogurt)*
  How much can you save? *(25¢)*
  Can you save on any size yogurt? *(No, only the 32 oz. size.)*
- Repeat this procedure for the second ad.

Tell learners to look at the questions.

- Have learners repeat the questions and answer orally. Clarify meaning if necessary.
- Ask learners to write the answers for the questions.
- Have partners read and answer the questions. Be sure each learner reads all the questions and all the answers once.
- Call on individual learners to read a question and answer. This could also be done with half the class reading the questions and half reading the answers.

Activity B Read the coupons. Answer the questions.

MANUFACTURER'S COUPON
EXPIRES 5-19-05

SAVE 25¢
When you buy any 32-oz. Yogurt

YOGURT

MANUFACTURER'S COUPON   EXPIRES 3-31-05

SAVE $1.00 on any 5
Tomatoes 14.5 oz. or larger
Limit one coupon per purchase.

expires = cannot be used after this date
expiration date = date when coupon expires
limit = no more than

1. Is there a limit on the tomato coupon? _Yes, there is._
2. Is there an expiration date on the yogurt coupon? _____
3. Are there expiration dates on the two coupons? _____
4. Are there limits on the coupons? _____

Read the questions and answers with a partner.

TASK 2 Look for Specials and Coupons

Work in your group.
What foods do you need in your homes?
Make a list for your group.
Find specials or coupons for the foods.
Tell about the specials and coupons.

This coupon has an expiration date.

There is a special on eggs this week.

Unit 5 Lesson 2 **77**

Answers
2. Yes, there is.
3. Yes, there are.
4. No, there aren't.

Use Customizable Master 1 (Bingo), plus food cards from the vocabulary cards for Unit 5. See instructions for playing bingo on p. 9.

Task 2

Provide supermarket ads or flyers from stores or newspapers so that learners can search in class for specials or coupons to use for this task.

- Ask learners to write three food items that they need at home.

- Have them find a coupon or ad for at least one of the items.
- Have learners practice talking about the items using the coupon or ad.

Assessment

Use Generic Assessment Master 6 (Oral Communication Rubric) to evaluate learner performance.

Assign Workbook p. 42, Exercises C–D, now.

Lesson 3: It's Lunch Time! 🔆www

Read the title and point out the lesson objectives below it.
- Tell learners that this lesson is about fast-food restaurants and going out to eat.
- Follow the suggestions on p. 5 for talking about titles.

Attention Box

If possible, display pictures of *hamburgers* and *fries.* Ask learners:
- Does this school (or learning center) have a *cafeteria?*
- Do you use it? Why or why not?
- Where can you buy *burgers?*
- Do you like *fries?*

This vocabulary should be understood, but learners should not be expected to produce the words at this point.

Question

Read the question aloud. List learners' answers on the board or a transparency. Tally responses and discuss how many people eat at home, at fast-food restaurants, at a work or school cafeteria, etc.

Listening Tip

- Ask learners how looking at the photo will help them understand what they hear. (Possible answers: *They will have a better idea of the context of the conversation. They will know what kinds of words the people might be using.*)
- Read the tip aloud.

Photo

Follow the suggestions on p. 4 for talking about the photo. Ask learners these questions:
- Where are the people?
- What do you see in the picture?
- What do you think is happening?

Write learners' answers on the board or an overhead transparency.

LESSON 3 💻 Work/School

It's Lunch Time!

◆ Order food in fast-food restaurants
◆ Learn about fast food in the US
◆ Use *or* in questions and answers

cafeteria
burgers = hamburgers
fries = french fries

Where do you eat lunch?

◆ Listening Tip 🎧 When you listen, look first. Think about what's happening. Look at the photo. Think. What's happening with Miyako and her friends at school? Listen to your teacher or the audio. You can read the words on page 119.

Miyako and her friends make lunch choices.

Talk or Write
1. Where is Miyako?
2. Where are her friends going?

What's Your Opinion? Should Miyako go with her friends?
❑ Yes ❑ Maybe ❑ No

78 *Unit 5 Lesson 3*

Listening

🎧 Play the audio or read the listening script on p. 119. Follow the suggestions on p. 5 for listening comprehension.

Talk or Write

This exercise helps learners become skilled at finding the main idea in what they hear.

Follow the suggestions on p. 6 for comprehension questions.

Answers
1. Miyako's at school.
2. Her friends are going to Hamburger Hut or Tacos to Go for a fast lunch.

What's Your Opinion?

Follow the suggestions on p. 6 for answering comprehension questions.

If learners answer *yes* or *maybe,* ask "Why?" (Possible answers: *It's a good chance to practice English or make new friends. Maybe she could take her lunch and just buy something to drink.*)

Vocabulary

Read the words in the student book. Follow the suggestions on p. 6 for introducing and reinforcing vocabulary.

Follow the suggestions on p. 6 for using vocabulary cards. Use the cards for the words in the Vocabulary box.

- To elicit prior knowledge, ask learners questions like these: Where do you go when you eat out? What foods do you eat?
- Write learners' answers on the board. If learners respond with the name of a fast-food restaurant, write *fast food* next to it.
- Introduce any words in the Vocabulary box that were not elicited from the group.
- Introduce the words in context (e.g., "Many people like to eat at fast-food restaurants such as ____. They are very popular.").

Class Chat

Use Customizable Master 2 (2-Column Chart). Follow the suggestions on p. 7 for customizing and duplicating the master. Make a copy for each learner. Follow the suggestions on p. 7 for Class Chats.

Grammar Talk

Follow the suggestions on p. 7 for introducing the grammar point.

- Explain that *or* can be used to indicate a *choice* or an *alternative*.
- In the first question, *or* is used as a choice. The answer is one of the choices *(at home* or *at work)*.
- In the second example, the answer includes two *alternatives*. The speaker shops at *either* Happy Mart *or* Smart Shop.

In the US

- Have learners read the passage to themselves.
- Read the passage aloud and have learners repeat each line after you.

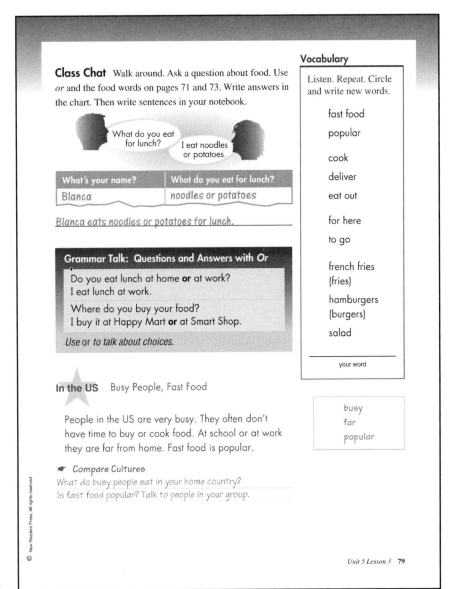

- Ask *yes/no* questions about some of the statements (e.g., Are people in the US very busy?).
- Ask information questions about the statements (e.g., Who is busy?).

Compare Cultures

Tally learners' responses to determine in which countries fast food is popular.

Assign Workbook p. 43, Exercises A–B, now or at any time during the rest of Lesson 3.

Activity A

Review the words in the box.

 Play the audio or read the listening script below twice.

- The first time, have learners listen. The second time, have them fill in the blanks.
- Have learners check their partner's work and read the selection to each other.

Listening Script

People in the US are very busy. They often don't have time to buy or cook food. At school or at work they are far from home. Fast food is popular. But there are problems with fast food. It often has a lot of fat, salt, or sugar. Too much fat, salt, and sugar are bad for people's health. Some fast-food restaurants are changing. Now they have salads or other healthy foods. Small changes in food choices can make big health differences.

Answers

1. buy
2. cook
3. Fast food
4. health
5. healthy
6. choices

Use Unit Master 49 (Thinking Skill: Food Pyramid) now or at any time during the rest of the unit.

Activity B

Follow the suggestions on p. 5 for listening comprehension.

Play the audio or read the listening script below.

Listening Script

Listen. Maria is at the fast-food restaurant.
Clerk: Welcome to Hamburger Hut. Your order please.
Maria: I'd like Fast Meal Number 3. Are there fries with that?
Clerk: Yes, there are. And to drink? Soda or coffee?
Maria: Orange soda, please.
Clerk: For here or to go?

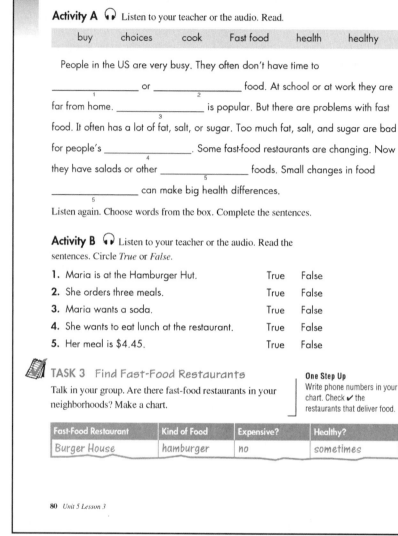

Activity A Listen to your teacher or the audio. Read.

| buy | choices | cook | Fast food | health | healthy |

People in the US are very busy. They often don't have time to

_____ or _____ food. At school or at work they are
　　　　1　　　　　　　　　　2

far from home. _____ is popular. But there are problems with fast
　　　　　　　　　3

food. It often has a lot of fat, salt, or sugar. Too much fat, salt, and sugar are bad

for people's _____. Some fast-food restaurants are changing. Now
　　　　　　　　4

they have salads or other _____ foods. Small changes in food
　　　　　　　　　　　　　5

_____ can make big health differences.
　　　5

Listen again. Choose words from the box. Complete the sentences.

Activity B Listen to your teacher or the audio. Read the sentences. Circle *True* or *False*.

1. Maria is at the Hamburger Hut.	True	False
2. She orders three meals.	True	False
3. Maria wants a soda.	True	False
4. She wants to eat lunch at the restaurant.	True	False
5. Her meal is $4.45.	True	False

TASK 3 Find Fast-Food Restaurants

Talk in your group. Are there fast-food restaurants in your neighborhoods? Make a chart.

One Step Up
Write phone numbers in your chart. Check ✔ the restaurants that deliver food.

Fast-Food Restaurant	Kind of Food	Expensive?	Healthy?
Burger House	hamburger	no	sometimes

Maria: To go.
Clerk: OK, that's $4.25.

Answers
1. True
2. False
3. True
4. False
5. False

Use Unit Master 50 (Grammar: Questions and Answers with *or*) now or at any time during the rest of the unit.

Task 3

Use Customizable Master 4 (4-Column Chart). Follow the suggestions on p. 7 for customizing and duplicating the master. Make a copy for each group.

Model questions for learners to ask in their groups.

One Step Up

- Provide phone books for learners to use in looking up phone numbers.
- Have partners practice asking restaurants if they deliver food.
- Then have learners call various restaurants to find out which ones deliver.

Assign Workbook p. 44, Exercises C–D, now.

Review Unit Skills

See p. 8 for suggestions on games and activities to review the vocabulary and grammar in this unit.

Unit 5 Project

Learners plan, prepare, and present a meal.

Get Ready

 Use Unit Master 51 (Unit 5 Project: Planning a Meal). Distribute a copy to each learner. Tell learners they will be planning a meal.

Follow these steps:
- Ask each learner to bring a recipe to class. Have each write on the master the foods he or she will need to make the recipe.
- Bring supermarket ads to class. Have learners look in the ads for the foods they need for their recipes.
- Write the foods and the prices. Ask if any food is on sale.
- For learners who do not have time or cannot cook, ask them to think about some food they like to order in a restaurant.
- Have them think about the food and make a list of what is in it. Then write the price they usually pay for it.

Do the Work

Buying the food or ordering it in a restaurant is a "reality check" for learners' price estimates.

The project can be done without this step. Use your own judgment as to whether learners have the time, money, and motivation to do this part of the project.

Present Your Project

Have learners fill in the sentences on the master before they make their presentations. The sentences they write can serve as notes for talking about their food.

Assessment

 Use Generic Assessment Master 6 (Oral Communication Rubric) or 7 (Written Communication Rubric) to evaluate learner performance.

UNIT 5 PROJECT

Planning a Meal

Do these things to plan, prepare, and present a meal.

Get Ready

Do these things:
- Find a recipe. Write it on the form from your teacher.
- What do you need to buy? Make a list of foods.
- Check the newspaper for food ads and coupons.

If you don't have time or can't cook, make choices:
- Can you order this food in a restaurant?
- Is it expensive in a restaurant?

Do the Work

If you have time and can cook:
- Buy the foods for the recipe.
- Make the food.
- Eat the food. Share it with family or friends.

If you don't have time or can't cook:
- Order restaurant food to go or to eat in the restaurant.
- What's in the food? Make a list.
- Write how much the food costs.
- Eat the food. Share it with family or friends.

Present Your Project

Talk or write about your food:
- Is it from a recipe or a restaurant?
- Read your food shopping list.
- Is the food healthy? Tell why or why not.
- Is the food cheap or expensive? Tell why or why not.
- Tell why you and your family like the food.

Remember?
cheap ¢ ¢
expensive $ $ $

share

One Step Up
Have a class party. Bring your food. Eat new foods. Talk about the foods. Talk about food in the US and other places. Have fun.

Technology Extra
Write your recipe on the computer. Make copies for the class.

Unit 5 Project **81**

One Step Up

Encourage learners to bring their food for the class to sample—either from a favorite restaurant or from home.

 Assign Workbook p. 45 (Check Your Progress).

 Use Unit Master 52 (Unit 5 Checkup/Review) whenever you complete this unit.

Unit 6: Call the Police!

Materials for the Unit

- Your keys
- Your personal photo album
- Examples of inexpensive items that are important to you
- Picture of a van
- Magazines with pictures of people
- Customizable Masters 2, 3, and 5
- Generic Assessment Masters 6, 7, and 10
- Unit Masters 53–58
- Vocabulary Card Masters for Unit 6

Call the Police!

Follow the suggestions on p. 5 for talking about the title.

- Read the four groups of unit goals listed below the title.
- Explain that in this unit learners will focus on crime-related issues such as protecting their home and valuables, reporting a crime to the police, and describing a suspect.

Question

Read the question below the arrow.

- List learners' answers on the board or a transparency.
- Answering this question may be challenging for some learners. Provide words if learners are struggling to express concepts but have limited vocabulary.

Photos

Follow the suggestions on p. 4 for talking about the photos. Ask learners, "What time do you go home from work or school every day?"

Ask these questions about the photo on the left:

- Who is she?
- Where is she?
- What is she doing?
- What time is it?

Ask similar questions about the photo on the right.

Caption

- Read the caption aloud.

UNIT 6

Call the Police!

Reporting a Crime

Home 1 · Community 2 · Work/School 3

- ◆ **Vocabulary** Home inventory words • Police report words • Describing people
- ◆ **Language** Past-tense statements with *be* • Past-tense statements with regular and irregular verbs • Past-tense questions with *be* and other verbs
- ◆ **Pronunciation** Long and short *i* sounds • Past-tense ending sounds
- ◆ **Culture** Neighborhood Watch programs in the US

important

Are your things safe?

Sara's a nurse at a hospital. She's going home. What is happening at her home?

Think and Talk

1. What's the problem?
2. Is your neighborhood safe?

What's Your Opinion? Is it important to buy insurance for your things?

☐ Always   ☐ Sometimes   ☐ Never

82 *Unit 6*

- Ask *wh-* questions about the caption.
- Be sure learners understand the connection between the two photos and are aware that the actions in both take place at the same time.

Think and Talk

Read the questions aloud. Explain that the questions refer to the two photos together. Have learners talk with their partners about the answers.

After learners answer question 1, ask, "How do you know?"

Answers

1. Answers will vary. (Possible answers: *Sara is going home from work. A man is stealing a television from her apartment.*)
2. Answers will vary.

What's Your Opinion?

Follow the suggestions on p. 6 for comprehension questions.

- Tell learners that insurance gives you money for losses from certain events (e.g., fires, storms, theft, accidents, sickness, death). Another kind of insurance helps pay for health care.
- Ask learners for what things they can buy insurance (e.g., home, car, health).

Picture Dictionary

Read the words in the student book. Follow the suggestions on p. 6 for introducing and reinforcing vocabulary.

Follow the suggestions on p. 6 for using vocabulary cards. Use the cards for the words in the Picture Dictionary.

<u>One Step Up</u>
- Explain that *lock* can be a noun or a verb. Here *lock* is a noun because it is a thing.
- Show your keys and say, "I lock my house with my house key."
- Then say, "When I lock my house, I put the key in the lock." Write this sentence on the board or an overhead transparency.
- Ask questions using *lock* first as a noun and then as a verb.

Gather Your Thoughts

Make a copy of Customizable Master 5 (Idea Map). Follow the suggestions on p. 7 for customizing and duplicating the master. Make a copy for each learner. Then follow these steps:
- Explain that these questions are about how to protect your things.
- Ask a learner the question in one of the peripheral circles. Write the answer in that circle. Have learners copy the answer into the same circle on their idea maps.
- Have the learner who answered your question ask the next learner another question from the idea map.
- Continue this way, giving every learner an opportunity to ask and answer questions.
- Write each answer in the idea map and have learners copy it into their own. Each learner's map should reflect the ideas of the whole group.

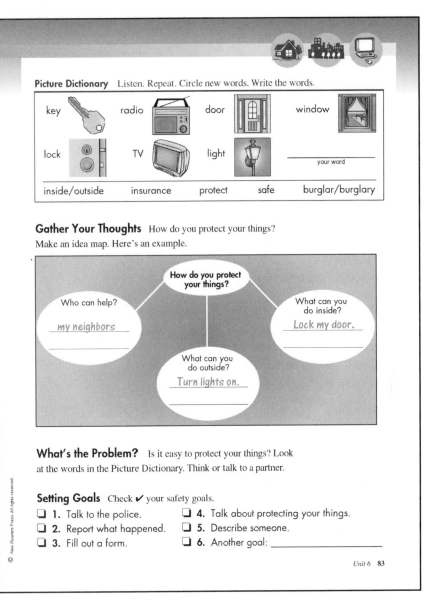

What's the Problem?

Follow the suggestions on p. 5 for identifying and analyzing problems.
- Read the question aloud. Have partners talk about the answer.
- Ask, "Is it easy or difficult to keep things safe in the US?" Tell learners to explain their answers.
- Ask, "Is it easy or difficult to keep things safe in your home country?" Have learners explain.

Setting Goals

Follow the suggestions on p. 5 for setting goals.
- Read the goals and discuss words that may be unfamiliar

(e.g., *police, report, fill out, form, describe*).
- Ask learners if anyone has another safety goal to share. Have them write in their notebook their most important personal goal for this unit.

<u>One Step Up</u>
Encourage proficient learners to orally share their most important goal with the class.

Lesson 1: What a Mess! www

Read the title and point out the lesson objectives below it.

- Tell learners that in this lesson they will make a list of valuable things in their home. Explain that *valuable* things cost a lot or are important to a person.
- Explain the word *mess*. Say, "This week, I didn't clean my house. My house is a *mess!*"

Question

Read the introductory question aloud. Then do the following:

- Write responses to the question on the board or a transparency.
- To illustrate *safe,* put your wallet on your desk. Say the wallet is not *safe* because someone can easily take it. Put the wallet away in your purse or pocket. Tell learners that it is now *safe*.

Attention Box

- Explain that a *burglar* is a person who takes things from homes or other places without permission.
- Things you cannot find are *missing*. Things a *burglar* takes are also *missing*.
- A person who finds a *burglary* has happened is *surprised* or *shocked*. Explain that *surprised* is usually a happy emotion, but *shocked* is not.

This vocabulary should be understood, but learners should not be expected to produce the words at this point.

Photo

Follow the suggestions on p. 4 for talking about the photo. Ask, "What do you see?" and "What's happening? How do you know?"

Reading Tip

- Read the tip aloud. Ask learners what each of the three punctuation marks mean. Point out the marks in the reading.

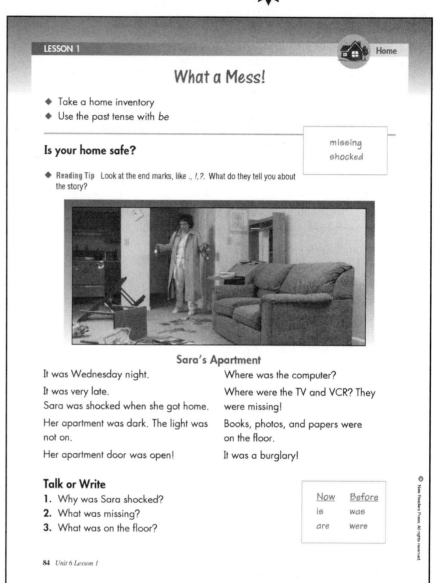

- Following the suggestions on p. 5 for reading comprehension.

Extension

Ask learners to look at unit and lesson titles for units 1–6 and find the punctuation marks *(?!)*. Write the titles on the board. Discuss why each has one of these marks.

Talk or Write

This exercise helps learners become skilled at reading for details.

Read the questions aloud. Follow up each by asking, "How do you know?"

Learners should not be expected to produce the past-tense verb forms, but introduce them aurally now.

Answers

1. Sara's apartment door is/was open.
2. Her computer, TV, and VCR are/were missing.
3. Books, photos, and papers are/were on the floor.

Extension

Ask learners to identify the sentence where they found each answer.

Vocabulary

Read the words in the student book. Follow the suggestions on p. 6 for introducing and reinforcing vocabulary.

Follow the suggestions on p. 6 for using vocabulary cards. Use the cards for the words in the Vocabulary box.

To convey the meanings *dark* and *light,* do the following:

- Turn classroom lights off and say *dark.* Turn the lights on and say *light.* Say, "At noon, it is *light.* At night, it is *dark.*"
- To illustrate *photo album,* show learners your own album and tell them, "A *photo album* is a book for photos."
- To convey the meaning of *quiet,* tell learners to talk loudly among themselves. Speaking over the din, say, "It's noisy." Then hold up your hand and say, "*Quiet,* please." When the talking stops, say, "It's *quiet.*"

Class Chat

Use Customizable Master 3 (3-Column Chart). Follow the suggestions on p. 7 for customizing the master. Make a copy for each learner. Follow the suggestions for Class Chats on p. 7. Tell learners to save their charts to use with Activity A.

Activity A

Ask learners to use the information in their Class Chat charts to write sentences in their notebooks.

Grammar Talk

Follow the suggestions on p. 7 for introducing the grammar point.

- Read the affirmative and negative statements together (e.g., *I was at school. I was not at work.*).
- Write *was not* and *were not* on the board or an overhead transparency.

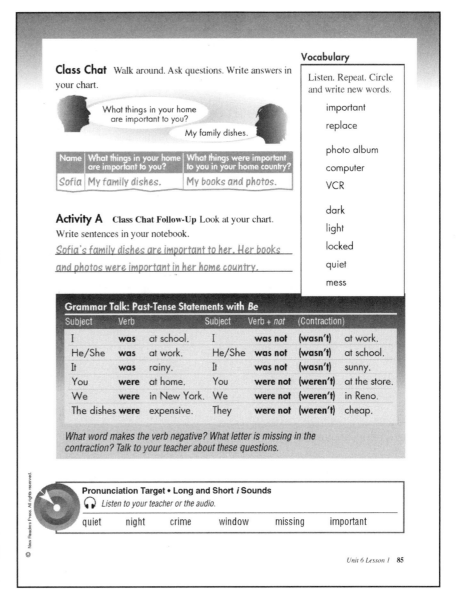

- Cross out the *o* in each *not* to show what is taken out to form the contractions. Then write *wasn't* and *weren't.*
- Ask questions to practice the past tense of *be* (e.g., Where *were* you last night? How *was* the weather yesterday?).

Answers

The word *not* makes the verb negative.

The letter *o* from the word *not* is missing in the contraction.

Pronunciation Target

Play the audio or read the words in the student book.

- Tell learners to listen for the long sound of *i (fine)* and the short sound of *i (it).*
- Have learners repeat the words as they hear them.
- Ask learners which words have the long *i* sound (*quiet, night, crime*) and which have the short *i* sound (*window, missing, important*). Write the words on the board or a transparency.
- Ask learners for other words with long and short *i* sounds. Write the words and use each in a sentence.

 Assign Workbook p. 46, Exercises A–B, now or at any time during the rest of Lesson 1.

Activity B

Ask learners to write the complete sentences using the past tense in their notebooks. Then have them read the sentences to their partners.

Tell learners to answer question 4 based on the story.

Answers
2. It was Wednesday night.
3. It was a burglary.
4. Where were her TV and VCR? *(Her TV and VCR were missing.)*

Use Unit Master 53 (Grammar: Dictation) now or at any time during the rest of the unit.

Activity C

Tell learners to place a check mark in front of those things their home has or that they currently do to make their home safe.

Have learners use *yes/no* cards to respond as you read each item (see p. 4).

Activity D

Refer learners to the photo of Sara's apartment on p. 84. Ask learners if they understand the meaning of the word *lost*. If not, explain or mime the meaning.
- After completing the activity, have learners check their answers with their partners.
- Read the completed passage all the way through. Then read each sentence and have learners repeat it after you.
- Ask comprehension *(yes/no* and *wh-)* questions about the reading.

Answers
2. burglary
3. computer
4. replace
5. important

 Assign Workbook p. 47, Exercises C–D.

Activity B   With a partner, change the verb to past tense.

1. Sara is at work.   *Sara was at work.* _____

2. It is Wednesday night. _____

3. It is a burglary. _____

4. Where are her TV and VCR? _____

Activity C   How do you protect your home? Check the boxes.
1. ❏ doors locked   ❏ doors open
2. ❏ light on   ❏ light off
3. ❏ one lock   ❏ two locks
4. ❏ key inside   ❏ key outside
5. ❏ window open   ❏ window closed
6. ❏ radio on   ❏ radio off

Activity D   Work with a partner. Use the words in the box to complete the story.

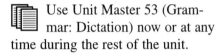

| burglary | computer | ✔ family | important | replace |

Sara has photos of her family in a book. She has a lot of _____ family _____
1

photos. Sara has other things in the book too. There are

letters from family and friends. But the photo album is a mess.

Sara also lost her computer in the _____. A _____ is
2   3

expensive. But Sara can _____ the computer. The photo album is
4

not expensive. But it is _____ to her.
5

TASK 1   Take a Home Inventory
Make a list of things in your home. What things were expensive?
What things are important to you? Why? Can you replace these things?

86   *Unit 6 Lesson 1*

Task 1

Use Customizable Master 2 (2-Column Chart). Follow the suggestions on p. 7 for customizing the master. Make a copy for each learner.
- Explain that some things are very important to us, although they do not cost much (e.g., a photo, a picture drawn by a child, a letter from someone you love).
- Show examples of your own important items to learners.
- Explain that if a burglar stole or broke any of these things, you would not be able to *replace* them, or get others.
- Ask learners to talk about things they cannot *replace*. Make a list on the board or an overhead transparency.

Lesson 2: Talking to the Police

Read the title, and point out the lesson objectives below it.

- Tell learners that this lesson will explain how to report a crime to the police. They will also learn how to talk about things that happened in the past.

Attention Box

This vocabulary should be understood, but learners should not be expected to produce the words at this point.

- Show learners a picture of a *van*. Explain that the car in the right-hand photo on p. 82 is a van.
- Explain that *ever = at any time*.

Question

Read the question aloud. Learners may find this question linguistically challenging because it involves past tense with *did*.

- Brainstorm reasons for talking to the police. List benign reasons (e.g., ask directions, car problems) as well as serious ones (e.g., reporting a crime).
- Ask learners, "Do you ever need to talk to the police?" Have them hold up their *yes/no* cards to answer (see p. 4). Tally the *yes* answers.
- Ask, "In your home country, did you ever need to talk to the police?" Have them answer with their cards, then do another tally.
- Finally, ask, "Did you ever need to talk to the police in the US?"
- Ask learners if any would like to share their reasons for talking to the police, but be aware of the sensitive nature of the question.

Photo

Follow the suggestions on p. 4 for talking about the photo. Ask, "Who do you see? Where are they? What is happening? How do you know?"

LESSON 2 — Community

Talking to the Police

- Report a crime
- Use past-tense verbs

ever
van

Did you ever need to talk to the police?

- Listening Tip 🎧 Listen to your teacher or the audio. You can read the words on page 119. Listen for the words that tell time or sequence: *first* and *then*.

Sara talks to the police.

Talk or Write
1. What happened at 9:50?
2. When did Sara come home?
3. What was missing?
4. Who saw the burglar?

Idiom Watch!
fill out =
complete the
information

What's Your Opinion? Do you help your neighbors protect their things?
❑ Always   ❑ Sometimes   ❑ Never

Unit 6 Lesson 2 **87**

Listening Tip

Read the tip aloud.

- Write the words *first, second,* and *third* on the board.
- Write the words *then* and *next.*
- Tell learners to listen for words like these. Such words help tell what happened when.

🎧 Play the audio or read the listening script on p. 120.

Talk or Write

This exercise helps learners follow time order.

Have learners write the answers to the questions and check them with a partner.

Answers

1. Mrs. Caruso saw a man. He put a TV in his van.
2. Sara came home at 10:00 P.M.
3. Several things were missing—a computer, a TV, and a VCR.
4. Her neighbor, Mrs. Caruso, saw him.

What's Your Opinion

Follow the suggestions on p. 6 for comprehension questions.

Vocabulary

Read the words in the student book. Follow the suggestions on p. 6 for introducing and reinforcing vocabulary.

Follow the suggestions on p. 6 for using vocabulary cards. Use the cards for the words in the Vocabulary box.

Class Chat

Use Customizable Master 3 (3-Column Chart). Follow the suggestions on p. 7 for customizing the master. Make a copy for each learner.

Follow the suggestions on p. 7 for Class Chats.

Grammar Talk

Follow the suggestions on p. 7 for introducing the grammar point.

- Point out that in past-tense statements, the negative form *did not* and its contraction *didn't* are the same for all forms, singular and plural.
- Read the sentences and have learners repeat.

Review each irregular form.
- Tell learners irregular verbs do not follow the usual rules; learners will need to memorize them.
- Read the present and past sentences for each irregular verb. Have learners repeat.
- Practice the past tense by asking questions (e.g., Where did you go yesterday? What did you wear yesterday?).

Answer
Most verbs in English use an *-ed* ending to show past tense.

Pronunciation Target

Play the audio or read the three sentences to learners.
- Write *-t, -d,* and *-id* on the board. Read the verbs again and ask learners which sound they hear

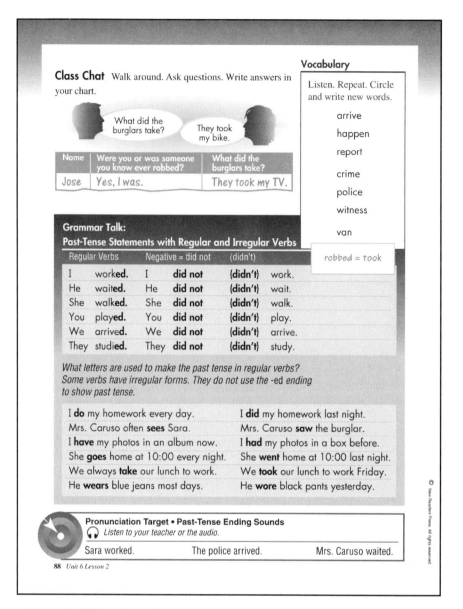

for each. Write the verbs on the board under the correct sound.
- Categorize other verbs, including the ones learned in this unit *(replaced, happened, protected reported),* in the same way.
- Follow this procedure with the remaining verbs in the Grammar Talk sentences *(walked, played, studied).* Read the complete sentence for each verb and have learners identify the sound.

Assign Workbook p. 48, Exercises A–B, now or at any time during the rest of Lesson 2.

Activity A

Ask learners to write their answers and read them to their partner. Have partners check each other's sentences for errors.

Answers
2. She <u>called</u> the <u>police</u>.
3. She <u>talked</u> to <u>Mrs. Caruso</u>.
4. Her neighbor <u>saw</u> a <u>van</u>.

Use Unit Master 54 (Grammar: A Day at School) now or at any time during the rest of the unit.

Activity B

Have learners read the Burglary Report silently.

• Ask learners *yes/no* and *wh-* detail questions like these:
Is the report number 29567? *(no)*
What is the apartment number? *(2)*
When was the burglary? *(July 8, 2004)*

• If learners have difficulty reporting the date in the last question, review and practice writing dates in words and numbers and in numbers only, with slashes separating month, day, and year.

Read the questions in the student book aloud.

• Tell learners they will do the role-play with their partners. One partner will take the role of the insurance agent and ask the questions; the other will be Sara and give the answers.

• Model the activity by reading the first question as the insurance agent. Have a learner answer the question as Sara. Then have partners complete the role-play.

• After the role-play, have learners write brief answers to the questions. Ask volunteers to write their responses on the board.

Answers
1. 9:30–10:00 P.M., July 8, 2004
2. a computer, a TV, and a VCR
3. at 182 Clare Avenue #2
4. Roberta Collins

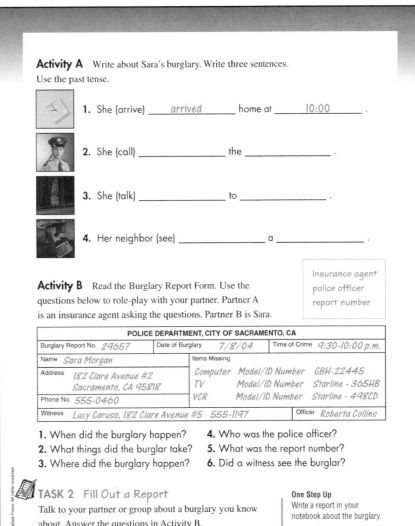

5. 29657
6. yes, Lucy Caruso

Assign Workbook p. 49 Exercises C–D, now or at any time during the rest of Lesson 2.

Task 2

Tell learners they can make up information if they do not know about a real burglary.

One Step Up

• Encourage more accelerated learners to tell the class about a burglary they have experienced.

• Learners may have difficulty relating action using past tense. Provide the past-tense forms when they cannot. Write the forms in a list on the board or an overhead transparency.

• Retell the story yourself by using the list of past-tense verbs as a guide. Then ask a learner to do the same.

Assessment

Use Generic Assessment Master 7 (Written Communication Rubric) to evaluate learner performance on One Step Up for Task 2.

Lesson 3: Wanted! www

Read the title and point out the lesson objectives below it.

- Explain that in this lesson learners will describe people. They will also ask and answer questions using the past tense.
- Tell learners that flyers with the word *Wanted* at the top are sometimes posted to tell about people *wanted* by police.

One Step Up

Introduce learners to the words *criminal* and *commit*. Say, "A person who *commits* a crime is a *criminal*." These higher-level words are not active vocabulary, but accelerated learners may find them useful in this lesson.

Attention Box

Read the words and have learners repeat them. Use each word in a sentence.

- Explain that a *suspect* is someone the police think has committed a crime.
- Tell learners that *suspect* can be a verb and a noun. Write sentences on the board or a transparency using it both ways. Show how the stress changes.

This vocabulary should be understood, but learners should not be expected to produce the words at this point.

Reading Tip

Ask learners where they see *Wanted* notices (newspaper, post office, supermarket).

First, have learners read the information above the description on the poster. Then ask these questions:

- Why are the police looking for this person?
- Who can you call if you find the person?
- What does the person look like?

Now tell learners to look at the description on the poster. What additional information does it give?

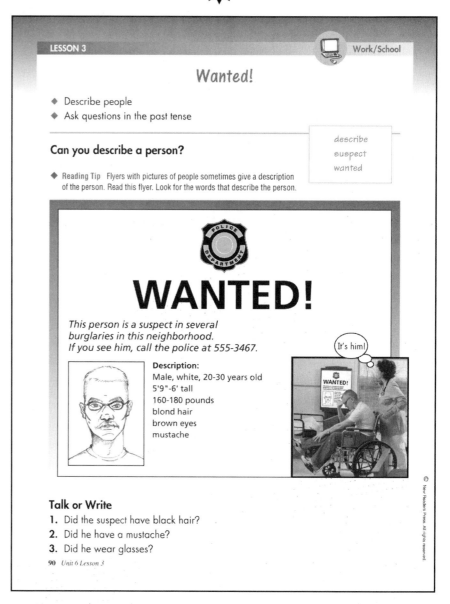

Extension

- Ask one or more learners with artistic talent to sketch an imaginary suspect wanted for a crime.
- Have other learners give details of the suspect's appearance. Ask questions to elicit details (e.g., Is the suspect a man or a woman? What does he or she look like? How old is the suspect?).
- Have learners write details under the drawing. Tell them to use the flyer in their books as a guide.
- Post the *Wanted* poster in your classroom.

Talk or Write

This exercise helps learners read and understand words that describe. Have learners discuss the answers with partners. Then ask volunteers to write their answers as complete sentences on the board.

Answers
1. No, he didn't.
2. Yes, he did.
3. Yes, he did.

Vocabulary

Read the words in the student book. Follow the suggestions on p. 6 for introducing and reinforcing vocabulary.

Follow the suggestions on p. 6 for using vocabulary cards. Use the cards for the words in the Vocabulary box.

Class Chat

Before the Class Chat begins, ask a volunteer to be a class "burglar." If possible, ask a staff member from your learning center.

- Allow learners only a few minutes to look at the volunteer.
- If the volunteer is a staff person, have him or her leave the room before learners begin the activity. If the volunteer is a learner, tell the other learners they may not look at the "burglar" once the activity begins.

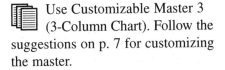 Use Customizable Master 3 (3-Column Chart). Follow the suggestions on p. 7 for customizing the master.

Grammar Talk

Follow the suggestions on p. 7 for introducing the grammar point. Review the formation of questions with *be* in past or present tense.

- Remind learners that, in questions in the present and past tenses, the subject and verb change (or *switch*) positions.
- To demonstrate, ask a learner, "Are you at school now?" Have the learner respond, "Yes, I am." Write the question and answer on the board.
- In the question, cross out *Are* and write *Were*. Then cross out *now* and write *yesterday*.
- In the answer, cross out *am* and write *was*. Read the new question and answer.

Follow the same pattern to present other verbs in the past.

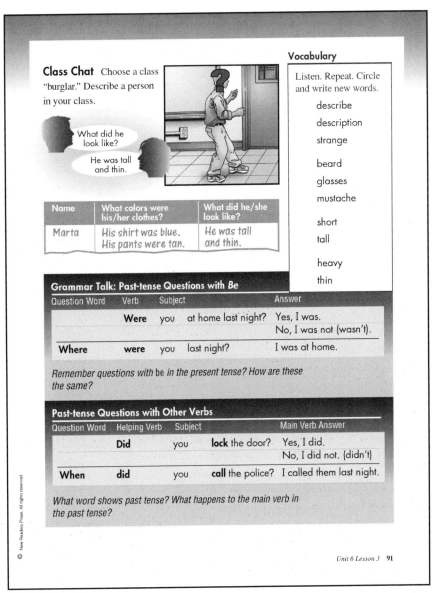

- Write the following sentence on the board or a transparency: *Do you lock the door every night?* Write a response from a learner.
- Repeat the question and answer in third person (e.g., *Does he lock the door every night?*).
- Circle *Do* and *Does* as words that show present tense. Cross them out and write *Did* to show how they change in the past tense. Remind learners that the past tense has only one form.
- Explain that *wh-* questions in past tense follow the same formula as in present tense: *wh-* word + helping verb + subject + main verb.

Answers

In questions with the verb *be,* the order of the words is the same in both present- and past-tense questions.

In past-tense questions with other verbs, *did* shows past tense.

In the past tense, the main verb is in the base form in the question and in the past tense in the answer.

Assign Workbook p. 50, Exercises A–B, now or at any time during the rest of Lesson 3.

Unit 6 *Lesson 3* **91**

Activity A

Tell learners to answer the questions in their notebooks. Then have them role-play the questions and answers with their partner.

Activity B

Tell learners they are going to read what Sara did last Tuesday. Read the seven entries as complete sentences.

Extension

Have learners write their questions on the board. Circle the verbs to reinforce the fact that these are simple forms of the verbs.

One Step Up

Tell learners to follow the model of Sara's time line.

- Explain that many of the events will be the same as Sara's (e.g., *Got up*), but others will be different. Say, "You probably did not talk to the police yesterday after you came home. Be sure to write what *you* did."
- Have learners tell the class about their day by reading the events as sentences.

 Assign Workbook p. 51, Exercises C–D.

 Use Unit Master 55 (Grammar: Past Questions and Answers) now or at any time during the rest of the unit.

In the US

Explain that a *stranger* is a person you and your neighbors do not know.

- Ask learners if they help their neighbors watch their homes. If so, what do they do?
- Ask if any learners have a Neighborhood Watch program in their neighborhood.

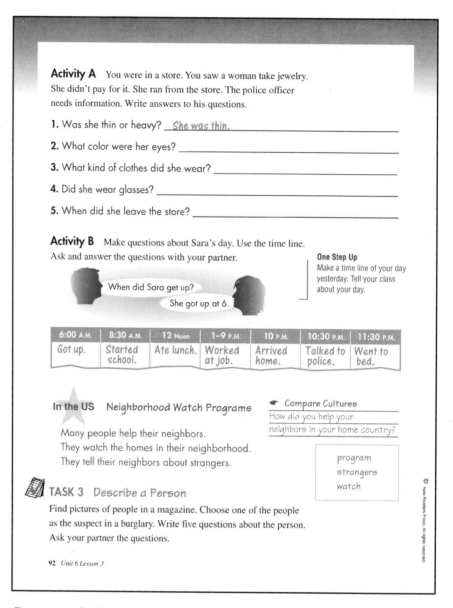

Activity A   You were in a store. You saw a woman take jewelry. She didn't pay for it. She ran from the store. The police officer needs information. Write answers to his questions.

1. Was she thin or heavy? _She was thin._

2. What color were her eyes? _____

3. What kind of clothes did she wear? _____

4. Did she wear glasses? _____

5. When did she leave the store? _____

Activity B   Make questions about Sara's day. Use the time line. Ask and answer the questions with your partner.

When did Sara get up?

She got up at 6.

One Step Up
Make a time line of your day yesterday. Tell your class about your day.

6:00 A.M.	8:30 A.M.	12 Noon	1–9 P.M.	10 P.M.	10:30 P.M.	11:30 P.M.
Got up.	Started school.	Ate lunch.	Worked at job.	Arrived home.	Talked to police.	Went to bed.

In the US   Neighborhood Watch Programs

Many people help their neighbors.
They watch the homes in their neighborhood.
They tell their neighbors about strangers.

☛ Compare Cultures
How did you help your neighbors in your home country?

program
strangers
watch

 TASK 3   Describe a Person

Find pictures of people in a magazine. Choose one of the people as the suspect in a burglary. Write five questions about the person. Ask your partner the questions.

92 *Unit 6 Lesson 3*

Compare Cultures

Ask what things learners did to help their neighbors in their home countries.

Task 3

Distribute magazines with pictures of people to each pair of learners.

- Tell learners to choose a picture of a "suspect" to write questions about.
- Have partners ask one another their questions.

One Step Up

Have partners write answers to one another's questions. Provide a small prize to the learner who writes the most descriptive sentences about a "suspect."

Assessment

 Use Generic Assessment Master 7 (Written Communication Rubric) to evaluate learner performance.

 Use Unit Master 56 (Game: Police Report Concentration) now.

Review Unit Skills

See p. 8 for suggestions on games and activities you can use to review the unit vocabulary and grammar.

Unit 6 Project

Learners plan, prepare, and make a home safety packet.

Get Ready

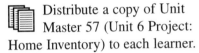 Distribute a copy of Unit Master 57 (Unit 6 Project: Home Inventory) to each learner.

Have learners think about the important things they have at home. Ask where they keep information about their things (e.g., purchase receipts, model or serial numbers, product warranties).

Show learners a serial number on an object in your classroom (e.g., overhead projector, CD player). Ask:
- Why is it good to have this information in a safe place?
- Who may need to see it? *(the police)*

Do the Work

Tell learners to make a list of things that are important to them.
- Have them make a copy and keep it in a safe place at home.
- Tell them to give another copy to a relative to keep.

Present Your Project

Have learners practice, or *rehearse,* their information with their group.
- Ask them to think about things that are similar or different on one another's lists.
- Tell learners why some of your things are important. Then ask about items on their own lists. (e.g., Did you bring them with you from your home country? Did a special person give you something?)

Peer Assessment

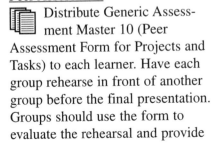 Distribute Generic Assessment Master 10 (Peer Assessment Form for Projects and Tasks) to each learner. Have each group rehearse in front of another group before the final presentation. Groups should use the form to evaluate the rehearsal and provide

suggestions for improvement prior to the final presentation.

Assessment

Use Generic Assessment Master 6 (Oral Communication Rubric) to evaluate learner performance.

Writing Extension

Ask learners whether friends, relatives, or neighbors keep keys to their car or home.
- Have them write sentences and read the sentences to their partners. Write some of the sentences on the board or an overhead transparency.

- Tell learners to use the Writing Checklist on p. 126 to check their sentences.

Technology Extra

Show learners how to make a four-column chart on the computer. Have them fill in their information. Tell them to keep the chart and add new information as they get new things.

Assign Workbook p. 52 (Check Your Progress).

Use Unit Master 58 (Unit Checkup/Review) whenever you complete this unit.

Home Safety Packet

Plan, prepare, and make a Home Safety Packet.

Get Ready
Think about the things in your home. Do you have a TV? Do you have a car? Do you have information at home about the things you buy?

Do the Work
Use the Home Inventory form your teacher gives you. Write a list of the important things you have. Put a copy in your desk at home. Think about how you protect your things. Write in your notebook.

Present Your Project
With your group, talk about your Home Inventory. How important are these things to you? Is there something that is not on the list? Why? Talk about how you protect your things. With your group, write what to do to protect your things. Share your group's ideas with the class. Make a class list of ideas.

HOME INVENTORY

Name		Brand/Model	
Car			
Bicycle			
Electronics:			
TV			
VCR			
CD Player			
Jewelry			

✎ **Writing Extension** Who has keys to your home? Who has keys to your car? Write sentences.

💻 **Technology Extra**
Make a table on the computer. Type or write your home inventory.

Unit 6 Project **93**

Unit 7: Succeeding at School

Materials for the Unit

- Pictures of soccer and basketball games and of a piano
- Pictures of other sports (optional)
- Magazine pictures representing things someone can do to succeed in school
- Local phone book
- Customizable Masters 2, 3, and 5
- Generic Assessment Masters 6, 7, and 10
- Unit Masters 59–65
- Vocabulary Card Masters for Unit 7

Succeeding at School

Follow the suggestions on p. 5 for talking about the title.

- Review the four groups of unit goals listed below the title.
- Explain that in this unit learners will focus on succeeding in school and helping their children succeed in school.

Attention Box

- Use the words in sentences.
- Use the pictures of *basketball*, *soccer*, and *piano* to introduce these words. Explain that *basketball* and *soccer* are sports. Talk about other *sports* and show pictures, if possible.
- Point to the photo of Minh working and tell learners this is an *ice cream shop*.

This vocabulary should be understood, but learners should not be expected to produce the words at this point.

Photos

Follow the suggestions on p. 4 for talking about the photos.

- Ask learners what they see and what Minh is doing.
- Read the photo caption aloud. Have all learners repeat each sentence together.

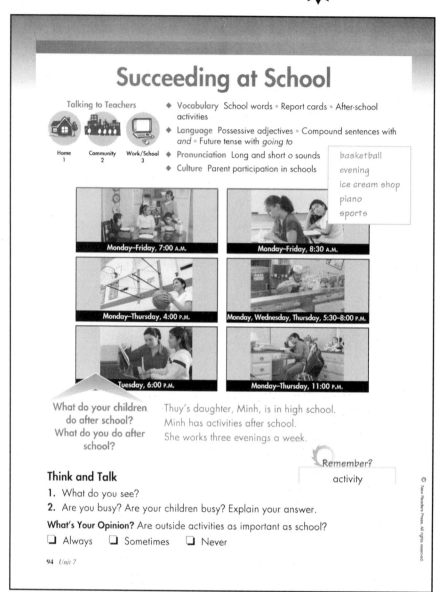

94 *Unit 7*

Extension

Ask these questions:

- Do you only go to school or do you work too?
- What other things do you do every day?

Model answers for learners by saying, "I go to work every day. After work, I pick up my children from school, clean the house, and make dinner."

Remember?

Direct learners to this box and review the word *activity* (p. 35).

Think and Talk

Read the questions and have learners talk to their partners about the answers.

Answers

1. Answers will vary. Write some on the board or an overhead transparency.
2. Answers will vary. Write some for learners.

What's Your Opinion?

Check to see if learners remember the adverbs of frequency (*always, often, sometimes, rarely, never*). Review these if needed.

Picture Dictionary

Read the words in the student book. Follow the suggestions on p. 6 for introducing and reinforcing vocabulary.

Follow the suggestions on p. 6 for using vocabulary cards. Use the cards for the words in the Picture Dictionary.

- Mime the adjectives *busy* and *tired*. For *tired*, point to the photo of Minh dozing.
- Explain that *homework* is school-work you do at home.

Extension

Tell learners that *housework* usually is work done to take care of your home and the people who live there (e.g., cooking, cleaning, laundry).

Gather Your Thoughts

Use Customizable Master 5 (Idea Map). Follow the suggestions on p. 7 for customizing and duplicating the master. Make a copy for each learner.

- Ask learners these questions: What do you do during the week? Are you busy?
- Write their answers on the board or an overhead transparency.

Have learners complete the maps in their groups, following these steps:

- Student A asks, "What do you do before school?"
- Student B answers, then asks Student C the same question.
- When all group members have asked and answered the question, repeat the procedure, this time asking, "What do you do after school?"
- Continue until all learners have asked and answered both questions. Learners' completed idea maps will reflect their group.
- When learners have completed their maps, compare the maps and make a class map.

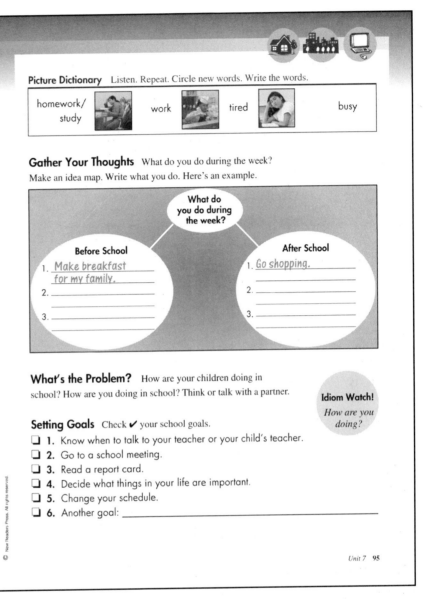

Picture Dictionary   Listen. Repeat. Circle new words. Write the words.

homework/ study   work   tired   busy

Gather Your Thoughts   What do you do during the week? Make an idea map. Write what you do. Here's an example.

What do you do during the week?

Before School
1. Make breakfast for my family.
2. _____
3. _____

After School
1. Go shopping.
2. _____
3. _____

What's the Problem?   How are your children doing in school? How are you doing in school? Think or talk with a partner.

Setting Goals   Check ✔ your school goals.
- ❏ 1. Know when to talk to your teacher or your child's teacher.
- ❏ 2. Go to a school meeting.
- ❏ 3. Read a report card.
- ❏ 4. Decide what things in your life are important.
- ❏ 5. Change your schedule.
- ❏ 6. Another goal: _____

Idiom Watch!
How are you doing?

Unit 7 **95**

Idiom Watch

Use the idiom *to be doing* in a question (e.g., How *are* you *doing?*). Tell learners this is like asking, "How are you?" Explain it can also refer to progress at work or school (e.g., I *am doing* well in English class.).

What's the Problem?

Follow the suggestions on p. 5 for identifying and analyzing problems. Ask these questions:

- Do you and your children have busy schedules?
- Do you know how you and your children are doing in school?

Then ask the questions in the book.

Extension

Ask learners *how* they know whether they and their children are doing well (report cards, daily or weekly grades, parent-teacher conferences, letters from teachers, their own progress in class, what their children say about their progress).

Setting Goals

Follow the suggestions on p. 5 for setting goals.

Extension

Poll learners to find out how many think each goal is the most important one. To do the tallies, have learners count off or ask a different learner to do the count for each goal.

Lesson 1: Reading a Report Card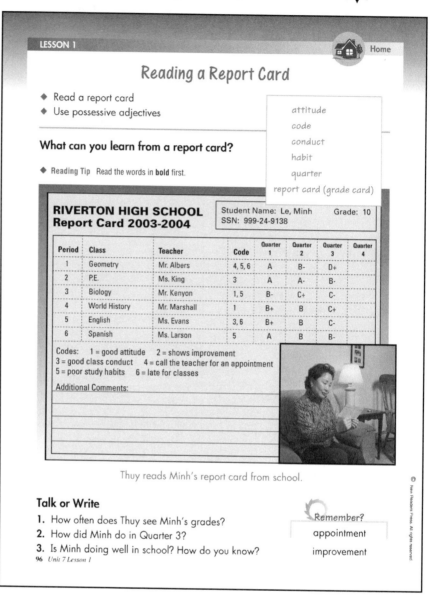

Read the title and point out the lesson objectives below it.

- Tell learners that this lesson is about reading report cards. Explain that parents need to know how their children are doing in school.
- Mention that many jobs give their employees reviews that are like report cards. It is important to know how to read them.
- Show assessment forms or rubrics from your program.

Follow the suggestions on p. 5 for talking about titles.

Attention Box

- Tell learners a student's *attitude* is how he or she thinks or feels about something. A good *attitude* means a person feels good about class and wants to learn.
- Explain that a *code* is a short way of showing something. In the report card shown, the *code* in the fifth column uses the numerals 1 to 6. Show learners what the *code* means at the bottom of the card.
- Tell learners that *conduct* is the way someone acts. Ask, "What is good class *conduct?*"
- To demonstrate *quarter,* draw a circle and label it *The School Year.* Divide the circle into four sections. Tell learners that each part of the circle is a *quarter.* Explain that this is one way to divide a school year.

This vocabulary should be understood, but learners should not be expected to produce the words at this point.

Question

Read the introductory question aloud. Show learners the *report* or *grade card* in their books.

Photo

Ask, "What do you see? What is Thuy doing? How do you know?"

Reading a Report Card

- Read a report card
- Use possessive adjectives

attitude
code
conduct
habit
quarter
report card (grade card)

What can you learn from a report card?

◆ Reading Tip Read the words in **bold** first.

RIVERTON HIGH SCHOOL
Report Card 2003-2004

Student Name: Le, Minh   Grade: 10
SSN: 999-24-9138

Period	Class	Teacher	Code	Quarter 1	Quarter 2	Quarter 3	Quarter 4
1	Geometry	Mr. Albers	4, 5, 6	A	B-	D+	
2	P.E.	Ms. King	3	A	A-	B-	
3	Biology	Mr. Kenyon	1, 5	B-	C+	C-	
4	World History	Mr. Marshall	1	B+	B	C+	
5	English	Ms. Evans	3, 6	B+	B	C-	
6	Spanish	Ms. Larson	5	A	B	B-	

Codes: 1 = good attitude   2 = shows improvement
3 = good class conduct   4 = call the teacher for an appointment
5 = poor study habits   6 = late for classes

Additional Comments:

Thuy reads Minh's report card from school.

Talk or Write
1. How often does Thuy see Minh's grades?
2. How did Minh do in Quarter 3?
3. Is Minh doing well in school? How do you know?

96 *Unit 7 Lesson 1*

Remember?
appointment
improvement

Reading Tip

Read the tip aloud. Have learners point to the bold words on the report card. Read across the row of heads, reviewing what each one means.

Follow the suggestions for reading comprehension on p. 5.

Talk or Write

This exercise helps learners become skilled at reading charts.

Possible Answers
1. four times a year
2. not well; her grades are low.
3. No, Minh is not doing well in school. We know from her grades and the codes.

One Step Up

Ask learners these questions about report cards in their home countries:
- Did you use letter grades or numbers in school?
- What kinds of classes did you have?
- How are report cards in your home country like report cards in the US? How are they different?

Vocabulary

Read the words in the student book. Follow the suggestions on p. 6 for introducing and reinforcing vocabulary.

Follow the suggestions on p. 6 for using vocabulary cards. Use the cards for the words in the Vocabulary box.

Tell learners this lesson talks about some classes, or *subjects,* taught in US high schools. Describe each subject. Use symbols to convey the meaning of *math* and *geometry.*

Class Chat

Use Customizable Master 3 (3-Column Chart). Follow the suggestions on p. 7 for customizing the master. Make copies for each learner.

If learners do not have children in school, they can complete column 3 for a child they know or with subjects they themselves would like to study.

Grammar Talk

Follow the suggestions on p. 7 for introducing the grammar point.
- Tell learners that possessive adjectives are like the apostrophe; they show ownership.
- Review the information in the grammar box. Point out that pronouns and adjectives must match (e.g., *I* and *my, you* and *your*). Write the pronoun–adjective combinations on the board or a transparency.

Answers
A noun that names a person, place, or thing follows a possessive adjective.

A possessive adjective tells who owns something or to whom something belongs.

Use Unit Master 59 (Grammar: Possessive Adjectives) at any time during the rest of the unit.

Class Chat What subjects did you study in school? What subjects do your children study in school? Walk around. Ask questions. Write answers in your chart.

What subjects did you study in school?

I studied Russian, math, and science.

Name	What subjects did you study in school?	What subjects do your children study?
Petra	I studied Russian, math, and science.	They study history, English, and science.

Vocabulary
Listen. Repeat. Circle and write new words.

subject

English

history

math (geometry)

physical education (P.E.)

science (biology)

Spanish

Grammar Talk: Possessive Adjectives (Review)

Subject Pronoun	Possessive Adjective	
I	my	I like **my** new teacher.
you	your	**You** can open **your** book now.
he, she, it	his, her, its	She does **her** homework every night.
we	our	We have **our** class picnic on Friday.
you	your	Do **you** have **your** English book?
they	their	**They** have **their** lunch at noon.

Minh's basketball game is on Friday. = **Her** basketball game is on Friday.

What follows a possessive adjective? What does a possessive adjective tell you?

Activity A Look at the report card on page 96 to answer the questions. Use possessive pronouns.

1. What is Mr. Albers's class? _His class is Geometry._
2. What's the name of the school? _Its name is Riverton High School._
3. What are Ms. King's and Mr. Kenyon's classes? _____
4. What period is Ms. Evans's class? _____
5. Who is Minh's geometry teacher? _____

Assign Workbook p. 53, Exercise A, now or at any time during the rest of Lesson 1.

Activity A

Tell learners to look at the report card on p. 96 to complete this activity.
- Model the activity by completing the first two questions on the board or a transparency. Have volunteers write the answers.
- After learners complete the activity, call on pairs to read the questions and answers aloud.
- If the answers are correct, have them write both questions

and answers on the board or transparency.

Answers
3. Ms. King's class is P.E., and Mr. Kenyon's class is Biology.
4. Ms. Evans's class is Period 5.
5. Minh's geometry teacher is Mr. Albers.

Assign Workbook p. 54, Exercise B, now or at any time during the rest of Lesson 1.

Activity B

- Remind learners that the words in the box are possessive adjectives.
- After learners complete the conversation, have partners each take a role and read the conversation together.
- Tell partners to reverse roles and read the conversation again.

Answers

2. your
3. her
4. His
5. your

One Step Up

Have a few pairs of learners read the dialogue in front of the class.

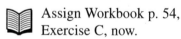 Assign Unit Master 60 (Thinking Skill: Solving Problems) now or at any time during the rest of the unit.

Task 1

Tell learners that in emergencies family members need to be able to find each other.

- Explain that, in such cases, it is good to have a list of contact information for every family member.
- Tell learners with no children to make the chart to give to family members or a friend.
- After learners complete their charts independently, review answers together.

Assessment

Use Generic Assessment Master 7 (Written Communication Rubric) to evaluate learner performance.

One Step Up

- Explain that in the US parents meet with teachers several times a year to talk about how their children are doing in school. Adult learners also meet with their teachers to talk about progress.

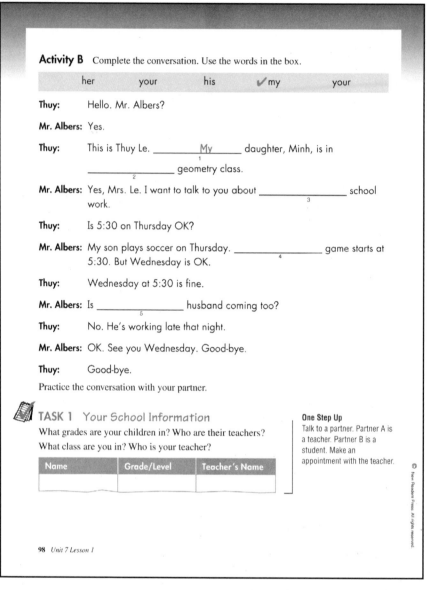

Activity B Complete the conversation. Use the words in the box.

| her | your | his | ✔ my | your |

Thuy: Hello. Mr. Albers?

Mr. Albers: Yes.

Thuy: This is Thuy Le. _____My_____ daughter, Minh, is in
_____ geometry class.
                    2

Mr. Albers: Yes, Mrs. Le. I want to talk to you about _____ school
                                                           3
work.

Thuy: Is 5:30 on Thursday OK?

Mr. Albers: My son plays soccer on Thursday. _____ game starts at
                                                 4
5:30. But Wednesday is OK.

Thuy: Wednesday at 5:30 is fine.

Mr. Albers: Is _____ husband coming too?
                    5

Thuy: No. He's working late that night.

Mr. Albers: OK. See you Wednesday. Good-bye.

Thuy: Good-bye.

Practice the conversation with your partner.

TASK 1 Your School Information

What grades are your children in? Who are their teachers?
What class are you in? Who is your teacher?

Name	Grade/Level	Teacher's Name

One Step Up

Talk to a partner. Partner A is a teacher. Partner B is a student. Make an appointment with the teacher.

At many schools, students *must* do this (it is a *requirement*).

- Tell learners that teachers want parents or adult learners to ask for meetings when there is a problem. Many schools have translators for people who need help with English.

Model the conversation with the class. Follow these steps:

- Take the part of the English teacher. Use the dialogue in Activity B as a model.
- Ask a volunteer to read Thuy's part, putting information about his or her own child in the blanks.

- Model the conversation again. This time have a learner make an appointment for him- or herself.
- Have partners read the dialogue to each other several times so that each one gets practice with each part.

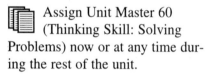 Assign Workbook p. 54, Exercise C, now.

Lesson 2: Making Decisions 🌐

Read the title and point out the lesson objectives below it.

- Tell learners that in this lesson they will learn about making decisions.

Follow the suggestions on p. 5 for talking about titles.

- Give examples to illustrate the expression *making decisions* (e.g., We need to *make a decision* about what to do.).
- Ask these questions:
  How do you make decisions?
  Do you make decisions for your family?
  How does your family make decisions?

Attention Box

- Use each term in a sentence.
- Use this paragraph to provide context for the two phrases: I *fix breakfast* for my family every day. In the morning I study English, and in the afternoon I work. I help at church and at my children's school. I have *too many* things to do!

This vocabulary should be understood, but learners should not be expected to produce the words at this point.

Photo

Ask learners what they see, what is happening, and how they know.

Listening Tip

Read the tip aloud. Then do the following:

- Point out the Talk or Write questions.
- Read the questions aloud, but do not ask for answers. Tell learners the listening exercise will answer these questions.

🎧 Play the audio or read the listening script on p. 120.
Follow the suggestions on p. 5 for listening comprehension.

LESSON 2   Community

Making Decisions

- Decide what's most important
- Make compound sentences with *and*

How busy are your children? How busy are you?

- Listening Tip 🎧 Look at the questions below the picture. Then listen to the conversation between Thuy and her sister-in-law. Listen to your teacher or the audio. You can read the words on page 120.

fix breakfast =
make breakfast

after
before
too many

Talk or Write

1. Why is Thuy worried about her daughter?
2. Who does Thuy want to talk to?
3. What activities does Minh have after school?
4. What does Minh do before school?

What's Your Opinion?   Is it good to be busy? Explain your answer.

Unit 7 Lesson 2 **99**

Ask these warm-up questions:
- Who is Minh? *(Minh is Thuy's daughter.)*
- What do you know about Minh? *(She is very busy, and she is not doing well in school.)*

Talk or Write

This exercise helps learners listen for sequence.

Possible Answers
1. Thuy is worried because Minh is always tired and has a lot of homework.
2. Thuy wants to talk to the principal.

3. Minh has a job, basketball, soccer, and piano.
4. Minh helps the other children get ready for school. She fixes breakfast for them.

What's Your Opinion?

To initiate discussion, ask volunteers to give their opinions.

Vocabulary

Read the words in the student book. Follow the suggestions on p. 6 for introducing and reinforcing vocabulary.

Follow the suggestions on p. 6 for using vocabulary cards. Use the cards for the words in the Vocabulary box.

Remember?

Review these words with learners by providing a contextualized example (e.g., I have a busy *schedule*. I work and study, and I *practice* the piano every evening.).

Class Chat

Use Customizable Master 3 (3-Column Chart). Follow the suggestions on p. 7 for customizing the master. Make a copy for each learner.

Follow the suggestions for Class Chats on p. 7.

- Tell learners that the slash mark (/) means there is a choice. Here, they can complete the chart for their children *or* for themselves.
- Have learners save their completed charts to use with Activity A.

Activity A

Have learners write sentences in their notebooks. Tell them to use the information from the Class Chat.

Grammar Talk

Follow the suggestions on p. 7 for introducing the grammar point.

- Read the first two examples. Tell learners they can use *and* to make one long sentence from two shorter sentences.
- Explain that *and* is usually used to join sentences with similar ideas.
- Ask learners how they answered the Class Chat question, "What time do you go to bed?" Use their responses to make more compound sentences with *and.*

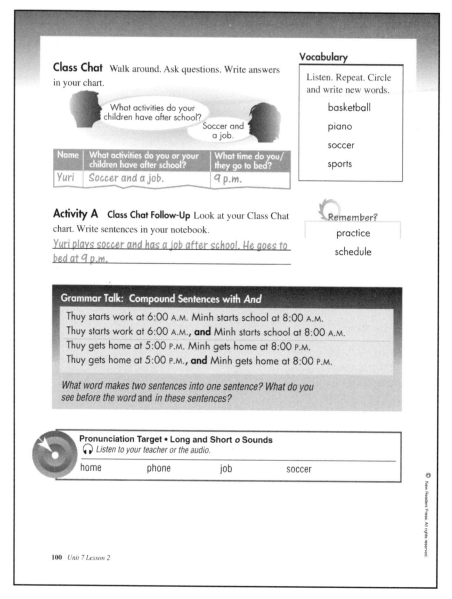

Answers
and; a comma

Use Unit Master 61 (Grammar: Using *and* to Join Sentences) now or at any time during the rest of the unit.

Assign Workbook p. 55, Exercise A, now or at any time during the rest of Lesson 2.

Pronunciation Target

Play the audio or read the words in the student book. Have learners repeat the words. Then do the following:

- Ask if the *o* sounds are the same. Ask how they are different.

- Point out the silent *e* on the end of the words with the long *o* sound.
- Ask learners what other words they know have long and short sounds of *o*. Remind them of words they already know with long *o* sounds *(piano, code)* and *shop* with a short *o* sound.

Assign Workbook p. 56, Exercises B–C, now or at any time during the rest of Lesson 2.

Use Unit Master 62 (Phonics: The Sounds of *o*) now or at any time during the rest of the unit.

Activity B

- Read the question at the start of the activity (*What did Thuy and Minh do last Saturday?*).
- Direct learners to the chart and ask, "What do you look for first in a chart?" (*information in bold*)

Help learners read the columns and then the rows. Then do the following:

- Write the first sentence on the board. Check for understanding.
- Point out that *soccer* is not repeated in the second part of the sentence.
- After learners complete the activity, have volunteers write sentences on the board.
- Read the first item again. Then ask volunteers to read the others.

Possible Answers

2. Minh did homework, and Thuy visited a friend.
3. Minh worked (was at her job), and Thuy cleaned the house.
4. Minh worked (was at her job), and Thuy helped the kids study.
5. Minh baby-sat, and Thuy ate out.

Activity C

Explain the meaning of *order of importance* (e.g., number one is the *most important;* number eight is *not very important.*)

- Give an example of what's *important* in your personal life (e.g., Even though I am very busy, I think helping my children with their homework is *important.*).
- Tell learners that their listing of importance for Minh's activities may not match other learners' lists. Point out that everyone has a different idea of what is important.
- After partners have talked about their lists, ask volunteers to share their lists with the class.

Activity B What did Thuy and Minh do last Saturday?
Talk and write.

Name	Day	9:00–11:00	11:00–12:00	1:00–3:00	4:00–6:00	6:00–9:00
Minh	Saturday	play soccer	homework	job	job	baby-sit
Thuy	Saturday	watch soccer	visit a friend	clean house	help kids study	eat out

1. 9:00–11:00 _Minh played soccer, and Thuy watched._
2. 11:00–12:00 _____
3. 1:00–3:00 _____
4. 4:00–6:00 _____
5. 6:00–9:00 _____

Activity C Make a list of Minh's activities in order of importance. Number 1 is most important.

| baby-sit | homework | school | work at the ice cream shop |
| basketball | piano lessons | soccer | help other children |

1. _____ 5. _____
2. _____ 6. _____
3. _____ 7. _____
4. _____ 8. _____

Talk with your partner. Do you and your partner agree?

TASK 2 *Make an Activities Chart*
List your activities in order of importance. Make a chart.

One Step Up
Show your chart to the class.
Talk about your answers.

Unit 7 Lesson 2 101

© New Readers Press. All rights reserved.

One Step Up

Ask learners why one activity was more important than another for them.

Task 2

Using Activity C as a guide, have learners list their own activities in order of importance.

- Help learners get started by listing a number of activities on the board (e.g., clean apartment, pay bills, do laundry, visit friends, shop for food).
- Use notebook paper or poster board for the charts.

Assessment

Use Generic Assessment Master 7 (Written Communication Rubric) to evaluate learner performance.

Unit 7 *Lesson 2* 101

Lesson 3: Parent-Teacher Meeting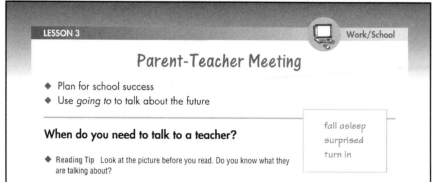

• Follow the suggestions on p. 5 for talking about the title. Then point out the lesson objectives listed below it.
• In this lesson, learners will learn about talking to teachers and planning for success in school.

Question

Tell learners to read the question silently. Then ask these questions:
• Do you talk to me or other teachers about your work?
• Do you talk to your children's teachers about their work?

Read the question aloud. Write learners' responses on the board or an overhead transparency.

Reading Tip

Read the tip aloud.
• Tell learners that looking at the picture before reading will help them understand what they read.
• The picture can tell them something about the people in the reading and where they are.
• They might also get ideas about what the people are talking about or the words they are using.

Photo

Tell learners to look carefully at the photo. Ask these questions:
• Where are the people?
• Who are they?
• What do you see in the picture?
• What is happening?

Put words on the board or a transparency as learners answer.

One Step Up

You may want to use an idea map that has the words *Thuy's Meeting* in the center circle and one of the questions in each of the larger surrounding circles. Learners' answers could be in smaller circles surrounding each of the questions.

LESSON 3 Work/School

Parent-Teacher Meeting

◆ Plan for school success
◆ Use *going to* to talk about the future

fall asleep
surprised
turn in

When do you need to talk to a teacher?

◆ Reading Tip Look at the picture before you read. Do you know what they are talking about?

Talking to the Teacher

Thuy has a meeting with Minh's geometry teacher, Mr. Albers. He tells Thuy these things. Minh had good grades in September, and she was a good student.

Now things are different. Minh is often late to class, and she has ten absences.

Sometimes Minh falls asleep in class, and she doesn't turn in her homework on time.

Thuy is surprised. Minh needs to pass this class. Thuy is going to talk with her. They are going to make changes in Minh's life.

Talk or Write

1. Who did Thuy have a meeting with?
2. How were Minh's grades in September?
3. Why is Minh having problems in class now?

102 *Unit 7 Lesson 3*

Reading

Follow the suggestions on p. 5 for reading comprehension.

One Step Down

This is a longer reading with challenging vocabulary. If necessary, break the reading into three parts. Stop after the first three sentences and again after the sixth. Check comprehension before continuing.

Talk or Write

This exercise helps learners read for cause and effect.

Answers

1. Thuy had a meeting with Minh's geometry teacher, Mr. Albers.
2. Minh had good grades in September.
3. Minh is often late to class. She has 10 absences. Sometimes she falls asleep in class. She doesn't turn in her homework on time.

Vocabulary

Read the words in the student book. Follow the suggestions on p. 6 for introducing and reinforcing vocabulary.

Follow the suggestions on p. 6 for using vocabulary cards. Use the cards for the words in the Vocabulary box.

To assess learners' knowledge ask questions like these:
- Who works at a school? *(teachers, the principal, counselors)*
- What happens if you do well in school? *(You succeed.)*
- What happens if you do well in a class? *(You pass.)*
- What happens if you do not do well? *(You fail.)*

Class Chat

Use Customizable Master 2 (2-Column Chart). Follow the suggestions on p. 7 for customizing and duplicating the master. Make a copy for each learner.

Follow the suggestions on p. 7 for Class Chats.

Grammar Talk

Follow the suggestions on p. 7 for introducing the grammar point.
- Explain that *going to* is used to talk about what you *will* do in the future. Draw a time line labeled *Past, Present,* and *Future.* Circle *Future* and write *going to* beside it.
- Read the first sentence to the class.
- Point out all the parts that make the sentence. Have learners read the sentence. Then read the rest of the sentences with them.

Answers
Be is the verb that comes before *going to.*

The base form of the verb follows *going to.*

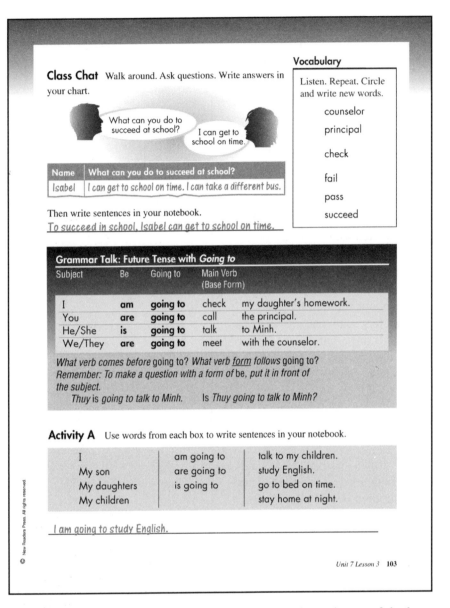

One Step Up
Have each learner ask and answer a question with *going to.* Model this pattern with a volunteer:

What are you *going to* do tomorrow?

Tomorrow I am *going to* study.

Assign Workbook p. 57, Exercise A–B, now or at any time during the rest of Lesson 3.

Activity A

Read aloud the words in each part of the box. Then do the following:
- Read the example. If learners have difficulty with this exercise, have them draw lines between the words in each part of the box to "map" the sentence. Model by drawing the box on the board or an overhead transparency.
- Have learners write their sentences in their notebooks.

Activity B

Have learners write sentences about themselves, their friends, or their families. Tell them these can be activities they actually will do or ones they want to do.

After learners complete the activity, ask several to write their sentences on the board or a transparency.

In the US

First, have learners read the passage silently. Then follow these steps:
- Read the passage aloud and have learners repeat each line.
- Ask *yes/no* and *either/or* questions about some of the statements (e.g., Do teachers write to students or parents?).
- Ask information questions (e.g., Who talks to parents?).

 Assign Workbook p. 58, Exercises C–D.

Task 3

Have learners choose if they want to work on a list of things they can do to succeed in school or things they can do to help their children succeed in school.
- Arrange work groups to accommodate these choices.
- Have a recorder in each group complete the list.
- Have a reporter in each group read the list to the class.
- Have the groups create posters of their lists using magazine pictures to illustrate their ideas.
- Encourage them to add a decorative border, a title, and their own pictures.

One Step Up

After learners display their posters, have them talk about the posters to the class.

 Use Unit Master 63 (Game: Make a Crossword Puzzle).

Activity B What are people in your family going to do this weekend? Write sentences with *and*.

1. _I'm going to go to the library, and my son is going to play basketball._
2. _____
3. _____
4. _____
5. _____
6. _____

In the US   Parents and Schools

Teachers in the US like to talk to parents about their children. Sometimes they write notes to the parents, and sometimes they call the parents. Parents need to call teachers to see how their children are doing.

Principals, counselors, teachers, and parents work together to help children succeed.

➤ Compare Cultures
How do parents and teachers work together in your home country? Do they talk about the children? When? Where? Talk with your group.

TASK 3 Success Planning Chart

What will it take for you to succeed in school?

1. In your group, make a list of things you can do to succeed in school.
2. Find pictures to show how you can succeed. Make a poster with your group. Put the poster on the wall of your classroom.

Review Unit Skills

See p. 8 for suggestions on games and activities you can use to review the unit vocabulary and grammar.

Unit 7 Project

Learners make a school information chart.

Get Ready

Have learners bring to class the information they will need: the name, address, and phone number of their adult learning center; the name, address and phone number of their children's school; any additional school information (e.g., registration forms, flyers, class schedules).

- If they do not have their school phone number, tell them to ask at the school office.
- If they do not know the address of a school, ask them how they can find out (e.g., look at the street sign, find the number on the building).
- Ask learners if they know the name of the person in charge of your school and the name of the principal at their children's school.
- Bring a local phone book in case learners have difficulty finding the information they need.

Do the Work

Distribute a copy of Unit Master 64 (Unit 7 Project: Make a School Information Chart) to each group. Give each learner a copy for each family member who goes to school.

- Have learners write their name (or child's name) in the chart.
- Refer them to Minh's report card for help making a schedule.
- Remind learners that in some schools, learners need to have notes for absences. Other schools want a phone call and a note. Ask what your school or their children's school wants.

Present Your Project

Peer Assessment

Distribute a copy of Generic Assessment Master 10 (Peer Assessment Form for Projects and Tasks) to each learner.

UNIT 7 Project

Make a School Information Chart

Do these things to make a School Information Chart.

Get Ready
Do these things:
1. Find the address and phone numbers for your school or your child's school.
2. Who are the teachers for your family?
3. Who has these jobs at your (or your child's) school:
   - Principal
   - Vice-Principal
   - Counselor

Do the Work
Complete the chart from your teacher with your information. Practice calling your school or your child's school. Write a note to your teacher or your child's teacher.

absent = not in class

Sample phone call

"Hello. My name's _____,
                        your name
and I'm _____'s
              your child's name
_____. He's/she's in
parent or guardian
_____'s class."
   teacher's name
"My child will be absent today. He/she is sick."

OR

"My child will be late today. He/she will be at school at _____."
                                              time

Sample note

Please excuse my _____,
                          son/daughter

_____
your child's name
She was home on _____
                        day and date
because she had _____
              a cold/a doctor's appointment, etc.
Sincerely,

_____ Date _____
  your signature

Present Your Project
Talk to your group or the class about your chart.

Technology Extra
Make a copy of your chart for your school on the photocopier.
Put the chart on the wall in your classroom.

One Step Up
Invite school employees to class to talk about their jobs. Ask questions and make a new chart.

Unit 7 Project 105

© New Readers Press. All rights reserved.

Follow the suggestions for peer assessment on p. 4.

Ask each group to practice its presentation with another group.

Have learners complete the assessment forms before the final presentations.

When groups present to the class, encourage active listening by asking learners detail and *wh-* questions.

Assessment

Use Generic Assessment Master 6 (Oral Communication Rubric) to evaluate the performances.

One Step Up

Invite personnel from your school as guest speakers. Ask them to tell who they are, what they do, and when learners should contact them. Remind the speakers that your learners have beginning-level listening skills. Help them prepare a short presentation using language accessible to learners.

Assign Workbook p. 59 (Check Your Progress).

Use Unit Master 65 (Unit Checkup/Review) whenever you complete this unit.

Unit 8: I Want a Good Job!

Materials for the Unit

- Audio- and videocassette tapes
- Class schedules from your school and other adult education centers
- Local phone books (one for each group)
- Customizable Masters 3–5
- Generic Assessment Masters 6, 8, 9, 10
- Unit Masters 66–71
- Vocabulary Card Masters for Unit 8

I Want a Good Job!

Read the title aloud.

- Review the four groups of unit goals listed below the title.
- Follow the suggestions on p. 5 for talking about the title.
- In this unit, learners will focus on employment and educational opportunities.

Attention Box

Help learners read the words in the box. Use each word in a sentence. This vocabulary should be understood, but learners should not be expected to produce the words at this point.

Photos

Because this is the last unit in the book and forms a bridge to the next level, the information provided in the photos is relatively complex.

- Spend some extra time on this page. Encourage learners to study the photos and caption and relate them to their own experience.
- Before discussing the photos, ask the questions below. List learners' responses on the board or an overhead transparency.

  Where do you work (or go to school)?

  Do you do your best every day? How?

  Do you try to improve every day? (Encourage learners to give personal examples.)

UNIT 8

I Want a Good Job!

Improving Your Skills

Work/School 1   Home 2   Community 3

- ◆ **Vocabulary** Employment words • Educational opportunities
- ◆ **Language** Can and can't • Compound sentences with but • A, an, the
- ◆ **Pronunciation** Long and short u sounds
- ◆ **Culture** Education can increase income

Do you have the job you want?

Cesar works at Best Computer Factory. Pilar volunteers at a library. They like their work, but they are ready for more responsibility.

Think and Talk

1. What's the problem?
2. Who tells you about job opportunities?

apply
award
factory
library
qualified
volunteer

106   *Unit 8*

Do you work well with others? (Ask for examples.)
- Explain the words *volunteer* and *responsibility.*
- Follow the suggestions on p. 4 for talking about the photos.
- Ask the following questions about each photo. Write learners' responses on the board or an overhead transparency.
  What do you see?
  What are the people doing?
  What are they thinking?

Think and Talk

Answers
1. Cesar is not sure if he's qualified for a supervisor job. Pilar is not sure if she's ready for a library clerk job.
2. Answers will vary. Write some on the board or a transparency.

Vocabulary

Read the words in the student book. Follow the suggestions on p. 6 for introducing and reinforcing vocabulary.

Follow the suggestions on p. 6 for using vocabulary cards. Use the cards for the words in the Vocabulary box.

Gather Your Thoughts

Start this activity by asking learners to think about what they do at home, at school, at work, and in the community. This will help them consider a wider range of possibilities.

- As learners report on their activities, write some on the board or an overhead transparency (e.g., *In the community, I play the guitar; at home, I bake cakes.*).
- Next, ask learners to think about *who* tells them how well they did on these activities (e.g., *members of my church; my children*).

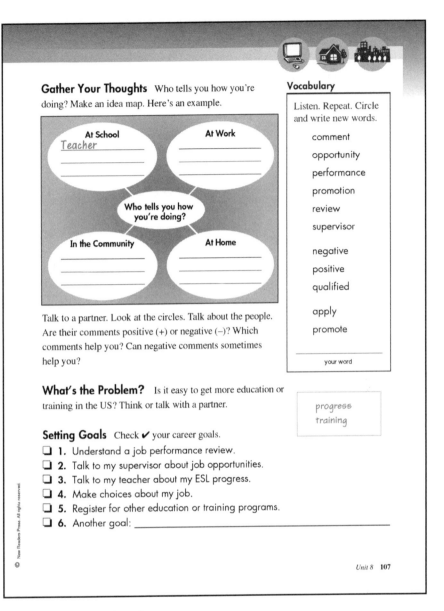

Use Customizable Master 5 (Idea Map). Follow the suggestions on p. 7 for customizing the master. Make one copy for each learner.

- Have learners work on their own to complete the map. Encourage them to include as many answers to the *Who* question as they can.
- Remind learners not to use people's names on their maps. Instead, have them use formal or informal titles (e.g., *the principal, my wife, my boss*).
- After completing their personal maps, have learners answer the questions below the map in their books. They can work either individually or in pairs.
- Ask for responses and write them on a class idea map on the board or a transparency.
- Have learners copy the class map and add to it during class discussion.

What's the Problem?

Follow the suggestions on p. 5 for identifying and analyzing problems. Ask learners to give reasons for their answers.

<u>One Step Up</u>

To elicit more information, ask learners for examples.

Setting Goals

Follow the suggestions on p. 5 for setting goals.

Lesson 1: Good for You!

Read the title and point out the lesson objectives below it.
- Tell learners that this lesson is about understanding how to read a performance review. Explain that a performance review is a report card for employees.
- Follow the suggestions on p. 5 for talking about titles.

Give examples of when to use the idiom *Good for you!* Provide two-line dialogues like these:
- I'm looking for a new job.
  Good for you!
- I got an *A* in my class.
  Good for you!

Attention Box

Use each word in a sentence. This vocabulary should be understood, but learners should not be expected to produce the words at this point.

Question

Read the introductory question aloud. Tell learners the reading will help them think about this question.

Photos

Remind learners to look at the pictures first. It can help them understand what the story is about.

To discuss the photos, ask these questions:
- What do you see in the pictures?
- What is this story about?

Reading Tip

Following the suggestions on p. 5 for reading comprehension. Read the story aloud. Then have learners read the story to one another.

Talk or Write

This exercise helps learners read to discover cause and effect.
- Follow the suggestions on p. 6 for comprehension questions.
- Encourage learners to give as many answers as possible for question 1.

Good for You!

◆ Talk about job skills
◆ Use *can* and *can't*

Do you want a job with more responsibility?

attitude
experience

◆ **Reading Tip**   Use the pictures to help you read.

Ms. Hunter is Cesar's supervisor. She congratulates him on his award for Employee of the Month. Cesar does very good work and is on time every day. He helps the other workers. People like to work with him.

Ms. Hunter wants to give Cesar a promotion. The job has more responsibility and more money, but Cesar needs a high school diploma or GED for that job.

Pilar works at the library as a volunteer. She doesn't get money, but she gets experience. She's a good worker and very responsible. Everybody likes her good attitude. Now she's thinking about a job with pay at the library.

Cesar and Pilar are going to get married. They want to make more money.

Talk or Write
1. Why did Cesar get an award?
2. Can Cesar apply for a new job at the factory?
3. Why did Pilar get an award?

108 *Unit 8 Lesson 1*

Possible Answers
1. Cesar got an award because he does very good work. He's on time every day. He helps other workers. He solves problems well. People like to work with him.
2. No. Cesar doesn't have his high school diploma or GED.
3. Pilar got an award because she's a good worker. She's very responsible. She has a good attitude.

Vocabulary

Read the words in the student book. Follow the suggestions on p. 6 for introducing and reinforcing vocabulary.

Follow the suggestions on p. 6 for using vocabulary cards. Use the cards for the words in the Vocabulary box.

- Ask if learners know what a *GED* is. Explain that people without a high school diploma can get a *General Educational Development* certificate by passing the *GED* test. This may help them get better jobs.
- Explain that a person who works for a company is an *employee* (e.g., Cesar is an *employee* of the computer factory.).
- Read the paragraph below to convey the meaning of *responsible, solve,* and *skills:*
  A responsible *employee comes to work on time, works hard, and wants to improve his or her* skills. *A responsible* employee *also tries to* solve *problems at work.*
- Congratulate your learners. Ask questions like these and say, "I *congratulate* you!":
  Who has a new job?
  Who got married this year?
  Who has a new baby?

Class Chat

Use Customizable Master 3 (3-Column Chart). Follow the suggestions on p. 7 for customizing and duplicating the master. Make a copy for each learner.

- Follow the suggestions on p. 7 for Class Chats.
- First, have partners practice asking and answering questions.
- Then tell learners to walk around the room and ask other learners questions. Have them write the answers in their charts.
- Tell learners to save their charts for use in Activity A.

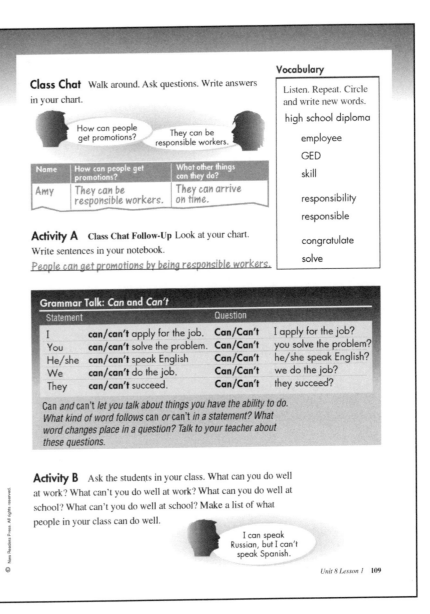

Activity A

Have learners use information from the Class Chat to write sentences in their notebooks.

Grammar Talk

Follow the suggestions on p. 7 for introducing the grammar point.

- Explain that finding a good job depends on your *skills*; it depends on the things you *can* or *can't* do.
- Tell learners that *can't = cannot.* Ask what letters are missing in the contraction. *(no)*
- Tell learners, "I *can* speak English. I *can't* speak French." Ask learners to give examples of things they *can* and *can't* do.

Answers

The base form of a verb follows *can* or *can't* in a statement.

The verb changes place in a question. (*Can* or *can't* moves in front of the subject.)

Use Unit Master 66 (Grammar: *Can* and *Can't*) now or at any time during the rest of the unit.

Activity B

Ask volunteers to write some of their sentences on the board.

Assign Workbook p. 60, Exercises A–B, now or at any time during the rest of Lesson 1.

Unit 8 *Lesson 1* **109**

Attention Box

- Read the words and definitions aloud.
- Give examples of *shifts* by asking learners about the hours they work.

This vocabulary should be understood, but learners should not be expected to produce the words at this point.

Activity C

- Explain that a *job performance review* is like a report card for employees.
- Read through the review with learners. Explain any new words.

Answers

1. Cesar is on time for work. He has a good attitude. He follows safety rules. He can work Machine C very well. He can't work Machine B well.
2. Cesar can work Monday through Sunday from 7 to 3. He can't work evenings or swing shift.
3. Answers will vary.
4. Answers will vary.

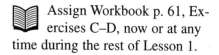 Assign Workbook p. 61, Exercises C–D, now or at any time during the rest of Lesson 1.

Task 1

Use Customizable Master 3 (3-Column Chart). Follow the suggestions on p. 7 for customizing and duplicating the master. Make a copy for each group.

- Have learners list in their notebooks all the jobs they can do.
- Have them list other skills they have (e.g., speaking another language, using a computer).
- Have learners work in groups to make a group chart.
- Assign a recorder or secretary to write information for each member on the group chart. Then assign a reporter to read the information to all learners.

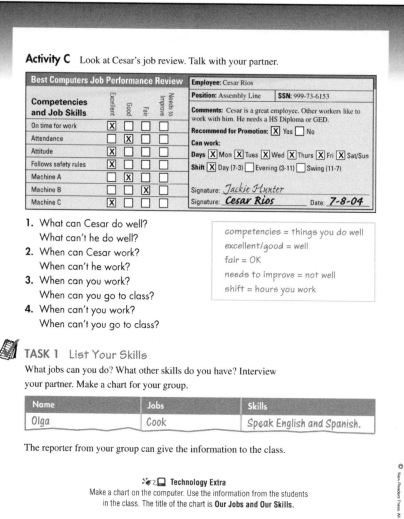

Activity C Look at Cesar's job review. Talk with your partner.

| Best Computers Job Performance Review | Employee: Cesar Rios |

Competencies and Job Skills	Excellent	Good	Fair	Needs to Improve
On time for work	X			
Attendance		X		
Attitude	X			
Follows safety rules	X			
Machine A		X		
Machine B			X	
Machine C	X			

Position: Assembly Line   SSN: 999-73-6153
Comments: Cesar is a great employee. Other workers like to work with him. He needs a HS Diploma or GED.
Recommend for Promotion: [X] Yes [ ] No
Can work:
Days [X] Mon [X] Tues [X] Wed [X] Thurs [X] Fri [X] Sat/Sun
Shift [X] Day (7-3) [ ] Evening (3-11) [ ] Swing (11-7)
Signature: *Jackie Hunter*
Signature: *Cesar Rios*   Date: *7-8-04*

1. What can Cesar do well?
   What can't he do well?
2. When can Cesar work?
   When can't he work?
3. When can you work?
   When can you go to class?
4. When can't you work?
   When can't you go to class?

> competencies = things you do well
> excellent/good = well
> fair = OK
> needs to improve = not well
> shift = hours you work

TASK 1 List Your Skills

What jobs can you do? What other skills do you have? Interview your partner. Make a chart for your group.

Name	Jobs	Skills
Olga	Cook	Speak English and Spanish.

The reporter from your group can give the information to the class.

Technology Extra
Make a chart on the computer. Use the information from the students in the class. The title of the chart is **Our Jobs and Our Skills.**

Assessment

Use Generic Assessment Master 6 (Oral Communication Rubric) to evaluate the presentations.

Technology Extra

Teach learners to create a three-column chart on the computer.

Extension

Have learners make one master chart with all their information. Title the chart *Our Jobs and Our Skills.*

Lesson 2: Planning a Future 🔆

Read the title and point out the lesson objectives below it.

- Tell learners that in this lesson they will talk about their future goals (the things they want to do in life) and make a goals chart.
- Read the introductory question aloud. Then ask these questions: Do you have a plan for the future? What do you need to do to reach your goals?

Attention Box

This vocabulary should be understood, but learners should not be expected to produce the words at this point.

Read these sentences to convey the meaning of *deserve:*
- I *deserve* to make more money.
- I *deserve* good grades.

Idiom Watch

- Ask learners if they already use *Hey!* or have heard other people use it. Provide these examples:
  Hey, come here for a minute.
  Hey, we don't have milk.
  Hey, Jim! How are you doing?
- Point out that *hey* is always used at the beginning of a sentence or by itself (e.g., *Hey! Be careful!*). Explain that *hey* is informal English and usually is used only with people we know well.

Photo

Ask these questions:
- Who are they?
- Where are they?
- What are they doing?
- Who is the waiter?" (*Ramon from Unit 4*)

Listening Tip

Read the tip aloud.

- Tell learners that they can understand many things in English without knowing every word.
- Explain that listening for main or "big" ideas is a good skill.

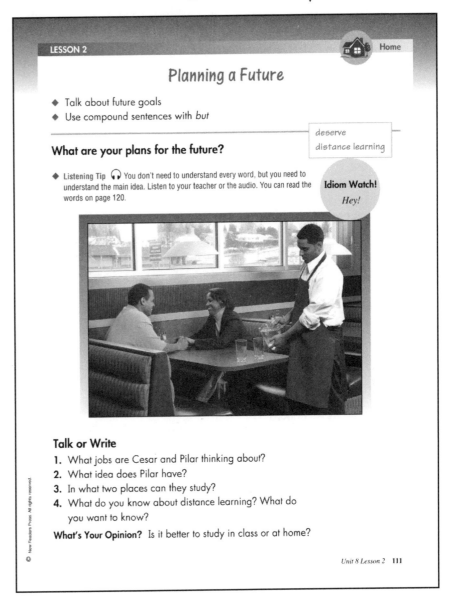

LESSON 2   🏠 Home

Planning a Future

- ◆ Talk about future goals
- ◆ Use compound sentences with *but*

What are your plans for the future?

deserve
distance learning

Idiom Watch!
Hey!

- ◆ Listening Tip 🎧 You don't need to understand every word, but you need to understand the main idea. Listen to your teacher or the audio. You can read the words on page 120.

Talk or Write
1. What jobs are Cesar and Pilar thinking about?
2. What idea does Pilar have?
3. In what two places can they study?
4. What do you know about distance learning? What do you want to know?

What's Your Opinion? Is it better to study in class or at home?

Unit 8 Lesson 2 **111**

🎧 Play the audio or read the listening script on p. 120. Follow the suggestions on p. 5 for listening comprehension.

Talk or Write

This exercise helps learners become skilled at finding the main idea.

Answers
1. Cesar is thinking about a supervisor job. Pilar is thinking about a clerk position.
2. Pilar has an idea for distance learning (learning at home).
3. They can study at school or at home.
4. Answers will vary.

What's Your Opinion?

Have learners respond by using their *yes/no* cards (see p. 4). Tally the answers. Ask learners to explain answers.

Extension
Draw a two-column chart with the heads *Study at Home* and *Study in School.* Have learners give positive (+) things about each alternative. Then draw a horizontal rule across the columns and have them give negative (–) things about each.

Vocabulary

Read the words in the student book. Follow the suggestions on p. 6 for introducing and reinforcing vocabulary.

Follow the suggestions on p. 6 for using vocabulary cards. Use the cards for the words in the Vocabulary box.

Class Chat

Use Customizable Master 3 (3-Column Chart). Follow the suggestions on p. 7 for customizing the master. Make a copy for each learner.

Follow the suggestions on p. 7 for Class Chats.

Circulate. Help learners generate at least two requirements for their jobs.

Activity A

Have learners write sentences using the information in their Class Chat charts.

Grammar Talk

Follow the suggestions on p. 7 for introducing the grammar point.

Read the sentences in the grammar box. Remind learners that in Unit 7 they made two sentences into one using *and*. Now they will make two sentences into one using *but*.

- Tell learners that *but* is used to combine two different ideas or to show a problem.
- Write these sentences on the board or a transparency:
  Cesar wants a supervisor job.
  He needs a high school diploma.
- Ask, "What does Cesar want? What does he need?"

Now join the two sentences into one sentence using *but*.

- Erase the period after the first sentence and change it to a comma.
- Change *He* to *he* and write *but* between the comma and *he*.

Answer

A comma is used before *but*.

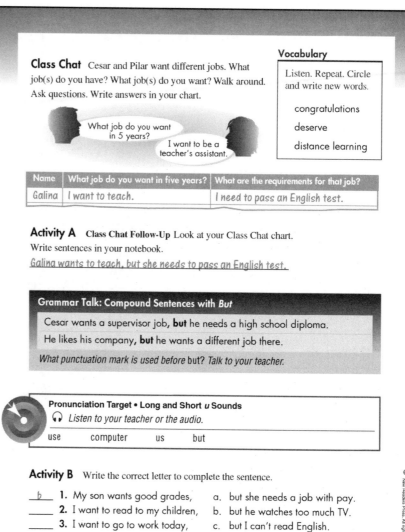

Class Chat Cesar and Pilar want different jobs. What job(s) do you have? What job(s) do you want? Walk around. Ask questions. Write answers in your chart.

What job do you want in 5 years?

I want to be a teacher's assistant.

Vocabulary
Listen. Repeat. Circle and write new words.

congratulations
deserve
distance learning

Name	What job do you want in five years?	What are the requirements for that job?
Galina	I want to teach.	I need to pass an English test.

Activity A **Class Chat Follow-Up** Look at your Class Chat chart. Write sentences in your notebook.
Galina wants to teach, but she needs to pass an English test.

Grammar Talk: Compound Sentences with *But*

Cesar wants a supervisor job, **but** he needs a high school diploma.

He likes his company, **but** he wants a different job there.

What punctuation mark is used before but? *Talk to your teacher.*

Pronunciation Target • Long and Short *u* Sounds
🎧 *Listen to your teacher or the audio.*

use   computer   us   but

Activity B Write the correct letter to complete the sentence.

_b_ **1.** My son wants good grades,   a. but she needs a job with pay.
___ **2.** I want to read to my children,   b. but he watches too much TV.
___ **3.** I want to go to work today,   c. but I can't read English.
___ **4.** Pilar likes her volunteer job,   d. but I have a bad cold.

112 *Unit 8 Lesson 3*

Pronunciation Target

🎧 Play the audio or read the words in the student book. Have learners repeat the words.

- Ask learners if the *u* makes the same sound in all the words.
- Ask learners what other words they know have these two sounds. Write them on the board or a transparency.
- Point out other *u* words in this unit (e.g., *future, supervisor,* and *opportunity*).

Use Unit Master 67 (Phonics: Long and Short *u* Sounds) now.

Activity B

Use the model to explain to learners how to do this matching exercise.

Extension

Have learners write the complete sentences in their notebooks.

Answers

2. c   3. d   4. a

Use Unit Master 68 (Grammar: Compound Sentences with *but*) now or at any time during the rest of the unit.

Assign Workbook p. 62, Exercises A–B, now or at any time during the rest of Lesson 2.

Activity C

Read the directions with learners and review the model.

- Tell learners to first answer each question with two sentences. The two sentences should suggest a problem or a difference.
- Circulate to help learners formulate their sentences.
- Have partners tell each other their sentences. Then tell partners to combine them into one using *but*.
- Ask learners to write some of their sentences on the board or an overhead transparency.

One Step Down

Before doing the activity, help learners generate ideas for each of the verbs (*have, want, need, like*).

Brainstorm ideas together and write them on the board or an overhead transparency. Use a word map for each verb to clarify the exercise.

Assign Workbook p. 63, Exercise C, now or at any time during the rest of Lesson 2.

Task 2

Make one copy of Customizable Master 4 (4-Column Chart). Add a vertical line to create five columns. Make a copy for each learner, but have learners work in groups.

- Read the directions with learners. Tell them they will ask each other the questions and use their partner's information to complete the chart.
- Read the model for the learners. Check for understanding.
- Model the activity by taking the role of the person asking the questions. Have a volunteer answer.

Assessment

Use Generic Assessment Master 6 (Oral Communication Rubric) to evaluate the presentations.

Activity C Talk to your partner. What do you have, want, need, and like? What's the problem? Use *but* to write one sentence for each verb.

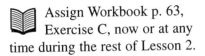
I have a computer at home. I don't know how to use it.

1. _I have a computer at home, but I don't know how to use it._
2. _____
3. _____
4. _____
5. _____

TASK 2 *Make a Goals Chart*

Work in a group. Think about the future.
What do you want to do?   OR   What do you want to be?
What do you need to do to make that happen?
Read the questions with a partner. Complete the chart.

One Step Up
Think about five years from now. Where do you want to be? What job do you want to have? Use the computer and write your future address and job.

	I can	I want to	I need to	My Goals
School	speak 3 languages	go to college	finish high school	I want to go to college, but I need to finish high school.
Work				
Family				
Community				

Talk to your partner. Tell him or her your information. Tell someone else in your group about your partner.

One Step Up

This activity should be fun for working and nonworking learners alike. Ask questions like these:

- If you are single, will you be married?
- If you are married, will you have children? How many? What will you name them?
- What country will you live in? What city or town?
- What job will you have?

If computers are not available, have learners write the information in their notebooks.

Lesson 3: Distance Learning 🔆

Read the title and point out the lesson objectives below it.

- In this lesson, learners will find out about opportunities to learn. They will read flyers and brochures as one way to find information about such opportunities.

Attention Box

Read the words. Use each in a sentence. Check for understanding.

This vocabulary should be understood, but learners should not be expected to produce the words at this point.

Reading Tip

Read the tip aloud. Direct learners' attention to the flyers.

- Read the caption under the illustration. Tell learners Pilar and Cesar found these flyers at the library.
- Ask learners to read the flyers and call out specific times and dates.
- As learners answer, write the times and dates on the board or an overhead transparency.

Follow the suggestions for reading comprehension on p. 5.
- Read the three flyers aloud.
- Have volunteers read all or part of each flyer. Ask questions to check for comprehension.

Talk or Write

This exercise helps learners become skilled at reading flyers.

Follow the suggestions on p. 6 for answering comprehension questions.

Answers
1. at home (with videos from Sierra Adult School; on cable TV); at Bayview Library (online)
2. ESL and GED classes
3. online at the Bayview Library or at home on cable TV

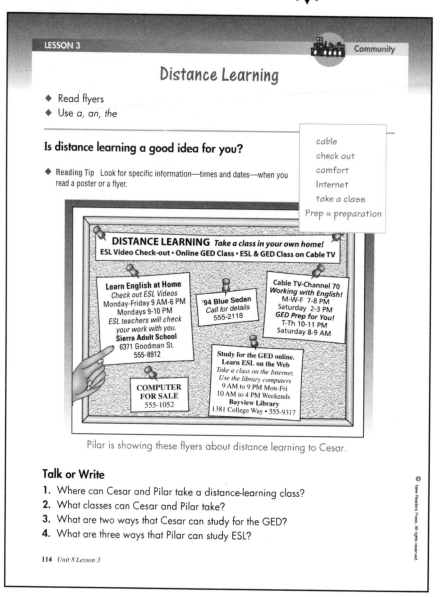

4. get videos from from Sierra Adult School; take an Internet class on Bayview Library's computers; study at home on cable TV

📖 Assign Workbook pp. 64–65, Exercises A–C, now or at any time during the rest of Lesson 3.

Vocabulary

Read the words in the student book. Follow the suggestions on p. 6 for introducing and reinforcing vocabulary.

Follow the suggestions on p. 6 for using vocabulary cards. Use the cards for the words in the Vocabulary box.

Introduce the words in context:

- Tell learners that many people pay money to rent movie *videos*. At a library, they can *check out* books and *videos*. They do not pay money to borrow them.
- Show learners examples of audio- and *videotapes*.
- Take a poll to talk about the words. Ask learners how many have *cable TV* and use the *Internet*. What do they watch on *cable TV?* What do they do on the *Internet?* Talk about your own experiences.

Class Chat

Use Customizable Master 3 (3-Column Chart). Follow the suggestions on p. 7 for customizing and duplicating the master. Make a copy for each learner. Follow the suggestions on p. 7 for Class Chats. Remind learners to save their charts to use for Activity A.

Grammar Talk

Follow the suggestions on p. 7 for introducing the grammar point.

Write examples of *a* and *an* as they appear with words beginning with consonant and vowel sounds. This concept should be understood, but learners should not be expected to have oral mastery of this distinction at this point.

<u>One Step Down</u>

Create a two-column chart on the board or a transparency. Write the heads *Vowels* and *Consonants* over the columns. Write the appropriate letters below each.

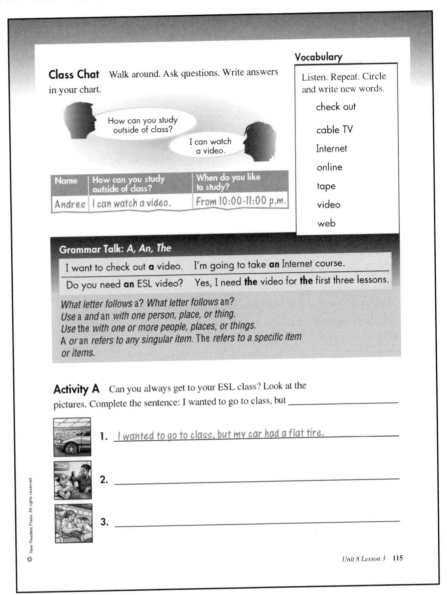

- Ask learners how many have studied or heard about vowels and consonants before. Have them respond by raising their *yes/no* cards (see p. 4).
- Have learners read aloud together all the vowels and then all the consonants.
- Tell learners to memorize the vowels. Erase the vowel column and have individual learners call out the vowels.

<u>Answers</u>

A consonant follows *a*.
A vowel follows *an*.

Use Unit Master 69 (Grammar: *A, An, The*) now or at any time during the rest of the unit.

Activity A

Do this activity with all learners, encouraging them and providing assistance as needed. Then review the questions again, asking volunteers to answer.

<u>Possible Answers</u>

2. I wanted to go to class, but my child was sick.
3. I wanted to go to class, but I had to work.

Activity B

Have learners work in pairs. Review the model. After they complete the activity, have individual learners each read a sentence. Tell learners to raise their hands when someone reads a word they do not know.

Answers

2. the	5. the	8. a
3. the	6. a	
4. an	7. an	

In the US

This culture section asks learners to synthesize information from a chart and a short reading. This important skill is assessed on the GED test.

- Have learners read the chart silently. Then read it to them and have them repeat each line.
- Explain the title, column heads, and any other vocabulary they may not know (e.g., *average = normal* or *mid-point; income = money earned from a job*).

Demonstrate numerical *averages*, gradually allowing learners to provide answers as they come to understand the English term.

Write the following equations on the board or a transparency:

- 6 + 10 divided by 2 = 8
  Say, "The average of 6 and 10 is 8."
- 60 + 80 divided by 2 = 70
  Say, "The average of 60 and 80 is ___." Let learners fill in the blank. *(70)*
- 100 + 110 + 150 divided by 3 = 120
  The average of 100, 110, and 150 is ___. *(120)*
- Ask *yes/no* questions about the information in the chart (e.g., Do people with a ninth-grade education usually make $59,000 a year?).
- Ask information questions about the reading and the chart (e.g., What is the average income for people with some college?).

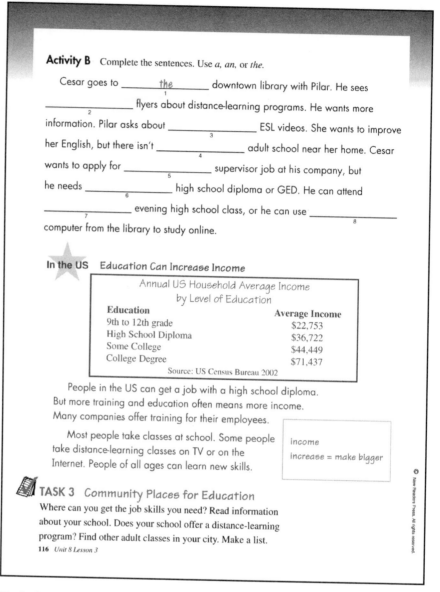

Activity B Complete the sentences. Use *a, an,* or *the.*

Cesar goes to ____the____ downtown library with Pilar. He sees _____ flyers about distance-learning programs. He wants more information. Pilar asks about _____ ESL videos. She wants to improve her English, but there isn't _____ adult school near her home. Cesar wants to apply for _____ supervisor job at his company, but he needs _____ high school diploma or GED. He can attend _____ evening high school class, or he can use _____ computer from the library to study online.

In the US Education Can Increase Income

Annual US Household Average Income by Level of Education	
Education	Average Income
9th to 12th grade	$22,753
High School Diploma	$36,722
Some College	$44,449
College Degree	$71,437
Source: US Census Bureau 2002	

People in the US can get a job with a high school diploma. But more training and education often means more income. Many companies offer training for their employees.

Most people take classes at school. Some people take distance-learning classes on TV or on the Internet. People of all ages can learn new skills.

income
increase = make bigger

TASK 3 Community Places for Education
Where can you get the job skills you need? Read information about your school. Does your school offer a distance-learning program? Find other adult classes in your city. Make a list.
116 *Unit 8 Lesson 3*

Task 3

- Place learners in groups.
- Provide each group with copies of your school's class schedule and those of other adult education centers (e.g., libraries, community colleges, community centers).
- Look up *Education* in the phone book to find other learning centers or their phone numbers and addresses. If these pages have large informative ads, point them out to learners.
- Ask comprehension questions about the ads and class schedules.

- Tell each group to make a list of places in their community that offer adult education and the kinds of classes they offer.
- Have each group use its list to create a poster about community adult education classes. Hang the posters in your classroom or school.

Review Unit Skills
See p. 8 for suggestions on games and activities to review the unit vocabulary and grammar.

Unit 8 Project

Learners plan and create a poster of their personal goals.

Get Ready

Tell learners to think about their goals.

- Read Cesar's time line with learners. Ask detail questions to check for comprehension.
- Tell learners to draw a horizontal line the width of a sheet of paper and create their own time line.
- Model a time line on the board with your own information.

Do the Work

- Use Cesar's information to show learners how they can create a simple resume from a time line.
- Have learners draft their resumes in their notebooks before creating the final copies.

Present Your Project

After they complete their time lines, have learners tell their group about them.

It is important for learners to become comfortable with saying they did a good job or can do something well.

- Tell learners that saying good things about yourself is an important skill in getting a job.
- Explain that this exercise helps prepare them for school and work interviews.

Some learners may not want to give their resumes to the whole class. As an alternative, limit distribution by having learners share their resumes only with their groups.

Peer Assessment

Distribute a copy of Generic Assessment Master 10 (Peer Assessment Form for Projects and Tasks) to each learner.

- Follow the suggestions for peer assessment on p. 4.

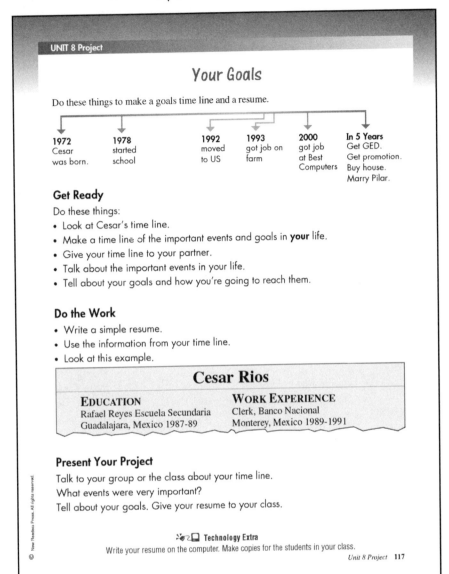

UNIT 8 Project

Your Goals

Do these things to make a goals time line and a resume.

| 1972 Cesar was born. | 1978 started school | 1992 moved to US | 1993 got job on farm | 2000 got job at Best Computers | In 5 Years Get GED. Get promotion. Buy house. Marry Pilar. |

Get Ready

Do these things:
- Look at Cesar's time line.
- Make a time line of the important events and goals in **your** life.
- Give your time line to your partner.
- Talk about the important events in your life.
- Tell about your goals and how you're going to reach them.

Do the Work

- Write a simple resume.
- Use the information from your time line.
- Look at this example.

Cesar Rios

| EDUCATION | WORK EXPERIENCE |
| Rafael Reyes Escuela Secundaria Guadalajara, Mexico 1987-89 | Clerk, Banco Nacional Monterey, Mexico 1989-1991 |

Present Your Project

Talk to your group or the class about your time line.
What events were very important?
Tell about your goals. Give your resume to your class.

Technology Extra
Write your resume on the computer. Make copies for the students in your class.

Unit 8 Project **117**

- Ask each learner to practice talking about his or her goals and experiences in front of a small group.
- Have learners complete the forms and study the comments before doing their final presentation.
- When groups present for the whole class, encourage active listening by asking learners questions about the presentations.

Assessment

Use Unit Master 70 (Project Assessment Form) to assess each learner's presentation. Make a copy of the master for each learner and place the completed form in the learner's portfolio.

Assign Workbook p. 66 (Check Your Progress).

Use Unit Master 71 (Unit Checkup/Review) whenever you complete this unit.

Self-Assessment

Give each learner a copy of Generic Assessment Masters 8 and 9 (Speaking and Listening Self-Check and Writing and Reading Self-Check). Go over the items together. The completed forms will become part of each learner's portfolio.

Listening Scripts

This section contains scripts for the content of the audiotape and audio CD for *English—No Problem!* level 1. Pronunciation cues are indicated in square brackets.

Warm-Up Unit
Are You Ready?

Lesson 2, Page 15
Welcome!
Listen to Tomas *[Toe-mas]* and his teacher.
Teacher: Welcome to English class, Tomas. Where are you from?
Tomas: I'm from Chile *[Chee-lay]*. Teacher, I need a pencil.
Teacher: Here's one. Bring a pencil tomorrow. And my name is Pat Allen.
Tomas: Hello, Mr. Allen.
Teacher: Now class, ready to write? OK, open your books. Do exercise A with your partners. Answer the questions.

Lesson 2, Page 16
Pronunciation Target: Syllable Stress
Listen.
late
<u>stu</u>dent
di<u>rec</u>tions

Lesson 3, Page 20
Activity A
Listen. Write the numbers.
Number one. How much are two notebooks? Two notebooks are six dollars.
Number two. How much are four pens? Four pens are eight dollars.
Number three. How much are ten pencils? Ten pencils are two dollars.
Number four. How much is the paper? The paper is two dollars and fifty cents.

Lesson 3, Page 20
Activity B
Listen to Tomas and the clerk. Put the conversation in order.
Tomas: I need to buy school supplies.
Clerk: What supplies do you need?
Tomas: I need a notebook and a dictionary.
Clerk: English or Spanish-English?
Tomas: Spanish-English, please.
Clerk: That's eight dollars and forty-five cents.
Tomas: OK. Here's ten dollars.
Clerk: And one dollar and fifty-five cents in change.

Unit 1
My Life Is Changing!

Lesson 2, Page 27
The Neighborhood
Listen to Nassim *[Na-seem]* and her husband.

Nassim: Lusala *[Lu-sah-la]*, I'm worried. My parents need help.
Lusala: They need to live here. What's the problem?
Nassim: This apartment is small with only two bedrooms.
Lusala: Apartments with three bedrooms in this neighborhood are expensive.
Nassim: Maybe I need a part-time job.
Lusala: No problem for you, Nassim! Your English is good.

Lesson 2, Page 28
Pronunciation Target: Question and Answer Intonation
Listen.
Is Nassim at home?
Yes, she is.

Unit 2
I Need to Plan a Party

Lesson 1, Page 37
Pronunciation Target: Present-Tense Endings
Listen.
wan<u>ts</u> *[-ts]*
like<u>s</u> *[-ks]*
write<u>s</u> *[-ts]*
nee<u>ds</u> *[-dz]*
agree<u>s</u> *[-z]*
en<u>ds</u> *[-dz]*

Lesson 3, Page 42
Changing Plans!
Listen to people talk.
Boris: Happy birthday, Pavel *[Pah-vel]*! This is a special cake for you.
Yelena: Oh, no! Here comes the rain! Boris, what can we do?
Boris: Let's go to the porch.
Rosa: Good idea. We can have the party there.
Yelena: Boris, take the cake. I'll take the presents.
Rosa: Kids, run to the porch.

Lesson 3, Page 43
Pronunciation Target: Long and Short a Sounds
Listen.
rain, cake, favor
plan, at, glad

Lesson 3, Page 44
Activity B
Listen. Write numbers one to seven to put the conversation in the correct order.
Miguel: Hello, Yelena *[Yell-ay-nuh]*. I am Miguel and this is Sylvia. We are Ben's parents.
Yelena: It's nice to meet you, Miguel and Sylvia. This is my husband, Boris.

Miguel: Hi, Boris. Thank you for inviting Ben to the party.

Boris: It's nice to have Ben here. Pavel *[PAH-vel]*, thank Ben for his present.

Pavel: Thanks for the backpack, Ben. It's great!

Ben: I'm glad you like it. Thanks for the cake. Mom, Pavel's dad makes great cakes.

Sylvia: Really? I need to call you, Boris. I need a cake for a church meeting next week.

Unit 3
How Do You Feel?

Lesson 2, Page 51
Making a Doctor's Appointment
Listen to Jim call the doctor.

Receptionist: Dr. Lee's office.

Jim: Hello, this is Jim Martin. I need an appointment with the doctor.

Receptionist: What's the problem, Mr. Martin?

Jim: I feel sick. My throat hurts, and I have a bad headache.

Receptionist: Do you have a fever?

Jim: Yes, my temperature's one-hundred-and-one degrees.

Receptionist: OK. The doctor can see you tomorrow, June tenth, at three P.M. *[P-M]*.

Jim: Tomorrow at three o'clock. Thank you.

Lesson 3, Page 55
Pronunciation Target: Intonation with Be *and* Wh- *[W-H] Questions*
Listen.
[Stress the rising intonation at the end of this question.]
Is your appointment at ↑three P.M.?↑
[Follow the arrows to stress the rising↑ and falling↓ intonations.]
When is your appointment *[ap-↑point-↓ment]?↓*

Unit 4
I Need a Budget!

Lesson 2, Page 63
Improving Your Job Skills
Listen to Ramon *[Rah-moan]* and his boss.

Ramon: Mr. Martin, I need to talk to you. I want to work more hours at the restaurant.

Mr. Martin: I'm sorry, Ramon. First you need to improve your service, your clothes, and your English.

Ramon: I'm studying English at school now.

Mr. Martin: That's good. But you speak only Spanish to the other workers.

Ramon: I'm trying to help them with their jobs.

Mr. Martin: You need to help the customers first. Those people need their bill. Remember—happy customers give good tips!

Ramon: OK, you're right. Thanks for the advice. I know I can do a better job.

Lesson 2, Page 64
Pronunciation Target: Long and Short e Sounds
Listen.
cheap
e-mail
need
rent
spend
expensive

Lesson 3, Page 68
Activity A
Listen. Use the words in the box to complete the conversation.

Ramon: I need to return these shirts.

Salesperson: What's the problem?

Ramon: They don't fit well. Is that shirt on sale?

Salesperson: No, it isn't. This shirt is on sale.

Ramon: Good! I need a medium in black.

Salesperson: OK. Anything else?

Ramon: No, thanks. That's it for today.

Unit 5
What's for Dinner?

Lesson 1, Page 73
Pronunciation Target: Intonation with Words in a List
Listen.
The store has apples↑, eggs↑, bananas↑, and ↓corn on sale.

Lesson 3, Page 78
It's Lunch Time!
Listen. Miyako *[Mee-yah-ko]* and her friends are at school.

Maria: It's lunch time! We're going to eat. Come with us.

Miyako: To where?

Maria: To Hamburger Hut or Tacos to Go for a fast lunch.

Miyako: Thanks, but I have my lunch today. I'm going to eat in the cafeteria.

Maria: Come on! The burgers and fries are really good.

Miyako: I know, but I'm trying to eat well and save money.

Maria: OK. See you in English class.

Lesson 3, Page 80
Activity A
Listen.
People in the US are very busy.
They often don't have time to buy or cook food.
At school or at work they are far from home.
Fast food is popular.
But there are problems with fast food.
It often has a lot of fat, salt, or sugar.

Too much fat, salt, and sugar are bad for people's health.
Some fast-food restaurants are changing.
Now they have salads or other healthy foods.
Small changes in food choices can make big health differences.

Listen again. Choose words from the box. Complete the sentences.
[Repeat sentences above.]

Lesson 3, Page 80
Activity B
Listen. Maria is at the fast-food restaurant.
Clerk: Welcome to Hamburger Hut. Your order please.
Maria: I'd like Fast Meal Number Three. Are there fries with that?
Clerk: Yes, there are. And to drink? Soda or coffee?
Maria: Orange soda, please.
Clerk: For here or to go?
Maria: To go.
Clerk: OK, that's $4.25 *[four twenty-five].*

Unit 6
Call the Police!

Lesson 1, Page 85
*Pronunciation Target: Long and Short **i** Sounds*
Listen.
quiet
night
crime
window
missing
important

Lesson 2, Page 87
Talking to the Police
Listen to Sara and the police officer.
Officer Collins: Ms. Morgan, we need you to fill out a police report. Please tell us what happened first.
Sara: I came home about ten p.m. When I arrived at the door, it was open.
Officer Collins: Then what happened?
Sara: I went inside, looked around, and I saw this mess!
Officer Collins: And then? Was anything missing?
Sara: Yes, several things—a computer, a TV, and a VCR.
Officer Collins: Did your neighbors see anything?
Sara: Yes, my neighbor, Mrs. Caruso, saw a man about nine-fifty p.m. He put a TV in his van.

Lesson 2, Page 88
Pronunciation Target: Past-Tense Ending Sounds
Listen.
Sara worked. *[-kt]*
The police arrived. *[-d]*
Mrs. Caruso waited. *[-ed]*

Unit 7
Succeeding at School

Lesson 2, Page 99
Making Decisions
Listen to Thuy *[Too-ee]* and her sister-in-law.
Thuy: Minh *[Min]* is always tired. Her school gives a lot of homework. I want to talk to the principal.
Karen: Maybe she has too many classes. Her counselor can change her schedule.
Thuy: Look at her report card.
Karen: Oh, Thuy. Her grades are not good this quarter. What is happening?
Thuy: Well, Minh is very busy this year. She has school, a job, basketball, soccer, and piano.
Karen: And does she help your other children get ready for school in the morning?
Thuy: Yes, Karl and I start work at six a.m. I need her to fix breakfast for the kids.
Karen: I understand why she's tired all the time.

Lesson 2, Page 100
*Pronunciation Target: Long and Short **o** Sounds*
Listen.
home
phone
job
soccer

Unit 8
I Want a Good Job!

Lesson 2, Page 111
Planning a Future
Listen to Cesar *[Say-sar]* and Pilar *[Pee-lar].*
Pilar: Congratulations, honey, on your award. You deserved it.
Cesar: You deserved your award too, Pilar. Let's celebrate our future!
Pilar: Are you thinking about the supervisor job?
Cesar: Yes, but I need a high school diploma or my GED *[G-E-D].*
Pilar: That's like me. The volunteer work was good experience, and now I want a clerk job with pay. But I still need to study more English.
Cesar: It's not easy to work and study. We need time for us too.
Pilar: Hey! I read a flyer at the library about learning at home. It's called distance learning.
Cesar: Great! Let's look at it. Maybe we can learn at home together.

Lesson 2, Page 112
*Pronunciation Target: Long and Short **u** Sounds*
Listen.
use
computer
us
but

Working with Maps

Use the maps in this appendix for those opportunities when learners initiate topics about their home countries or about items in the news.

US Map

Use this US map to show learners where their state and city are located. Ask them what state they live in, what other states they know about, and in what states they have friends or relatives.

Here are some other activities you can do with the map:

- Use the map when appropriate to show where the characters in the student book live or where learners think they live.
- Addresses are referred to throughout the student book and workbook in the stories, school registration forms, medical forms, and elsewhere. Refer learners to the US map at each of these points. Ask them to find the city and/or state on the map.

World Map

Use a world map as a way to welcome new learners into your class. If you have a world map on the wall of your classroom, you can make a wall display.

- Take a Polaroid picture of each learner. Learners can write their names at the bottom of their pictures. Using a piece of yarn, pin one end of the yarn to the town they live in now and pin the other end to the town they came from,

along with the picture of the learner. As new learners join your class, add their pictures to the map in the same way.

- Use the world map when appropriate to show where the characters in the student book were born.
- When talking about the weather (e.g., in the Warm-Up Unit and in Unit 2) refer learners to the world map. Ask: *Is it rainy in your home country today? How is the weather today in Mexico? How is the weather today in Ukraine? Is it warm or cold?*
- Refer learners to the world map when presenting the "Compare Cultures" portion of each unit.

The US

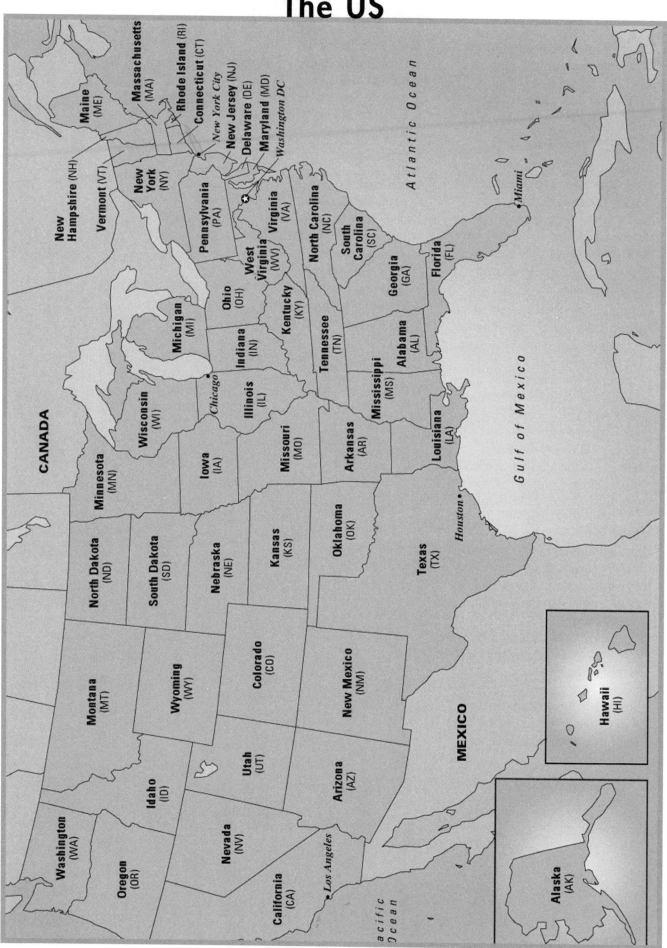

The World

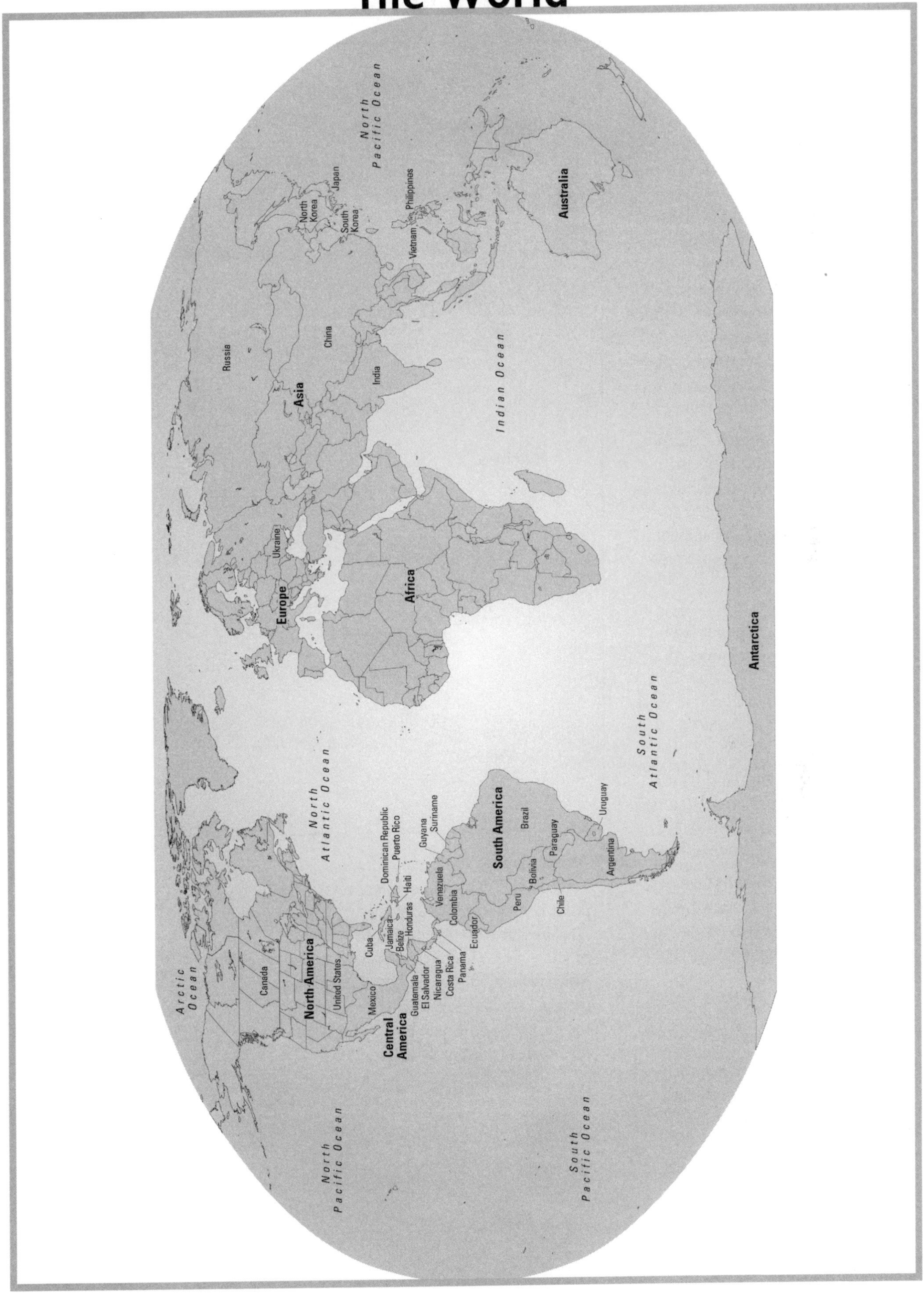

Arctic Ocean

North Pacific Ocean

North Atlantic Ocean

North Pacific Ocean

South Pacific Ocean

South Atlantic Ocean

Indian Ocean

Asia

Russia

China

India

North Korea

South Korea

Japan

Vietnam

Philippines

Australia

Europe

Ukraine

Africa

Antarctica

North America

Canada

United States

Mexico

Cuba

Jamaica

Belize

Honduras

Central America

Guatemala

El Salvador

Nicaragua

Costa Rica

Panama

Dominican Republic

Puerto Rico

Haiti

Guyana

Suriname

Venezuela

Colombia

Ecuador

South America

Brazil

Peru

Bolivia

Chile

Paraguay

Uruguay

Argentina

Alphabet and Numbers

Alphabet

Beginning-level learners benefit from periodic review of the alphabet. As you monitor learners' writing, you can refer learners who are still having difficulty with letter formation to this page.

- Indicate which letters you would like them to practice by writing the letters on a small piece of paper. Learners can then match the letters that you wrote with the letters on the page.
- If learners have personal copies of the book, you can also assign writing practice for homework.

Use the alphabet on this page as a whole-class listening activity to assess learners while presenting the Warm-Up Unit:

- Call out a letter of the alphabet and ask learners to point to the letter.
- Have individual learners say the letters while a volunteer from the class writes the letters on the board.
- As a variation, learners can work with partners to say and identify the letters.

In the Warm-Up Unit and Unit 1, learners learn to print and sign their names. Refer them to this page when presenting these topics.

Use the alphabet to help learners read multiple-choice questions. Write the letters inside circles on the board and have learners "bubble in" the answers.

Numbers

Use this page to assess learners' previous knowledge of numbers when presenting the Warm-Up Unit.

- Call out numbers, and have learners point to the numbers they hear.

- As a variation, spell out a number (T-W-E-N-T-Y) and have learners point to the correct number.
- Use the numbers for dictation practice. Say a number and have learners write the word. To check their accuracy, have learners spell the number while you or a volunteer writes it on the board.

Alphabet and Numbers

The Alphabet

A	B	C	D	E	F	G	H	I	J	K	L	M
N	O	P	Q	R	S	T	U	V	W	X	Y	Z

a	b	c	d	e	f	g	h	i	j	k	l	m
n	o	p	q	r	s	t	u	v	w	x	y	z

Numbers

0 zero	1 one	2 two	3 three	4 four	5 five	6 six	7 seven	8 eight	9 nine	10 ten
11 eleven	12 twelve	13 thirteen	14 fourteen	15 fifteen	16 sixteen	17 seventeen	18 eighteen	19 nineteen	20 twenty
21 twenty-one	22 twenty-two	23 twenty-three	24 twenty-four	25 twenty-five	26 twenty-six	27 twenty-seven	28 twenty-eight	29 twenty-nine	30 thirty
	40 forty	50 fifty	60 sixty	70 seventy	80 eighty	90 ninety	100 one hundred
	200 two hundred	300 three hundred	400 four hundred	500 five hundred	600 six hundred	700 seven hundred	800 eight hundred	900 nine hundred	1,000 one thousand

124 *Alphabet and Numbers*

Months, Days, and Holidays

Months and Days

In the US, dates are written in a different order than in most learners' home countries. Using the US system is an important skill to learn.

- Explain that months are often represented by a number. Have learners practice writing each month with a number (e.g., 1. January, 2. February).
- Say "Month 4" and have learners tell you the name (April) or write it on the board.
- Write today's date on the board (e.g., 12/25/04) and write *month-day-year* above it.
- Read a date for the learners (e.g., December 25, 2004) and have them write the date using numbers in the correct order.
- Then reverse the process and dictate the numbers. Have learners write the full date.

Calendar

Working with a calendar is a good way to review days and numbers. The calendar should be reviewed throughout the series whenever appropriate (filling out forms, writing time lines, etc.).

For continual reinforcement, write the date on the board every day (or have a learner do it) and ask: *What month is this? What day is it? What's the date?*

Use the calendar on this page for the following activities:

- Read a specific date (e.g., August 14th) and ask learners to tell you what the day is (e.g., Saturday).
- Spell a number from one to thirty-one and ask learners to say the correct day.
- Say a day (e.g. Monday) and ask learners to look at the calendar and write the dates that fall on that day (e.g., 2, 9, 16, 23, 30).

Months and Days

	Months	Abbreviations	Days	Abbreviations
1.	January	Jan.	Sunday	Sun.
2.	February	Feb.	Monday	Mon.
3.	March	Mar.	Tuesday	Tues.
4.	April	Apr.	Wednesday	Wed.
5.	May	May.	Thursday	Thurs.
6.	June	Jun.	Friday	Fri.
7.	July	Jul.	Saturday	Sat.
8.	August	Aug.		
9.	September	Sept.		
10.	October	Oct.		
11.	November	Nov.		
12.	December	Dec.		

August 2004

Sun.	Mon.	Tues.	Wed.	Thurs.	Fri.	Sat.
1	2	3	4	5	6	7
8	9	10	11	12	13	14
15	16	17	18	19	20	21
22	23	24	25	26	27	28
29	30	31				

US Holidays

Day	Date
New Year's Day	January 1
Martin Luther King Day	January 15*
Presidents' Day	third Monday in February
Memorial Day	May 30*
Independence Day	July 4
Labor Day	first Monday in September
Veterans Day	November 11
Thanksgiving	fourth Thursday in November
Christmas	December 25

* Observed on the closest Monday.

Months, Days, and Holidays 125

US Holidays

Tell learners that this is a list of official holidays in the United States.

- If you have a calendar in your room, ask different learners to see if those holidays are listed on the calendar and what the exact date is for the current year.
- Ask if anybody knows any information about the holidays. Write some vocabulary words on the board as learners respond.
- At the beginning of each month, ask the learners what holidays are in that month.

Write the name of a holiday on one card (e.g., *New Year's Day*), and a date on a second card (e.g., *January 1, 2004*). If you have more learners, you could add a third card by writing the date in numbers (e.g., *1-1-04*) and a fourth by drawing a holiday symbol.

- Hand out one card to each learner. Have learners walk around and stand together in teams for each holiday.
- Then have each team get together in chronological order starting with the January holidays.

Verb Tense Review and Writing Checklist

Verb Tense Review

Past-tense verbs are presented in Unit 6. As learners work on the various activities using the past tense, remind them they can reference this page for the irregular past forms.

Use flash cards to practice irregular past-tense forms:

- Pass out vocabulary cards for the verbs. Have learners write the irregular past-tense forms on the back of the cards.
- If learners finish activities early, they can use the cards with their partners. One partner reads the verb, and the other has to give the past-tense form.

Practice using the irregular past-tense forms with this activity:

- Write this sentence on the board: *What did you ___ yesterday?*
- Ask learners to complete the question with one of the verbs in the list.
- Then have the learners' partners write responses (e.g., I bought food yesterday.).
- Reverse the roles and repeat the activity.

Writing Checklist for Sentences

Refer learners to this checklist for any activity that requires writing.

- Review the questions with the learners and explain what each one means. You may choose to have learners check only one or two of the questions at first and then add more as they progress.
- After learners complete the checklist for a writing activity, have them assign one point for each question they can answer with a *yes*.
- Learners can track their progress using the checklist.

Verb Tense Review

present	past	present	past
buy	bought	see	saw
drive	drove	send	sent
eat	ate	spend	spent
fit	fit	take	took
give	gave	tell	told
make	made	wear	wore
ride	rode	write	wrote
run	ran		

Writing Checklist for Sentences

- ❑ 1. <u>Did</u> I capitalize the first word of every sentence?
- ❑ 2. Did I end every sentence with a period (.), question mark (?), or exclamation point (!)?
- ❑ 3. Did I ~~used~~ use correct grammar?
- ❑ 4. Did I check my ~~speling~~ spelling?
- ❑ 5. *Is my handwriting neat and easy to read?*

Topics

Grammar and Pronunciation

A

a, an, 115

C

can and *can't,* 109
commands, 31
compound sentences
  with *and,* 100
  with *but,* 112
contractions
  negative, with *be,* 25
  with *be,* 13
  with past-tense
    statements with *be,* 85
  with past-tense
    statements with regular
    and irregular verbs, 88
  with present continuous
    statements, 61
  with present-tense verbs,
    37
  with present-tense *wh-*
    questions with *be,* 52
  with *yes/no* questions and
    answers, 43

F

frequency adverbs, 40
future tense with *going to,*
  103

I

intonation
  with questions and
    answers, 28
  with *be* and *wh-*
    questions, 55
  with words in a list, 73

L

like, like to, 64

N

need, need to, 19, 64
nouns
  count and non-count, 73
  plurals of regular, 19

O

object pronouns, 49

P

past tense
  questions with *be* and
    other verbs, 91
  statements with *be,* 85
  statements with irregular
    verbs, 88
  statements with regular
    verbs, 88
possessive
  adjectives, 16, 97
  nouns, 16
prepositions
  of location, 28
  of time, 38
present continuous
  statements and questions,
    61
present tense
  verbs, 37
  wh- questions with *be,* 52
  wh- questions with other
    verbs, 55
  yes/no questions and
    answers, 43

Q

question words, 52–53
questions and answers with
  or, 79

S

sounds
  of long and short *a,* 43
  of long and short *e,* 64
  of long and short *i,* 85
  of long and short *o,* 100
  of long and short *u,* 112
  of past-tense endings, 88
  of present-tense endings,
    37
subject pronouns with *be,*
  13
syllable stress, 16

T

the, 115
there is, there are, 76
this, that, these, those, 67

W

want, want to, 64
wh- questions,
  with *be,* 52–53
  with other verbs, 55

Y

yes/no questions and
  answers with *be,* 28